Interplay of Cultural Narratives in Martinique
French, African, and Indian Journeys toward a Pluralistic Society

Mahadevi Ramakrishnan
and R. Scott Smith

Interplay of Cultural Narratives in Martinique: French, African, and
Indian Journeys toward a Pluralistic Society

Authors: Mahadevi Ramakrishnan and R. Scott Smith
Cover and Layout: Carribean Studies Press
Cover Picture: Jessica Pearce

Library of Congress Control Number: 2015939307

For more information, please contact:

Caribbean Studies Press
2725 NW 19th Street,
Pompano Beach, FL 33069
Telephone: (954) 968-7433
E-mail: caribbeanstudiespress@earthlink.net
Web: www.caribbeanstudiespress.com

ISBN: 978-1-62632-370-4

Contents

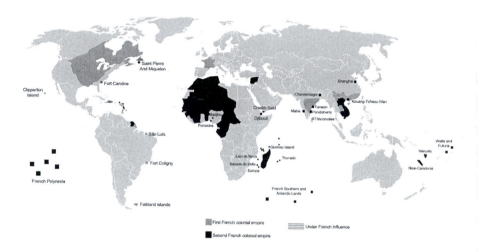

Figure 1. Map of France's 1st and 2nd colonial empires
(adapted by Educa Vision, Inc.)

Preface

Martinique, an island whose signature dish is *colombo,* a variation of a South Indian curry delicacy, but where breakfast is classically French (*croissants* and *café au lait*); where the signature headdress for women, called *madras* (former name for Tamil Nadu, a South Indian state), is a plaid pattern based on African motifs. The welcome sign at the airport is in Creole and French (*"Nou kontan wè zot"* and *"Bienvenue en Martinique"*). No single signifier of cultural identity referenced above speaks to the depth of the journeys and experiences of Martinicans today. From our visits to the island, we have observed that Martinicans are, first and foremost, citizens of the French Republic (despite being 4,200 miles away from France), but most will readily admit that they are Martinican by culture. French is the official language and yet most Martinicans express themselves freely in Creole within informal settings, even though it is still stigmatized in many circles as "unrefined." Since the late 20th century, however, Creole has been enjoying an ascendance of legitimacy and value, gradually expanding beyond casual use into literary and public discourse. What is striking about Martinique is this dizzying array of cultural inputs that coexist in a veritable braided society, in which it can be genuinely difficult to tell where one cultural strand ends and another begins.

We were both drawn to explore Martinique from different professional and personal backgrounds. One of us (Mahadevi Ramakrishnan) teaches French at Colgate University in Hamilton, NY and is originally from South India. Her main interests are in language acquisition through cultural immersion and the process of adaptation to different cultural contexts. The other (R. Scott Smith) teaches Psychology at Utica College in Utica, NY and is African American.

He is a community psychologist investigating the processes of reciprocal acculturation between host communities and new members. Both of us have research interests in resettlement and acculturation processes as well as intercultural communication. The combination of our professional and personal backgrounds drew us to explore the intricacies of how the interplay of history, language, psychology, economics, and culture shapes identities, particularly the adaptation of immigrants to a new community and vice versa.

Together we have researched institutional and cultural adaptations related to the influx of a large number of refugees into Utica, a small community of roughly 60,000 inhabitants in upstate New York from 2006-2008. Having studied the resettlement process of refugees who left their homeland under duress and the reaction of the host communities to their presence, Martinique piqued our curiosity about the effects of other contexts for resettlement. In contrast to the refugee populations in Utica, whose emigration was exigent, the history of immigration to Martinique over 350 years starting in the 1600s (as with most Caribbean islands), involved varying degrees of choice, depending on the emigrants' situation. Our visits to Martinique from 2011-2014 led us to reflect on what factors may have led to the preservation, loss, or transformation of one's original culture in a braided society such as Martinique or, for that matter, in any situation where multiple cultures interact. To answer such questions seemed to us to hinge on contexts of migration and resettlement, relationships that we scrutinize in more detail in Chapter 1.

The Caribbean island of Martinique, today an official part of France, is an exemplary case study on three levels. It illustrates:

a. a peculiarity in the post-colonial path it took relative to most former colonies, in that Martinique chose to be politically and legally integrated with France as an Overseas Department,[1] unlike the

---

[1] Along with Guadeloupe and French Guiana in the Caribbean and Reunion in the Indian Ocean.

majority of colonies that chose to become independent;

b. extensive efforts in the development and preservation of the Creole language and culture in the true sense of its Latin root *creare*, "to create"; and

c. the extraordinary hybridization of Carib, French, African, Indian, Chinese, Syrian, and Lebanese cultural narratives within an approximately 400 square-mile area.

Literature in English about Martinique is relatively sparse. To our knowledge, our work seems to be the only one that explores the evolution of Martinique's hybrid identity (from the beginnings of colonization to the present) in the contexts of emigration and resettlement for the aforementioned three most researched ethnic groups on the island.

Organization of the Book

Chapter 1 provides a panoramic overview of important factors in migration and resettlement, and explores what an interdisciplinary inquiry into Martinique entails. As we analyze the circumstances under which different cultural groups resettled in Martinique, each wave has undoubtedly punctuated the process of cultural evolution. Through this lens we delineate what we see as the distinctions between cultural hybridization and creolization.

Chapter 2 focuses on what is known about the indigenous Carib people as the original host community and their social organization. The context of early European exploration of the Caribbean, European perceptions of these indigenous peoples, and their mutual exchanges provide a framework for understanding the genesis of cultural hybridization in Martinique.

Chapter 3 delves into the circumstances of France's foray into colonialism with a focus on the role of the buccaneers, corsairs, and explorers (voluntary migration). The economic, religious, and political underpinnings for the exploration and settlement of Martinique are also a major consideration.

Chapter 4 turns to discussion on the transition from tobacco to sugar, the development of the institution of slavery, and the birth of the plantation society. The architecture of French socioeconomic and religious dominance, necessary for the colonial enterprise, was constructed during this period. The involuntary migration of enslaved Africans to Martinique and the process of creolization, creating a new culture and language, are highlighted.

Chapter 5 summarizes the varied adaptive responses of enslaved Africans and *gens de couleur* (mixed-race individuals) to the dominance of the French Plantocracy. These responses ran the gamut from subtle forms to defiant and sometimes violent forms.

Chapter 6 scrutinizes the inter- and intra-group dynamics among enslaved Africans, gens de couleur, the White Plantocracy, and the mainland French as plantation society faced numerous challenges to its dominance. The mounting pressures in Martinique and France to abolish slavery and the complexities of emancipation are also detailed.

Chapter 7 is dedicated to chronicling the narratives of the third-largest ethnic group in Martinique's history, Indian indentured workers. The socioeconomic ramifications of the abolition of slavery formed the setting in which their little-known stories unfolded.

Chapter 8 begins with further exploration of two other groups of post-abolition indentured workers: the Congolese and the Chinese. An in-depth inquiry into the path Martinique took to Departmentalization is framed within Martinique's post-abolition struggles, two world wars, and the Négritude movement.

Chapter 9 covers the unintended consequences of Departmentalization and the responses of Martinique's intellectuals via post- Négritude identity movements to political and cultural assimilation to France. The mutual attempts of Martinique and France to recognize Martinique's "right to difference" while remaining an integral part of France is addressed in this chapter as well.

Chapter 10 concludes the book with an exploration of what future interdisciplinary research on Martinique might involve; a recap of evidence for the roles of emigration and resettlement contexts as mediators for cultural evolution; an overview of Martinican pluralistic society; and finally views of contemporary Martinicans about themselves, their history, and their future.

The target audience for this book includes undergraduate and graduate students, faculty, and researchers at universities and travelers interested in learning about the local culture and history of places they visit. The book (in its entirety or specific chapters) is of particular interest to faculty teaching introductory and intermediate courses in Africana Studies, Anthropology, Caribbean Studies, Cross-cultural Psychology, Diversity Studies, Ethnic Studies, French and Francophone Studies, Geography, History, Intercultural Communication, Linguistics, and Sociology.

To help students navigate nearly 400 years of complex intertwined history, we have devoted a section to reflective questions at the end of each chapter. These questions are intended to facilitate students' understanding of the information, critical thinking about the interdisciplinary nature of the material, and appreciation of the synergy among disciplines. Furthermore, due to extensive use of discipline-specific terminology and foreign terms (French, Indian, African, and Carib), we have included a glossary at the end of each chapter. Unless otherwise noted, all translations are by Mahadevi Ramakrishnan.

Acknowledgments

We would like to thank our daughters for allowing us to test their patience and understanding during the writing of this book ("Which chapter are you on? Just Chapter 2? You're not finished *yet*?!?"). Our family members in Cupertino, CA have been unfailingly supportive from day one, so we thank them as well. A special thanks goes to Tom Nelson, who urged us to follow through on this project "because you don't want to have regrets later on that you didn't"; Dr. Anamaria Iosif-Ross for providing encouragement throughout the process, from sharing her publishing experiences to providing feedback on drafts; and to Dr. Helen Blouet, who also provided helpful review of earlier versions.

Our deepest gratitude to colleagues at both Colgate University and Utica College for their financial support that enabled us to travel to Martinique several times to interview, visit, and interact with scholars, students, friends, and locals in various parts of this beautiful island. Christian Goodwillie, director of Special Collections and Archives, Mark Tillson, Special Collections coordinator, and Kathy Collett, archivist at Hamilton College's Burke Library were unfailingly helpful to us in navigating the treasure trove of the Beinecke Lesser Antilles Collection. Thanks also go to Lily Cossey, our photographer, for taking the time out of her busy schedule to digitize the illustrations. Our appreciation goes out to Ray Beckett of the Maritime Gallery, Jean Benoist, Library of Congress, Bibliothèque Nationale de France, and UNESCO for permission to reprint other images.

We are most indebted to our friends and colleagues from Martinique, most of whom are affiliated with the University of the French West Indies, Martinique, Schoelcher Campus. Without their time and expertise we would never have been able to complete our work: Jean Bernabé, linguist and director of GEREC-F (Groupe d'Etudes et de Recherches en Espace Créolophone et Francophone); Raphaël Confiant, dean of the School of Arts & Sciences and political scientist; Marie-France Degras, geographer and activities coordinator at CIRECCA (Centre International de Recherches, d'Echanges et de Cooperation de la Caraïbe et des Amériques); Patrice Domoison, ethnologist; Michel Dispagne, linguist; Gerry L'Etang, anthropologist; René Morelot, assistant director of CIRECCA; François Rosaz, geographer; Marie-José Saint-Louis, translator and linguist; Juliette Sméralda, sociologist; and Christine Warner, language coordinator, School of Law.

A very special thanks goes out to Ms Warner's law students for their candid and enthusiastic responses about their island and its people. Thanks also to the Colgate University students who traveled to Martinique, especially Spencer Nehrt, who taught English in La Trinité from 2013-2014, for his insights on Creole language use in primary schools in Martinique. Finally, we extend our profound appreciation to everyone else we encountered on our visits to Martinique, who shaped our understanding of this exemplary mosaic culture.

Chapter 1

Emigration, Resettlement, and Cultural Evolution
An Interdisciplinary Approach

...what happened in the Americas was of immense suddenness. In two or three centuries, Slap! Three, four, five, six, or seven different peoples, of different races, with different Gods, different languages, were forced to create a future together in a context of extreme violence.[1]

—Patrick Chamoiseau
Martinican author

Throughout history, displacement of people has been a constant occurrence: "the history of the world is a history of emigration" (Jean Bernabé, personal communication, March 2013). Whether seeking better opportunities or better education, escaping war, natural disasters, religious persecution, or simple greed for wealth and power (and a host of other reasons), people have emigrated and resettled in new environments and continue to do so. The resettlement of emigrants in any environment inevitably sets in motion a reciprocal chain of human adaptive responses, affecting the intra-group and inter-group dynamics of the host community and the newcomers alike. With continued interaction between these groups over time, evolution of their cultural narratives becomes equally inevitable; elements of one's original culture may be preserved, others may be lost, and some may be transformed or fused with those of other cultures.

This book explores the history of resettlement and development

---

[1] Chamoiseau, Confiant, Bernabé, & Taylor, 1997, p. 136.

of cultural identities on the Caribbean island of Martinique from 1635 to the present. Particular attention is given to three variables: the cultural narratives of the three major cultural groups (French, African, and Indian), their reciprocal influences, and most importantly, their respective adaptive strategies to the process of resettlement. The narratives of the original host community in Martinique, the native Caribs, their interactions with early European explorers, and their critical role in cultural hybridization are also examined. Our key premise is that investigating the contexts of emigration and resettlement can help us understand the evolution of cultural narratives of both host communities and immigrant groups.

Figure 2. Map of Martinique c. 1800. (Courtesy of www. themaritimegallery.co.uk)

Host Communities in the Context of Martinique's History

Beginning in the 1500s, the **New World** (especially the Caribbean), with its indigenous populations as the original host communities, became an environment of European exploration and subsequent colonization, eventually involving millions of people displaced from Europe, Africa, Asia, and the Middle East. The term "host community" is broadly construed for our purposes with respect to Martinique (and perhaps most other colonial societies). A host community does not require numerical superiority or geographic localization, although that is the case with instances of immigration or refugee resettlement. In the paradigm of colonization, however, the definition of host is somewhat fluid. The original host community where colonization occurs is usually numerically dominant and socioculturally established, as were the original inhabitants of Martinique, the island Caribs. French colonists in time supplanted the Caribs and established themselves as the socioeconomically dominant host community in Martinique. Mainland France and its social ecology can be considered the "distant" host community. Despite its geographic distance from Martinique, France's socioeconomic influence has reverberated throughout Martinique's history.

In all host communities, distant or otherwise, there are bound to be mutual adaptations between them and newcomers. Through every phase of Martinique's history, which is intimately tied to that of France, the latter had to adapt its perceptions and policies to those of the island natives, enslaved Africans, Indians, and French settlers and their descendants in Martinique, especially during periods of unrest. Colonial enterprises in Martinique and elsewhere in the Caribbean served as France's "laboratories for social, economic, political and cultural experiments" (Aldrich, 2002, p. 935). Thus, the role of mainland France as the distant host community is a recurrent theme echoing throughout this book.

Contexts of Immigration to Martinique

Immigration to Martinique since the earliest European explorers can be conceptualized in one of three ways: voluntary, involuntary by force, and voluntary under exigent and sometimes dubious conditions. The European explorers of the 15th and 16th centuries, specifically the French, were mostly aware of potential benefits and risks of their journey and voluntarily chose to come to Martinique (and could return at will). This was true of state-sanctioned and private entrepreneurial expeditions led by sons of nobles and feudal lords who lacked an inheritance. Also thrown in the mix were adventurers, explorers, buccaneers, and merchants.

In contrast, Africans from the western and central regions of the continent were involuntarily brought to Martinique under unspeakable conditions to provide free labor for French planters under equally unspeakable conditions. Unlike European colonizers, the enslaved Africans had no clue as to what was in store for them and had no hope of return to their native lands.

The first wave of indentured workers that resettled in Martinique starting in the 1630s was primarily from France. After the abolition of slavery in 1848, the largest group of indentured workers came from India, and small contingents arrived from China and Congo as well. With respect to these various waves of indentured workers, there is evidence that, although they all signed contracts to travel to faraway lands to escape challenging conditions in their homeland for a contracted period of time and then return, they were often misinformed about the risks and benefits of their migration. This misinformation was sometimes a deliberate deception by employers and sometimes a result of limited understanding by desperate people willing to take a leap into the unknown to escape dire situations. Hence, we term their emigration voluntary under exigent circumstances.

Creolization and Hybridization

It is through the incremental and unavoidable process of mixing or "cross-pollination" (Garraway, 2005, p. 44) of the cultural narratives of all the aforementioned groups, and the identities emerging from this process, that we interpret cultural hybridization (or blending of cultures) in Martinique. Subsumed in the larger framework of hybridization is the process of **creolization**. The European slave trade resulted in an "anthropological rupture" (Bernabé, 2013, p. 32) of enslaved people from their original culture, and was the dynamo that energized creolization.

We interpret anthropological rupture as the violent, abrupt uprooting of people from Africa and the traumatic process of resettlement, involving the total devaluation and subsequent negation of African culture and the threat of brutality at any attempt to express it. In short, the forceful involuntary context of migration, and the equally coercive context of resettlement, produced cultural changes that were qualitatively and quantitatively distinct from hybridization. Qualitatively, the psychological impact of having one's humanity eradicated, and a new status and cultural norms imposed, required the enslaved to create a new way of making sense of their world.

Quantitatively, this rupture led to greater loss of the African cultural matrix than is seen in the cultural hybridization in Martinique of the French or Indians. Thus, creolization is logically limited to societies with a history of slavery, as on the island of Martinique. Because of this, after the emancipation of enslaved Africans in 1848, Martinique can be interpreted as in a state of "neo-creolization" (Confiant, 2003), or "post-creolization" with continuing hybridization (Bernabé, personal communication, March 18, 2014).

The development of a **Creole** language (linguistic creolization) is a signature feature of Martinican culture. The French and the enslaved Africans came from diverse regions and provinces of their respective homelands, so there was no way to presume the intelligibility of their respective languages (Confiant 2009). Creole, the *lingua franca* in Martinique, can be thus described as "a signifying system composed, very crudely, of a preponderantly French-derived vocabulary married to a syntax and morphology of basically African origin" (Burton, 1995b, p. 137).

As Bernabé (2013) notes, Creole language is not prevalent in all former slave societies, which can be largely attributed to the density of the slave population in relation to the European population. Where the enslaved population outnumbered the enslaving population, Creole languages emerged (e.g., Martinique, Guadeloupe, French Guiana, Haiti, Réunion, Mauritius, Seychelles, Jamaica, etc.). Nevertheless, even without a slave majority, Creole cultures (cultural creolization) developed in slave societies, especially in religious, artistic, and culinary domains. In addition to a distinct Martinican Creole language, *quimboiserie* (herbalism, magic, and spiritual practices from West African traditions), drumming, and storytelling are important aspects of Creole culture in Martinique. *Santería* in Cuba, Puerto Rico, and the Dominican Republic; *Condomblé* and *Capoeira* in Brazil; as well as jazz and blues in the United States are all considered examples of cultural creolization without an accompanying linguistic component, as described by Bernabé (2013).

It is important to note that the processes of creolization and hybridization both involve cultural reciprocation, that is, all parties contribute to and are affected by each other's contributions. The following three observations illustrate this concept in more detail and provide a preview of what we consider the underlying structure of Martinique's contemporary braided culture. The first example of cultural reciprocation is the correlation between spiritual and religious belief systems and the colonizers' religion. Features of West African spiritual traditions appear preserved to a greater extent in colonies where Catholicism was the dominant religion; Haiti or Cuba are examples of this correlation. This is presumably because Catholic ritual and beliefs, such as the worship of saints, were more congruent with the "animistic and fetishistic" features of some African spiritual traditions. The "anti-animistic and anti-fetishistic" (Bernabé, personal communication, March 18, 2014) propensities of Protestant colonies made it more challenging for these West African traditions to thrive there; the United States is an example of this correlation.

The second example of cultural reciprocation is the development of Creole languages. Establishing and managing the plantation economy created a pressing need for French slave-masters and enslaved Africans to communicate with each other. Their mutual efforts to develop a system of communication formed the genesis of Creole.

The third example is herbalism, the practice of using local plants for medicinal and spiritual purposes, imported from Africa (also known as quimboiserie). This practice of the enslaved in Martinique was also resorted to by the French to compensate for the lack of physicians and medical knowledge.

The process of creolization has been conceptualized in various ways in Martinique and other regions where slavery existed; certainly there is validity in these perspectives. Some viewpoints equate creolization with cultural hybridization (and even as a precursor of globalization) and consider the process as ongoing. Creolization certainly is a form of hybridization. However, the magnitude and monstrosity of the system of slavery that forced cultural blending and evolution begs for a distinction from cultural hybridization.

Interdisciplinary Approach to Cultural Evolution in Martinique

Analyzing the processes of creolization (linguistic and cultural) and hybridization resulting from the context of emigration and resettlement can assist in understanding the multilayered, dynamic complexity of contemporary Martinican culture and identity. Some critical elements to consider are the following, although not all elements necessarily affect cultural change to the same extent:

- circumstances of emigration,
- characteristics of the emigrants,
- narratives of their journeys,
- newcomers' impact on the host community and the host community's response to them,
- reciprocal adaptations of both groups to each other and their environment over time, and
- changes in inter- and intra-group dynamics with multiple waves of newcomers, each with a unique context of emigration and resettlement.

To investigate relationships among these elements, this book is informed to varying degrees by disciplines ranging from history to sociology to psychology to linguistics, to name a few, thus affording a clearer and more textured insight into the interweaving of disparate cultural strands that created the tapestry of Martinican identity today. A brief discussion about how we understand interdisciplinary inquiry follows.

Martinique and other Caribbean cultures historically developed in the context of multicultural contacts; thus, multiple levels of analysis are required because of the "...overwhelming evidence for the intrusion of outside forces" (Trouillot, 1992, p. 34). Exploring the interplay of cultural narratives in Martinique requires attention to the chronology of events in Europe and the greater Caribbean (such as Columbus's voyages and the French and Haitian revolutions) beginning in the 1500s. Social stratification in Martinique created by the systems of slavery and indentured workers is associated with historical events, as well as being intimately linked to the economics of cheap labor and huge profits, that is, the sugar economy. In order for these institutions to thrive, hundreds of thousands of human beings had to be uprooted from their homelands and disconnected from their original languages and cultures and adapt themselves emotionally, cognitively, and behaviorally to a new environment, bringing psychological dimensions to the fore. When the structures of social institutions and interactions are deliberately crafted to the detriment of any group, interactions are oppressive (García-Ramírez, de la Mata, Paloma, & Hernandez-Plata, 2011), creating the architecture of social dominance. Social institutions (government, industries, churches, schools, etc.), neighborhoods, and organizations are all levels at which intergroup contact occur, and how that contact is structured sets the stage for the nature of those interactions. The oppressive system of slavery led to the loss of the original languages of enslaved Africans, and the urgent need for communication yielded Creole, a common language between alien groups, further linking social, psychological, and linguistic factors.

The web of interconnections outlined above represents merely a small part of the dense network of interdisciplinarity that this case study of Martinique affords. Plunging into the study of Martinique using any single discipline or combination has been undertaken by many scholars and should create opportunities for many more; however, to our knowledge, this book may be the only work in English that spans the entirety of Martinique's history in the context of its cultural evolution. This book also reflects an experiential, participatory, and ethnographic approach, drawing on our travels in Martinique and detailed records of personal observations, conversations, and interviews, both formal and informal.

Complex phenomena such as cultural evolution can be researched from several levels of analysis, and there is ample evidence suggesting this is useful for deeper and broader comprehension of such phenomena. Because of the richness of Martinique's history, inlaid with the narratives of its diverse ethnic groups, and the extensive time period covered, our book does not claim to cover the full spectrum of analysis. Nor is it possible for us to be exhaustive and encyclopedic here in covering several centuries of history. Nevertheless, our research indicates that to fully comprehend contemporary Martinique's braided culture, an interdisciplinary approach spanning Martinique's entire history is indispensable. We also hope that our book serves as a solid overview of Martinique that is useful both as an introduction for those unfamiliar with the island and as a catalyst for new research on Martinique that delves further into any of the disciplinary strands this book incorporates.

Methods and Rationale for Sources

To faithfully represent the "diversality" (Glissant, 1989, p. xxx) of cultural voices in contemporary Martinique, we endeavored to gather sources for research that were comparably diverse from academic works, ethnographic inquiry, and popular culture. Primary and secondary sources spanning multiple disciplines (in French, English, and in translation) were used extensively. Publications from the Regional Council of Martinique and the legislative archives of the French National Assembly were useful for information and local perspectives on historical events. Articles from the French, Martinican, and Caribbean press were helpful in assessing recent cultural discourse and perceptions of current events in Martinique and the Caribbean. Finally, websites such as potomitan.info served as an archive of literary and scholarly works on Creole language and culture.

Given that so many of our primary and secondary sources were not written by Martinicans, we feel impelled to give voice to what Martinicans from various walks of life say about their history, culture, and current experience. To that end, semi-structured interviews were recorded with Martinican scholars and students, most of whom were associated with the University of the French West Indies, Martinique. Many Martinicans, from retired teachers to teachers in training, from cab drivers to vendors in the market in St. Pierre, from grassroots environmental activists to the caretaker of a local Hindu temple, also contributed through extensive discussions with us. In addition, we used participant observation and photography to document and reflect on the experiences of Martinicans. Recognizing that our informant sample was limited, we strived to present perspectives of both older and younger Martinicans; women and men; classic and contemporary sources; scholarly and general perspectives; and artistic, academic, and journalistic approaches to capture the many strands of Martinique's culture.

The next chapter explores who the original inhabitants of Martinique were and the process of cultural hybridization that started with encounters between these original inhabitants, the Caribs, and Europeans settlers; an "Antillean laboratory," as Confiant puts it, of cultural hybridization that presaged modern globalization. A striking feature that is reflective of this laboratory is the amalgamation of social and environmental ecology on this island. Ninety per cent of all trees and plants currently found in Martinique (bamboo, sugar cane, breadfruit, banana, etc.) were imported. Today's banana and sugarcane plantations supplanted the original environment that early French explorers found there (Confiant, personal communication, March 17, 2014). Similarly, the majority of Martinicans have ancestors who were not indigenous to the island, just like the vegetation, a further illustration of Martinique's complex interconnectedness.

Glossary

host community - Established community that receives immigrants, refugees, indentured workers, or slaves as settlers.

Caribs - Native American people who inhabited the Lesser Antilles and areas of the neighboring South American coast at the time of Spanish conquest. The Caribbean Sea was named for them.

cultural hybridization - Process of cultural change and blending resulting from two or more cultural groups living and working in the same community over time.

New World - Caribbean islands and the Americas opened to European exploration and exploitation by Christopher Columbus in 1492.

creolization - Cultural hybridization in the context of slavery.

Creole - (Spanish, *"Criollo"*; French, *"Créole"*) Refers to people, language, or other cultural features emerging from the colonial experience in the Caribbean and Americas; may also include islands in the Pacific and Indian oceans (see Chapter 3).

quimboiserie - (French, *"quimbois"* is presumed to come from the French phrase *"tiens bois,"* or "holds/controls wood," linking it to botanical origins). Herbalism and magico-spiritual practices derived from West African traditions.

Reflective Questions

1. Discuss the authors' perception of the concept of cultural hybridization. How is it distinct from the concept of creolization?

2. Can the concept of hybridization be applied to contemporary globalization and the resettlement of people in many parts of the world? Give examples.

Chapter 2
Caribs, Early Europeans, and the Genesis of Hybridization in Martinique

*For me, the research or study of our Carib roots
is an integral part of our [Martinican] culture.[2]*

—François Rosaz
Martinican geographer

Because cultural hybridization is a fluid and indeterminate process, we can assume that the true genesis of hybridization in the Caribbean predates formal settlement and colonization of these islands. However, prior to the voyages of Christopher Columbus, there is little to no documentation about the Caribbean and its indigenous people, which limits knowledge of pre-Columbian hybridization.

First, this chapter explores some early European sources, from Columbus on, that shed light on the social ecology of the indigenous inhabitants of the Caribbean. It is in this framework that reciprocal adaptive responses between Europeans and indigenous people were established. Second, the socioecological contexts in Europe that facilitated exploration (especially Spanish and French) of the Caribbean are examined. Third and most important, this chapter posits the interchange of cultural narratives between indigenous people and Europeans during the 16th and 17th centuries as a wellspring of cultural hybridization on the island of Martinique.

---

[2] *Pour moi, la recherche ou l'étude de nos racines Caraïbes fait partie intégralement de notre culture* (François Rosaz, personal communication, March 19, 2014).

Indigenous People and Earliest
Spanish Accounts

Christopher Columbus's ambition in 1492 to reach the East through the Atlantic Ocean in search of silk, gold, and spices generated the first documented European explorations of the Americas and interactions with indigenous inhabitants of this region (Butel, 2002). Although he did not succeed in his original ambition, Columbus never failed to exalt to the Spanish monarchy the profitability of monopolizing the resources of the Caribbean islands, especially the usefulness of its people. On October 12, 1492, the first Caribbean island Columbus set foot on was San Salvador (a Bahamian island), and the first inhabitants he met in the Caribbean are thought to have been the **Tainos** of the **Greater Antilles**[3] (called **Arawaks** in the **Lesser Antilles;**[4] Confiant, personal communication, March 17, 2014; American Journeys Collection, 2003).

The Tainos/Arawaks

Columbus recounts that the natives received him calmly without belligerence and were very pleased with the gifts he provided. He perceived them as generous, sharing what they had in exchange for meager trinkets; the loyalty engendered by even small gifts, such as caps and glass beads, was quite striking to him (American Journeys Collection, 2003). It was during his fourth expedition in 1502 that he landed on Martinique's shores at Le Carbet (Delphine and Roth, 2009).

---

[3] Cuba, the Cayman Islands, Jamaica, Hispaniola (Haiti & Dominican Republic), and Puerto Rico.
[4] Anguilla, Antigua & Barbuda, St. Martin, Montserrat, and St. Barthélemy, Guadeloupe, St. Christopher & Nevis, Dominica, Martinique, St. Lucia, Barbados, St. Vincent & the Grenadines, Grenada, Trinidad & Tobago, plus various islands, including what are now the Virgin Islands.

Figure 3. Map of the Antilles c. 1730 (Courtesy of www.themaritimegallery. co.uk.)

Because Columbus sought gold, he constantly inquired about it and mentioned it 21 times in his journals in the first 10 days of his arrival in the Caribbean islands (Arciniegas, 1946). The natives seemed cooperative, pointing him in the direction where they thought it might be found. Over time, even though this information did not yield what he was looking for, Columbus developed a favorable impression of the inhabitants. This laid the foundation for a trusting relationship, and the indigenous people even requested Columbus's help to fend off other indigenous tribes whom they feared because, as he understood it, these other tribes ate their enemies. He chronicles the following local narrative: "far away, there were men with one eye, and others with dogs' noses who were cannibals, and that when they captured an enemy, they beheaded him, and drank his blood, and cut off his private parts" (American Journeys Collection, 2003, p. 57). This was the beginning of the persisting theme of cannibalism about this group of indigenous people known as the Caribs, largely from the Lesser Antilles.

The Caribs

There is much controversy about the accuracy of characterizing the Caribs as cannibals. Various theories include the Caribs engaging in cannibalism within their own group as well as outside of it, cannibalism as a ritualistic practice in attacking enemies, and others asserting that such accounts were contrived by the Spanish to justify killing natives and seizing their lands. Available anthropological research supports no widespread cannibalism among the Caribs, and only one eyewitness report of the practice from a French missionary, Raymond Breton (who resided in Dominica for several years from 1641). However, ritual practices of chewing and biting enemy body parts to impart fortitude and valor, offering roasted limbs as gifts, or displaying enemy body parts as badges of courage and honor were reported by several 17th century chroniclers (Petitjean Roget, 1980; Boucher, 1992; Sweeney, 2007).

The favorable impressions that Columbus formed of the indigenous people were frequently tinged with condescension and paternalism, however. The recurring threads of exploitability, vulnerability, and overall inferiority of the "Indians" are found throughout Columbus's journals from his first expedition. He saw them as gullible people with no laws, no gods or religion, and dependent on the Spaniards for protection and salvation. Particularly because of his perception that they lacked religious convictions or practices, Columbus believed that converting these natives to Catholicism would be a simple matter (American Journeys Collection, 2003), a premise that in the end was not supported. The following quote from a translation of Columbus's journals sums up his attitudes and intentions with stark clarity:

They have no arms and are without war-like instincts... and are so timid that a thousand would not stand before three of our men. So that they are good to be ordered about, to work and sow, and do all that may be necessary, and to build towns, and they should be taught to go about clothed and to adopt our customs. (American Journeys Collection, 2003, p. 101)

Reading Columbus's impressions and interpretations of the Caribbean islands and people, we wonder how much of his report was tempered by the failure of his original mission: finding a quicker route to Asia for acquiring gold and spices. He might have emphasized the lucrative potential of this New World and its people as a substitute for the concrete riches he was charged to find. It is important not to underestimate the sociocultural and linguistic barriers that limited Columbus's understanding of the indigenous people and their culture, a significant impediment that he was quite aware of (American Journeys Collection, 2003). It is thus likely that Columbus's accounts are not without misinterpretations and misconstrued observations. Nevertheless, these missives defined the social ecology of the indigenous people for future European explorers and shaped the dynamics between them.

Later French Accounts

In the late 16th century, Montaigne discussed ethnocentrism in his essay "Of Cannibals." His interpretation of barbarism (as that we are not familiar with) puts a more human face on regarding indigenous people savages and barbarians (Confer, 1968; Montaigne, 1877/2012). But the most significant and detailed sources for understanding the people and early history of the Caribbean were by French missionaries and explorers of the 17th century: Bouton, Labat, Breton, DuTertre, and Rochefort. Some were contemporaries of the French pioneers, and they referred to the indigenous people as Caribs rather than as Columbus's term, "Indians." Their ethnographic observations of indigenous customs and interactions with Europeans were documented several generations later than Columbus's. There is ample evidence that this period (1492-early 1600s) saw considerable cultural exchange between Europeans and Caribs, diminishing the sociocultural and linguistic barriers that Columbus faced when he first encountered the indigenous people.

However, we can extrapolate from this evidence that in-depth descriptions of Carib culture in these early French accounts may not reflect "pure" Carib culture prior to European influence, because the more reliable and important accounts were published well over 100 years after initial encounters between the two cultures. Furthermore, all these accounts were by Europeans, thus observed and interpreted through the lens of European contexts, rendering them susceptible to bias just as Columbus's chronicles (Boucher, 2008); regrettably, neither the Caribs or Arawaks were in a position to transmit their narratives in their own voices and perspectives. Nevertheless, the information provided by French ethnographers is primarily what researchers have resorted to in studying the history and culture of the Caribs.

Development of Indigenous Host Communities

How and when these indigenous people arrived in the Caribbean islands is unclear. There are only hypotheses whether they originated from South America or North America, with neither proposition having sufficient data for conclusive support. It is clear, however, that the Caribs and Tainos/Arawaks were and are the most-studied indigenous groups of the Caribbean. French pre-colonial and colonial testimony focused primarily on the Caribs as the indigenous hosts, linguistically and ethnically similar across the Lesser Antillean islands. Although they came from different islands, Caribs appear to have supported each other and fought against European aggression as a unified and homogenous group: "When the French attacked Guadeloupe, St. Vincent sent hundreds of warriors to help, but they were defeated.... When the French invaded Martinique in 1635 the Caribs sent 1500 warriors from Dominica and St. Vincent, but were defeated again" (Sweeney, 2007, p. 11).

Despite several defeats, the Caribs were never fully dominated by any European power and were the last group standing in opposition to European expansion; in fact, they provided refuge from the Spanish to the last of the Tainos in the Greater Antilles (Boucher, 1992; Sweeney, 2007). Caribs were ultimately exiled from Martinique to the islands of St. Vincent and Dominica toward the end of the 17th century, thus cutting off further infusion of Carib cultural narratives in the flow of hybridization. Today, there are no more than 3,000 Caribs in Dominica, most of mixed ancestry (Confiant, personal communication, March 17, 2014).

The actual Carib population in Martinique before the arrival of the French is unknown. However, some factors permit us to extrapolate that the Carib population might have been 1,300 or more in Martinique in 1660. This estimate is based on census data of 1660, which indicated the non-French population of Africans, *gens de couleur* (people of mixed race), and Caribs at 2,683. Given that there were approximately 300 enslaved Africans in Martinique between 1639-1640 and that the slave trade did not start in earnest until around 1651, it can be estimated that enslaved Africans constituted at most 50% of that 2,683 census figure (Petitjean Roget, 1980). The gens de couleur population could not have been significant considering that the number of women (African or French) was minimal.

There are several theories about how Caribs became the dominant indigenous group in the Caribbean, most of which relate to their interactions with Arawaks in the Lesser Antilles. These theories range from conquest (Carib invasion of Arawak lands, murder and enslavement of men, and kidnapping of Arawak women and children); to gradual intermingling (trading, conflicts, and migration); and European propaganda about Carib cannibalism (to provide a pretext for Europeans to massacre indigenous people and occupy their territory). Because there are few documented accounts of initial encounters between Europeans and indigenous groups in the Caribbean, it is important to explore available information in the context of reciprocal human relations and adaptive responses during this period. Using this context for analysis, we can say there was extensive contact and interaction, both violent and peaceful, among the Arawak and the Caribs. This interaction resulted in the blending of cultural narratives, especially the linguistic aspect, over time diminishing distinctions between the two groups (Allaire, 1977; Boucher, 1992; Gullick, 1980; Hulme, 1986; Rouse, 1948; Sweeney, 2007; and Taylor, 1949).

The cultural generalizations made by Columbus (non-belligerent, generous, hospitable, gullible, irreligious and ready for conversion, etc.) tended to be more applicable to the Tainos of the Greater Antilles, the host community he encountered on first reaching the Caribbean. Generalizations characterizing the Caribs as hospitable, warlike, cannibalistic, and intrepid hunters and seamen, etc. tended to refer to people of the Lesser Antilles, who were the host community first encountered by the French. European perceptions of Caribs and their culture served as a backdrop to their intergroup relations.

European Exploration and the Struggle for Dominance in the Caribbean

Socioecological Factors Supporting Spanish Imperialism

Following his initial expeditions, Columbus is said to have reported that the natives in the New World were "sufficiently disposed to embrace the Catholic faith and be trained in good morals" (Davenport, 1917, p. 76), as stated in the Papal Bull of May 4, 1493, issued by Pope Alexander VI. The same Papal Bull also bestowed upon Spain's monarchy and its successors the exclusive right to occupy, own, rule, and exploit as they saw fit the territories in the New World, "100 leagues towards the west and south from any of the islands commonly known as the Azores and Cape Verde" (Davenport, 1917, p. 77). Anyone who dared trespass these boundaries without permission of the Spanish monarchy faced excommunication (Petitjean Roget, 1980, p. 27). This contributed to Spain's economic and military hegemony in the Caribbean throughout the 1500s; even so, other European powers challenged Spain's monopoly and attempted to gain a foothold in the region.

As a direct result of its vast influence, Spain engaged in numerous crusades to fill its coffers and expand its empire from Cuba, Hispaniola (now the Dominican Republic and Haiti), and Puerto Rico in the Greater Antilles to Central and South America. Spain's imperial ambitions resulted in the annihilation of a substantial portion of the native population, brutal plundering of the Aztec and Inca empires, and the debut of the Atlantic slave trade to satisfy the increasing need for manual labor (Butel, 2002; Petitjean Roget, 1980; Boucher, 2008). Spain's interest in the New World was less focused on the Lesser Antilles because of the lack of gold, mountainous terrain, and the formidable Caribs, whose tactics resembled modern guerilla warfare (Confiant, personal communication, March 17, 2014), which dissuaded the Spanish from greater investment in this region (Roberts, 1942). However, the strategic position of the Lesser Antilles between the Greater Antilles, South America, and the Atlantic Ocean made for a convenient way station for Spanish ships to replenish food and water and to rest and recover (Petitjean Roget, 1980), thus providing some of the earliest records of European interactions with the native Caribs.

Socioecological Factors Supporting French Imperialism

Charles I of Spain (r. 1516-1556), also known as Charles V, ruler of the Holy Roman Empire (r. 1519-1556), and François I of France (r. 1516-1547) were contemporaries who waged continual territorial wars in Europe during the first half of the 16th century. The expansion of Spain and the Holy Roman Empire in Europe and the New World was a threat to France's monarchy. François I contested Spain's dominance throughout his reign, and is said to have questioned the authority of the Papal Bull of 1493, stating "the sun shines on me just the same as on the other; and I should like to see the clause in Adam's will that cuts me out of my share in the New World" (Arciniegas, 1946, p. 118). France was envious of the riches that Spain was bringing back from the New World and eager to share in the looting, although it lacked the naval prowess to challenge Spain directly or undertake similar imperial enterprises. Thus, France resorted to more surreptitious means of undermining Spain's growing empire in the Americas.

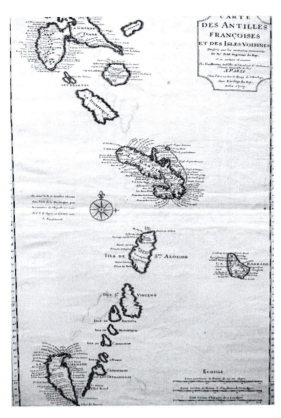

Figure 4. Map of the French Antilles 1717. (Courtesy of the Beinecke Lesser Antilles Collection, Burke Library, Hamilton College, NY.)

Letters of marque or authorization from French royalty or its representatives to rob Spanish ships in the New World were issued to **privateers**. On their return to France, these privateers shared the booty with their benefactors, a mutually advantageous arrangement. This thinly veiled, state-sponsored form of piracy unleashed a slew of privateers (predominantly from ports in Normandy and Aquitaine), who sought personal fortune and adventure at the expense of the Spaniards. Hoffman (1980) points out that from 1535 to the end of Francis I's reign (1547), as many as 66 Spanish vessels were seized by French privateers. Privateers were not only pillaging Spanish ships, however, but some were also engaging in illegal trade with the Spanish. They left French seaports to load their ships with enslaved people from the African coast of Guinea and sold them to the Spanish in Colombia, Venezuela, and other parts of mainland South America to help develop Spanish colonies in the New World (Butel, 2002).

In an effort to ease rising tensions and conflicts in Europe and the New World, France and Spain signed the **Treaty of Cateau-**

Cambrésis in 1559. Certain clauses in this treaty suggested a division of overseas territories so that beyond a certain point, known as the *ligne des amitiés* or line of friendship, south of the Tropic of Cancer and west of the Azores (Petitjean Roget, 1980, p. 43), the safety of any vessel from any country could not be guaranteed. Incursions before that boundary would be grounds for military retaliation. It was not until 1598 that the line of friendship was formally codified with the **Treaty of Vervins**, marking Spain's concession of absolute rights to lands of the New World (Petitjean Roget, 1980).

As international obstacles to France's imperial designs were surmounted, a domestic quagmire had been brewing since the 1560s: religious conflicts with the **Huguenots**, a branch of Calvinist Protestant Christianity, mostly of Anglo-Saxon/Norman origin (Gray, 1983). These civil struggles further depleted the political and monetary resources of the French monarchy, complicating competition with the Spanish for profits in the Caribbean. France's embroilment in increasingly more intense religious conflicts for the remainder of the 16th century significantly slowed its exploration in the New World. On one hand, granting letters of marque to privateers advanced the French monarchy's goal to challenge Spanish enterprises in the Caribbean (Butel, 2002). Ironically, most of these accomplished mariners were from the region of Normandy, which was also a stronghold of the Huguenots; hence, on the other hand, this may have contributed to empowering and enriching the Huguenots, fueling domestic religious tensions.

The **Treaty of Bergerac** and the **Edict of Poitiers** signed in 1577, and the **Treaty of Nérac** signed in 1579, were earlier efforts to establish peace between the religious groups in France that coalesced into the **Edict of Nantes** in 1598 (Sutherland, 1988; Champeaud, 2001). This historic edict asserted that France was a Catholic nation that tolerated some Protestant rights (but only in specific areas for limited periods) and helped to slow the pace of religious persecution and retaliation. The Edict was not satisfactory to either Catholics or Protestants and religious hostilities continued through the 17th century (Turchetti, 1991; Boucher, 2008). The Edict of Nantes, in conjunction with the Treaty of Vervins (formally recognizing the line of friendship) signed the same year, did however provide a political opportunity for the French monarchy to expand its empire in the New World.

Interactions between the Carib Host Community and Europeans

Some of the earliest encounters of the indigenous Caribs with Europeans were with the Spanish. Although Spain was far more interested in the larger islands of the Greater Antilles, and never truly expanded its colonial enterprise into the smaller islands of the Lesser Antilles, the impact of Spanish encounters with the Caribs was hardly negligible. Spanish massacres and their spread of diseases drastically reduced the Carib population in the Lesser Antilles (Hubbard, 2002).

Despite Spanish brutality and violence unleashed upon the Caribs for over a century, it is noteworthy that the Spanish never successfully subjugated them (Roberts, 1942), and, in fact, there is evidence of cooperation. In the early 17th century, the Europeans' desperate need to survive the harsh New World environment and the Caribs' desire to improve their day-to-day lives galvanized the process of hybridization. Caribs benefitted from using European metal implements and sails on their dugout canoes for lengthy sea ventures, and from more potent alcohol (Boucher, 2008). Europeans (especially the Spanish) had many occasions to be grateful for Carib hospitality, illustrating the reciprocity of adaptive behavior:

The Caribs were visited by the Spanish who often stopped

for refreshments to and from their long journeys... they left
their animals, mostly pigs, and planted banana trees and
sugar cane. Sometimes, they also left behind their sickly,
who were cared for by the Carib Indians with whom they
had made peace.[5] (Rochefort, 1658, as cited in Petitjean
Roget, 1980, p. 396)

The introduction of tobacco in Europe and its impact on the
pace of hybridization cannot be underestimated. Although Columbus
mentioned the use of tobacco by indigenous people on the island of
San Salvador as early as 1492 (Petitjean Roget, 1980, p. 37), it was
not until the mid-1500s that the alluring effects of this plant gripped
Europe. The word "tobacco" was borrowed from the indigenous
Tainos of St. Domingue (Haiti) and introduced to France in the 1570s
by the ambassador to Portugal, Jean Nicot (hence, nicotine; Petitjean
Roget, 1980). For the next several decades, as the value and the
lucrative potential of tobacco burgeoned, opportunities for legal and
illegal trade between *l'amont* (land of the civilized), and *l'aval* (land
of the savages)[6] emerged, spawning frequent intercultural encounters.
Expeditions to trade with and take land from the Caribs for cultivating
tobacco proliferated, some financed by the King of France and
others by private financiers. The European perception of themselves
as civilized, and the Caribs and other indigenous people as savages,
sparked the drive to impose European culture to civilize them; this

---

[5] *...estoit fort visitée des espagnols qui y prenoient souvent leurs rafraichissements
en allant en en retournant de leurs longs voyages...laissé des animaux, des porcs
principalement et planté des bananes et de la canne à sucre. Ils y laissoient aussi
quelquesfois leurs malades qui étoient traitez par les indiens caraîbes avec lesquels ils
avaient fait la paix à cette condition.*

[6] *L'amont* and *l'aval* were terms used in the treaties, contracts, letters of marque,
and commissions of the day to refer to the place of origin (Europe) and to the
faraway lands beyond the Tropic of Cancer (the Caribbean), respectively. The
terms had a connotation of superiority of the former (*l'amont* or mountain)
over the latter (*l'aval* or valley; Petitjean Roget, 1980, pp. 23-28).

drive eventually was entwined with other motives for colonization.

French interests in the Caribbean from the outset were focused on trade and commerce (legal and illegal) for fortune, adventure, and geopolitical advantage. Evangelism was not a French objective until after the first quarter of the 17th century; although it began as an ancillary motive, religious conversion became pivotal in its own right (Peabody, 2004; Boucher, 2008). The French and Europeans in general found it extremely challenging to Christianize and otherwise Westernize the Caribs. Even after 30 years of missionary work by **Dominican Friars** starting in 1635, it appears that they were barely able to convert more than a score of Caribs to Christianity (Boucher, 2008 p. 39). There are indications that both the clergy and colonial plantation owners felt that the gift of salvation, given to the Caribs through conversion to Catholicism, created a kind of obligation, or at least reciprocity. The French appeared to expect repayment of this favor by having the Caribs cede rights to their land and natural resources (Garraway, 2005). The Caribs' resistance to both conversion and this sense of entitlement surely contributed to resentment by the French and more aggressive policies toward the Caribs by 1560.

In contrast, Caribs were far more receptive to European languages. By the mid- 1600s, a form of pidgin called *baragouin* (an "ancestor of Creole"), a mix of Carib, French, Flemish, English, and Spanish, was noted by the chroniclers Breton, Dutertre, and Labat. Baragouin was considered "the unique tool of communication between the indigenous Caribs and the early European colonizers"[7] (Etienne, 2003, para. 3).

There were also French and Spanish words added to the Carib language. For example, Carib words such as *carta, camicha, caniche, cabayou*, etc. were discerned by Breton as acquired from Spanish (Petitjean Roget, 1980; Baker, 1995). The extent of European linguistic

---

[7] *l'unique outil de communication entre autochtones caraïbes et conquistadors et colons européens.*

influence can be attributed to increased intercultural contact and the value Caribs placed on trade, espionage, and understanding European intentions in the Caribbean. An interesting example is the word "Carib" itself, which does not appear to have been generally used by this group to refer to themselves, at least not among themselves (Sweeney, 2007). This term acquired self-ascribed connotations of a fierce warrior or rebel, along with cannibalism. It is interesting that the word Arawak people used to refer to their foes, *caniba* ("manioc people"), is the root for both *cannibal* and *Caribbean,* though pronounced differently (Sweeney, 2007, p. 4). European characterizations of Caribs were appropriated by indigenous groups (i.e., the Tainos/Arawaks, as well as the Caribs themselves) either to disparage other groups in order to forge strategic alliances with Europeans, or as a self-affirming facade to discourage European encroachment (Garraway, 2005). This pattern of cultural reciprocity apparent in early European-Carib relations was greatly influential in the development of Caribbean identities and continued cultural hybridization.

Conclusion

From the first contact on, major shifts in Europe echoed in the Caribbean. The economic, political, and religious contexts of 16[th]and 17th century Europe framed exploration and subsequent colonization of the Caribbean. Columbus's quest for gold and spices, François I's challenge to Spain's monopoly in the Caribbean, and the papacy's desire to convert indigenous people and expand Christian monarchies forced open the doors to the Caribbean and the rest of the New World, justifying the European presence.

The recurring problem of relying on European perspectives of Caribbean indigenous people because of the absence of their own accounts makes a thorough understanding of their pre-Columbus culture challenging. Garraway (2005, p. 11) posits that the lack of non-European textual voices requires scholars to critique European narratives in ways that transcend the context of the times. As an example, Columbus's failure to reach the Far East, which may have affected his accounts of Caribbean people, always looms large in research on these groups. Nevertheless, European perspectives are the only available records of their interactions with the Caribs, so researchers are limited to European interpretations of this original host community.

The skills and knowledge of Martinique's environment that the Caribs shared facilitated European resettlement and the subsequent development of the plantation economy with enslaved Africans. Equally noteworthy is the Caribs' adaptation to the European presence and, in the process, how the concept of host evolved to be most inhospitable to the Caribs, as we see in the following chapter. The reverberations of early reciprocal acculturation between Europeans and Caribs serve not only as a reference for the genesis of hybridization, but also as a backdrop for the French colonial enterprise of the 17th century. Several transitions brought major changes in cultural narratives in Martinique, the most significant being the end of this *pas de deux,* the supplanting of the Carib original host community by French pioneers and the start of the African slave trade.

Glossary

Taino - Indigenous people found mostly in the Greater Antilles, sometimes called the Arawak.

Greater Antilles - Four largest islands of the Antilles—Cuba, Hispaniola, Jamaica, and Puerto Rico—lying north of the Lesser Antilles chain. They constitute nearly 90 % of the total land area of the Caribbean.

Arawak - Indigenous people found mostly in the Greater Antilles, sometimes called the Taino.

Lesser Antilles - Long arc of small islands in the Caribbean Sea extending in a north-south direction from the Virgin Islands to Trinidad and then east-west from Margarita to Aruba off the northern coast of Venezuela.

gens de couleur - (French, "people of color") Specifically free, mixed-race (primarily European and African) individuals.

letters of marque - Commissions or warrants granted by a monarch for what would otherwise be acts of piracy.

privateers - Privately owned armed vessel commissioned by a belligerent state to attack enemy ships, usually vessels of commerce. Privateering was carried on by all nations until the 19th century. Frequently it was impossible to restrain privateers within the legitimate bounds of their commissions. Thus, it was often difficult to distinguish between privateers, pirates, corsairs, and buccaneers, many of whom sailed without commissions.

Treaty of Cateau-Cambrésis - April 3, 1559 agreement marking the end of the 65-year (1494-1559) struggle between France and Spain for control of Italy, with the result that Habsburg Spain became the dominant power in Italy for the following 150 years.

ligne des amitiés - (French, "line of friendship") Geographic boundary (south of the Tropic of Cancer and west of the Azores) beyond which safety from attacks by other European vessels or pirates could not be guaranteed by any European ruler; international confrontations north and east of the boundary were grounds for war.

Huguenots - Protestants in France in the 16ᵗʰ and 17ᵗʰ centuries, many of whom suffered severe persecution for their faith.

Edict of Nantes - Law promulgated at Nantes in Brittany on April 13, 1598 by Henry IV of France. It granted a large measure of religious liberty to his Protestant subjects, the Huguenots.

Edict of Poitiers - Ratification in September 1577 of the Treaty of Bergerac that allowed Huguenots free exercise of their religion, but only in the suburbs of one town in each bailiwick (*"bailliage"*), and where it had been practiced before the outbreak of hostilities.

Treaty of Nérac - Reauthorization of the Edict of Poitiers, notable for the length of the negotiations between the Huguenot leader, Henry of Navarre, and the Catholic leader, Queen Catherine de Médicis; the treaty confirmed and secured rights declared in the Edict of Poitiers.

Treaty of Vervins - The Peace of Vervins (1598) by which Spain recognized Henry IV as King of France.

l'amont - (French, "toward the mountain or the source") Term implying the source of civilization; where sailing expeditions began.

l'aval - (French, "toward the valley or the lowlands") Term implying barbarous or uncivilized lands; the destination of sailing expeditions.

Dominican Friars - Also known as Black Friars, one of four orders of the Roman Catholic church, founded by St. Dominic in 1215.

baragouin - (From French) Unintelligible and incomprehensible language.

caniba - (Arawak) Term for the indigenous people of the Lesser Antilles known as Caribs.

Reflective Questions

1. What factors may have influenced Columbus's observations of the Caribbean and its native people, and how did his accounts affect later European perceptions of them?

2. In what ways did Europeans adopt Carib customs and language, and vice-versa? Provide examples of this reciprocal acculturation.

3. How were the exploration and colonization of the Caribbean shaped by socioecological conditions in Europe? What role did the papacy play?

Chapter 3

The Dawn of French Colonialism and the Slave Trade

Genesis of Creolization

In Martinique today, we are a colony. We are not a colony in the classic sense of the word, of course, but we are a colony because in this country, everything is decided by the French... the important thing is that we do not have power in our own country.[8]

—Raphaël Confiant
Dean of the School of Arts & Sciences
University of the French West Indies Martinique

The French colonial enterprise began on the island of St. Christophe (more commonly known as St. Kitts), which eventually became part of the British empire in the 18th century. This island is crucial to understanding French colonialism, not only because it was their first colony, but also because the journey and experience of these settlers informed future colonial expeditions (particularly in Martinique). This chapter addresses the intermediate phase (1627-1660) between the exploration and settlement phases of French colonial history.

No chronicle of the French empire in the Caribbean is intelligible without reference to both Captain d'Esnambuc and Cardinal Richelieu, introduced in this chapter. Both figures were critical in the colonization of St. Christophe and Martinique, as well

---

[8] Raphaël Confiant, personal communication, March 17, 2014.

as to the concept of French plantation society. The **Company of St. Christophe,** established and financed by Richelieu and his entourage in 1626 to colonize Caribbean islands, is also explored in this chapter. The evolving dynamics between financiers of the company and pioneer colonists, and the effect on their respective adaptive strategies, group identities, and the French mercantile system, are integral to this intermediate phase. Pivotal lessons for building a thriving colony are a major topic, especially because Martinique and the rest of the French empire in the Caribbean were built on the experiences of colonizing St. Christophe, continuing the process of cultural hybridization discussed in Chapter 2.

The claiming of Martinique in 1635 by d'Esnambuc, an effectively planned and executed scheme, marks the beginning of French colonialism in earnest. The increasing demand for land and labor culminated in the expulsion of Caribs from Martinique and the advent of contracted labor from France, the *engagés*. The inefficiency of the engagé system, along with the continued demand for cheap labor, inexorably devolved into the system of slavery. The emergence of Creole during this process as a language of compromise among Caribs, French, and Africans is also addressed. This period in French Caribbean history witnessed the transition from the cultivation of tobacco to sugar, although tobacco profits were far from exhausted. With the Caribs no longer in the equation, the French became the socioeconomically dominant host community during expansion of the slave trade. The shift in host communities and the influx of a new ethnic group, the enslaved Africans, triggered a renegotiation of cultural identities and development of a new hierarchical structure that remained in place until the abolition of slavery in Martinique in 1848.

D'Esnambuc and Cardinal Richelieu

Pierre Belain d'Esnambuc of Normandy, considered the founding father of the French colonial enterprise in the Caribbean, officially established the first French colony on the island of St. Christophe (St. Kitts) in 1627. D'Esnambuc, a *flibustier* (originally from the Dutch *vryjbuiter,* meaning "freebooter"; Garraway, 2005, p. 100), was one of several independent military contractors operating under a royal commission. The primary goals of granting these commissions were to get rid of pirates and other lawless vagabonds who ravaged the seas beyond the line of friendship, and to boost French trade and expansion in the Caribbean.

The waters of the Caribbean and its islands were hardly foreign to d'Esnambuc, who had been frequenting this region since 1620. His father was a nobleman bankrupted by religious conflicts, leaving many debts for his children. D'Esnambuc, as the youngest son "whom the law of primogeniture had left without an income" (Roberts, 1942, p. 32), took to the seas at the age of 18 in search of fortune, as did many in his situation. His contract of May 1, 1623 spelled out his responsibilities as he left from Le Havre as "Captain and Chief Navigator under God of the ship *l'Espérance* [Hope]" to sell and exchange goods from France in return for novelties, including fauna found on his voyage to "Peru, Brazil and other islands" (Butel, 2002, p. 25).

During one such mission in 1625 (there is controversy regarding the date of this event; see Hubbard, 2002), d'Esnambuc's vessel suffered considerable damage in a skirmish with Spanish warships and had to make an emergency docking at St. Christophe. From all accounts, d'Esnambuc graciously accepted the hospitality of the Englishman Sir Thomas Warner, who had established a small settlement there and was involved in cultivating tobacco. Following his successful tobacco trading from Saint Christophe, d'Esnambuc returned to France and

Figure 5. Statue of Pierre Belain d'Esnambuc, Fort de France. (Photo by authors, March 2013.)

sought backing from Cardinal Richelieu, King Louis XIIIth's chief minister, to invest in tobacco production there (Butel, 2002).

D'Esnambuc's proposition was in line with Richelieu's foreign policy objectives because the cardinal's focus was to build France's navy as a way to bolster French prestige, to destabilize Spain's growing empire in Europe and the New World, and to expand overseas commerce. Richelieu saw the Caribbean, along with South America, Canada, West Africa, and Madagascar, as an avenue to achieve these aims; thus, as the self-appointed Grand Master of Navigation and Commerce, he founded a number of chartered companies with varying rights and responsibilities to conduct trade, and even to colonize

(Crouse, 1940; Boucher, 2008). Seeing the potential for profit from the Caribbean trade (especially in tobacco) based on the experiences of the flibustiers, entrepreneurs, and entities such as the **Dutch West Indies Company,** several other investors in Richelieu's entourage and outside the royal court were persuaded to support a larger-scale venture (Crouse, 1940; Butel, 2002).

As mentioned, Richelieu invested heavily (about one third of the total capital) in the Company of St. Christophe, which he helped found in 1626. He commissioned d'Esnambuc and Urbain du Roissey to start a French settlement (*"Une résidence de Français,"* Butel, 2002, p. 26) on the island of St. Christophe. The charter for this colony had three aims: religious, political, and economic. To elaborate, the first was spreading the Roman Catholic faith among the Caribs; the second was claiming the island (and any others they found) for the King of France; and the third was gathering and trading goods, as well as growing tobacco and other crops for profit. Realizing these aims required *inhabiting* the island, literally, establishing the *habit* of occupation, thus generating specific French terminology to describe their group identity and draw distinctions between mainland France and the colonies (i.e., *Habitation, habitués, habitants, vieux habitants*; Petitjean Roget, 1980). This first French settlement in St. Christophe became the "nursery" of all future French colonization in the Caribbean.

Colonization of St. Christophe

D'Esnambuc recruited some 300 men from the northern seaport of Le Havre, and du Roissey enlisted about 200 in the northwestern port of Brittany; they arrived in the spring of 1627 to settle St. Christophe (Crouse, 1940; Butel, 2002; Boucher, 2008). Most of these recruits left France in search of better prospects; some were seeking fortune and adventure, others merely looking for work to pay off debtors, and yet others looked for upward mobility and land ownership.

Challenges for the Pioneer Colonists

In general, these prospective settlers were not seafarers and were thus unprepared for the rigors of such a protracted ocean journey (Tapié, 1975; Petitjean Roget, 1980), which was merely the beginning of many challenges for the fledgling colonial effort. Insufficient provisions, sickness during the voyage resulting in attrition of almost half by the time they landed, and the care needed by remaining settlers to survive hampered the early phase of settlement. The impact of the voyage across the Atlantic on many settlers is captured poignantly in Garraway's (2005) haunting description:

> Divorced from all social reality outside the ship itself, and traveling in a timeless, unending ocean toward an unknown world, the travelers experience a loss of all boundaries— between life and death, sanity and insanity, health and sickness, rich and poor, noble and non-noble. Oscillating uncontrollably between fear of death and delusions of grandeur, they feign illness, hallucinate, and perform rituals of social travesty, reimagining themselves as royalty. (p. 125)

In Chapter 1, the impact of the journey to Martinique on the subsequent cultural evolution of various groups was mentioned. Clearly, the distance, hardships, and length of the voyage affected all migrants to Martinique to different extents and in different ways. Based on available accounts, we can surmise that, for the most part, the more grueling and hazardous the conditions of emigration from their homeland, the stronger the resilience and social bonds grew among that emigrant group. For French engagés, the tradition of *matelotage*, or the bond between shipmates, was a solid foundation for developing colonial society in Martinique. When an engagé finished the term of his contract, he would often pool resources with another former engagé, purchase a plot of land to cultivate, and hire other indentured workers (or even buy slaves). This tradition had such social standing that in some cases it was deemed equivalent to the rights of wives to estates (Garraway, 2005).

The harsh environment with its tropical heat, rugged terrain, powerful hurricanes, venomous snakes, and deadly diseases took a devastating toll on the early settlers. The colonists' discovery of how tobacco cultivation depletes the soil posed another hurdle (Boucher, 2008), ultimately prompting them to eye larger islands and the production of other crops (i.e. sugar), which was a transformative phase of the French colonial economy. To further complicate matters, the Company of St. Christophe was incapable of providing timely resupplies of food, men, and other reinforcements. Any reinforcements that came were modest, and in one instance, tragic. One account describes that a resupply ship from France with about 600 men disembarked in St. Christophe, with the majority severely ill and exhausted from the difficult journey. Some survived, but about 30 were left to die on the beaches, only to be devoured by land crabs (Butel, 2002). Both du Roissey in 1627 and d'Esnambuc in 1629 had to return to France to plead for more assistance. Labor shortages hampered the pioneer colonists throughout this intermediate period, in stark contrast to the English colonists who were better organized and supported. Between the start of the French colony on St. Christophe in 1627 and that of Martinique and Guadeloupe in 1635, there were fewer than 2,000 French colonists in all; the English numbered more than 5,000 on St. Christophe alone (Butel, 2002).

Thus, undependable supplies of goods and labor, compounded by challenging conditions of the new environment, proved unprofitable for the Company of St. Christophe, whose financiers gradually distanced themselves from the colony. This compelled desperate settlers to trade illegally with the Dutch in order to survive, and also left them vulnerable to attacks from the Spanish navy, which was still powerful in the region (Crouse, 1940; Boucher, 2008). It became clear to Richelieu and d'Esnambuc that more people and resources were needed to capitalize on the opportunities that the islands presented (Petitjean Roget, 1980). France's foray into mercantilism in the Caribbean was off to a fitful start.

Learning to Adapt

Although this initial mission had difficulties from the outset, we need to mention two factors that aided d'Esnambuc and the colonists in coping with their hardships: strong relations with the Englishman Thomas Warner (who had established a small settlement there) and with the Caribs. The daily survival lessons learned from the Caribs, and the hospitality and assistance provided by Warner, served as lifelines that prevented d'Esnambuc and his men from perishing. The steadfast respect established between d'Esnambuc and Warner led to a mutually beneficial arrangement unusual in its extent of cooperation. The treaties drawn up by these two even specified that hostilities between their respective sovereigns would not be cause for conflict between them, an arrangement seldom seen in this era (Crouse, 1940, Butel, 2002). And even though a major part of d'Esnambuc's and Warner's collaboration was fighting off the Caribs, they both learned that pursuing more amicable relations with the indigenous people was more productive in the long run. Working hard to develop constructive interactions with the Caribs and benefiting from their knowledge of the environment were crucial in cultural hybridization, helping to set the foundation for a successful colony. As Butel (2002) notes,

> Thus, the colonization of St. Christophe served as an apprenticeship. The pioneers learned from the Indians some useful lessons regarding housing, food, hunting and most importantly, navigating the islands. St. Christophe became the base of operations for colonists' migration to the other islands of the Antilles.[9] (p. 27)

Furthermore, St. Christophe appears to have provided an early blueprint for a new system of social hierarchy: the plantation society that served as the backbone of the French colonial enterprise for the next two centuries. Plantation society was based on amassing wealth from land ownership, use of hired migrant labor from France, and the production and sale of tobacco and other goods. The pioneer colonists returned frequently to the Netherlands, England, and France, not only to sell their products, but also to bring back more engagés (contracted labor) from the French countryside to work their fields in St. Christophe. They were brought (sometimes under deceptive pretexts) for a contractual period of three years. At the end of that period, some engagés extended their contract while some chose to return to France; in other instances, they were granted plots of land or purchased their own. Former engagés who became landowners and successfully turned a profit sought more land and more labor, so the cycle repeated itself, creating additional layers of hierarchy in the nascent colonial society of St. Christophe (Petitjean Roget, 1980).

Although the Company of St. Christophe with its first French settlement was mostly a failure, the lessons learned from its travails were not lost on Cardinal Richelieu, nor was the potential profitability

---

[9] *Enfin un apprentissage de la colonization se fit à Saint-Christophe. Ses pionniers y reçurent des Indiens d'utiles leçons sur le logement, la nourriture, la chasse et surtout la navigation à pratiquer aux îles. La colonie fut une base de migration des colons vers les autres Antilles.*

of the colonial enterprise. In February 1635, seeking to reinvigorate the ailing company, Richelieu prevailed on Louis XIII to authorize a new venture, the **Company of the Isles of America**. This new incarnation offered greater funding and autonomy to its financiers, Richelieu again principal among them. The new company's objectives were to expand France's colonial ambitions to other islands in the Lesser Antilles by shipping at least 4,000 Catholics within a 20-year period to the region. In the company's charter the French word *"colonies"* is used for the first time, replacing the more generic term "islands" (Butel, 2002). The beginnings of French assimilation policies can be seen in the renewed emphasis on converting indigenous people to Catholicism and in ensuring that all settlers were French and Catholic (Crouse, 1940; Petijtean Roget, 1980).

Colonization of Martinique

The early settlement phase of Martinique (1635-1660) saw three milestones in French Caribbean history: the shift from tobacco to sugar production, permanent banishment of the Caribs to the islands of St. Vincent and Dominica, and the advent of slavery. The same year the Company of the Isles of America was founded, Liénart de l'Olive and Jean du Plessis, two experienced adventurers who had spent time in St. Christophe, were commissioned by Richelieu to colonize Martinique, Dominica, or Guadeloupe (Butel, 2002). They landed on Martinique in June 1635, claiming it for Louis XIII at a site midway between present-day St. Pierre and Fort de France. Four Dominican friars, who accompanied l'Olive and du Plessis on this expedition, officiated at the planting of the cross. These four friars, Pierre Pelican, Nicolas Bréchet, Pierre Gryphon, and the distinguished linguist Raymond Breton, were sent expressly to spread the Catholic religion.

Deciding that Martinique was not ideal for colonization

because of its mountainous terrain, they continued to Guadeloupe and proceeded to settle there. D'Esnambuc was displeased that, despite his being named Governor General of St. Christophe and future colonies by the king, the company entrusted l'Olive and du Plessis with this new colonial mission. Thus, d'Esnambuc set out to claim and colonize Martinique under his own aegis (Crouse, 1940; Butel, 2002). On September 1, 1635 Captain d'Esnambuc landed on Martinique at the Roxelane River, just north of present-day St. Pierre. On September 15, 1635, he formally annexed Martinique in the name of the King of France (Delphin & Roth, 2009). The care taken by d'Esnambuc in selecting his crew and provisions, as well as his leadership, helped ensure a smoother and swifter path to successful development of Martinique as a colony than St. Christophe in 1627.

D'Esnambuc's experience in the Caribbean, specifically in St. Christophe, gave him keen insight into life on the islands, and his shrewd political instincts were evident in a letter he sent to Cardinal Richelieu a couple of months after he took possession of Martinique. He wrote of having stationed some 150 men in Martinique, which he felt offered a strategic advantage over the Spanish, with whom Louis XIII had declared war in May 1635. D'Esnambuc also informed Richelieu of his plan to occupy the island of Dominica to keep the English from overrunning the French in the Caribbean (Petitjean Roget, 1980). He appeared to select men familiar with the climate (though not all) and the work involved in tropical tobacco cultivation. As added insurance, most settlers were either related to d'Esnambuc or had a bond of loyalty to one another. These seasoned colonists shared the goal of building a successful colony in Martinique and a common understanding of how to do it (Boucher, 2008; Petitjean Roget, 1980).

D'Esnambuc outfitted his ships with provisions that readily enabled his settlers to feed and shelter themselves while they established cash crops. From the lessons learned in St. Christophe, he chose to pursue a policy of peaceful engagement with the Caribs whenever possible, with minimal or no encroachment on their lands. This policy continued in Martinique until 1649, long after D'Esnambuc's death (Petitjean Roget, 1980). Unfortunately, d'Esnambuc did not live to see the full flourishing of his project in Martinique, as he died late in 1636. By 1637, the Company of the Isles of America, realizing the need for proper capitalization of their project in order for success, authorized women, arms, and a cannon to be sent from France to fortify the colony of Martinique (Petijean Roget, 1980).

Ousting the Caribs

Shortly before d'Esnambuc's death, he appointed his nephew Jacques Dyel du Parquet governor of Martinique, who continued the policy of peaceful cohabitation with the Caribs and negotiated demarcation of the French and Carib territories, which the French observed during the early years of the colony (Boucher, 2008). The French occupied the western part of the island (the Caribbean side) and the Caribs the eastern part (the Atlantic side). The Jesuit missionaries settled along the boundary (Petitjean Roget, 1980). Because the northeastern side of Martinique was closest to Europe, French ships disembarked there first. The greater convenience of docking in the area the French called **Capesterre** made this Atlantic side of the island, a Carib domain, an area the colonists probably coveted.

Many examples of cultural reciprocity between the Caribs and the French began to be documented at this time. For example, during his governorship and subsequent proprietorship of Martinique,[10] du Parquet is noted to have adopted Carib adornments and hairstyles

[10] Because of serious losses, directors of the Company of the Isles of America started to liquidate their assets in 1649, selling them to the governors of their colonial possessions and anyone else willing to purchase them. Du Parquet then bought Martinique as well as the islands of St. Lucia, Grenada, and the Grenadines in 1650 (Crouse, 1940).

when meeting with them, and Carib chieftains would don European hats or other such clothing when calling on French officials (Boucher, 2008). The following account from the missionary Maurile de St. Michel speaks further to how the early French settlers adapted their eating habits to the new environment:

> Here, instead of bread made from wheat, we eat bread made from the cassava plant, which is very common and abundant. Instead of beef, we eat lamentin [the manatee], which is a sort of sea cow caught along the shore. Instead of chicken, we eat lizards, from which a very good soup is made.... (Roberts, 1942, p. 40)

Other examples of adaptation were the influence of French and Spanish on terms in the Carib language noted in Chapter 2, and Carib words that were adopted by the French, such as buccaneer (*boucanier*) and hurricane (*ouragan*; Garraway, 2005). A majority of the names for trees and plants in Martinique are derived from the Carib language, even though most are not native to the island (Confiant, personal communication, March 17, 2014). Du Parquet's fair treatment and cultural understanding of the Caribs was highlighted by many chroniclers of the period. Upon his death in 1658, the outpouring of affection and grief from all three communities, the Caribs, French colonists, and enslaved Africans, was said to be remarkable (Butel, 2002).

Relations between the Caribs and the French were not uniformly tranquil, however. As is common in most intergroup encounters, Carib responses to the French may have been influenced by past interactions with other Europeans or by what they heard about Europeans from other Caribs.[11] Du Parquet shared his uncle's approach to the Caribs:

---

[11] There was extensive communication and contact among bands of Caribs on all the islands of the Lesser Antilles, as discussed in Chapter 2.

initial cooperation and friendliness backed with decisive military strength. He had similar results as well: periods of largely peaceful interactions punctuated by occasional clashes. The fear engendered by these shows of force, and the attitude of cooperation and coexistence that d'Esnambuc and du Parquet encouraged, probably went a long way to foster greater stability of intergroup relations in Martinique than most colonies. Nonetheless, significant clashes with the Caribs took place in 1654 and 1657, primarily due to the colonists' *"faim de terres,"* or hunger for land, that led them to occupy the neighboring islands of Grenada and St. Lucia (Butel, 2002). After du Parquet's death in 1658, tensions appear to have flared between the Caribs, wealthy colonists, and leadership in Martinique (Boucher, 2008).

Discontent was also brewing among the colonists, many of whom had by this point accumulated wealth and power. Not surprisingly, resentment over taxes and fees that du Parquet implemented became a point of contention. When he became proprietor of Martinique in 1650, it was no longer possible to deflect anger at taxation onto the company. Following his death, du Parquet's wife, Marie, became the acting governor of a Martinique in turmoil. Powerful colonists rebelled and vied for control of Martinique's government and affairs. Some organized along regional factions, either siding with associates of du Parquet, primarily from Normandy, or aligning with the entourage of Mme. du Parquet from Paris (Butel, 2002), while others saw the opportunity to open hostilities against the Caribs, with an eye toward occupying the strategic Carib stronghold of Capesterre on the Atlantic side.

A subsequent decision by the **Colonial Council of Martinique,** under the leadership of Madame du Parquet, to declare war on the Caribs in 1658 struck a final blow to Carib attempts to remain in Martinique. By the spring of 1660, a treaty was negotiated by the French and British Caribbean governors (with assistance from two missionaries), whereby the roughly 6,000 Caribs would be confined to the islands of St. Vincent and Dominica, and the rest of the Lesser Antilles would be divided between the French and British (Crouse, 1940; Peabody, 2002).

The position of host community held by the Caribs was involuntarily ceded to the French, and the cultural space left by the Caribs was rapidly filled by the next wave of newcomers to Martinique, enslaved Africans. Nevertheless, as Confiant points out about the Caribs, "they have disappeared but have left something for us," including a small but important linguistic legacy and their knowledge of the islands (Confiant, personal communication, March 17, 2014).

The Shift to Sugar

Before colonization of Martinique, tobacco prices had been slipping; tobacco from St. Christophe was sold at 10 *livre tournois* (or l.t., a currency that preceded the franc) per pound in 1629, 1.2 l.t. per pound in 1635, and less than .2 l.t. per pound toward the end of 1639 (Butel, 2002). Engagés hired to work on the plantations for a 36-month term were unable to pay for their return journeys and so renewed their contracts to work the fields for another three years. The problem of falling tobacco prices became severe enough to warrant an injunction in St. Christophe by 1639 to forego planting tobacco for a year (also because of soil depletion caused by tobacco cultivation), and instead plant coffee, cotton, indigo, *roucou* (red coloring derived from seeds of tropical *achiote* trees), and other food crops (Butel, 2002).

Although injunctions such as this spread across the Lesser Antilles fairly quickly, few planters heeded them, and many continued illegal tobacco trade with the Dutch. Tobacco was the primary cash crop in Martinique, Guadeloupe, and St. Christophe until 1642. Despite the colonists' reluctance to abandon tobacco as a cash crop, there is evidence of considerable interest in sugar for some time before it became the major industry in the Caribbean; in 1635, when Du Plessis and L'Olive were commissioned by the Company of the Isles of America to colonize Martinique, Guadeloupe, or Dominica, one of their charges was to cultivate cotton and sugar (Petitjean Roget, 1980). Thus, awareness that sugar was the future of prosperity was at the forefront of the minds of the governors of the French colonies even in the 1630s (Crouse, 1940).

Disappointed with its tobacco revenues, the company turned toward the Dutch sugar enterprise and attempted to hop on the sugar train (Petitjean Roget, 1980). Well aware that unlike tobacco production, which required "a relatively modest investment; *un investissement relativement modeste,"* (Butel, 2002, p.38) sugar production required ample machinery and labor, the Company of the Isles of America in 1643 authorized the purchase and delivery of 60 enslaved Africans to Guadeloupe to cultivate cane for sugar production. Soon, the wealthy inhabitants of Martinique, including colonists, several filibustiers, and even missionaries embarked on developing plantations for the potentially lucrative production of sugar for European markets ("Patrimoine de la Martinique," 2014).

Throughout the 1640s, French colonists were dilettantes of sugar production; the word *"sucrerie,"* or sugar mill, appeared in the correspondence of early chroniclers for the first time in 1648 (Petitjean Roget, 1980). There is evidence of a sugar mill located to the north of Saint Pierre in Martinique as early as 1652; about 30 slaves were employed in this operation, which was run by the Jesuits. However, in 1654 the serendipitous arrival in Guadeloupe of Dutch refugees from Brazil, who had mastered the art of refining sugar, was a turning point. At roughly the same time, a 642-acre plantation owned by the Du Parquet family in St. Pierre was operating a sugar mill with slave labor. Although the end of tobacco culture and the rise of sugar culture was apparent, tobacco, once the king of crops in Martinique, thrived as late as 1671; that year there were 264 tobacco plantations versus 232 sugar plantations and refineries (Crouse, 1940; Butel, 2002).

Advent of Slavery

The use of enslaved African laborers existed as early as the late 1400s; the Portuguese used enslaved Africans on sugar plantations in Cape Verde, the Azores, Sao Tome, etc. along the West African coast. The earliest mention of enslaved Africans in the French Caribbean predates France's first colony in St. Christophe in 1627. D'Esnambuc on his voyage in 1625 mentions that the English and a few French living in St. Christophe were using slave labor for tobacco cultivation. The 40 or so enslaved Africans, probably acquired from Spaniards, are the first known French-owned enslaved Africans in the Caribbean (Munford, 1986).

There are several reasons why France did not enter the slave trade as early as the English, who preceded them by almost three generations (Ferguson, 2008). The use of slaves in French colonies was hampered by an ancient ordinance by Louis X in 1315 granting freedom from servitude to anyone "...throughout our kingdom... at good and suitable conditions" (Peabody, 1996, p. 28). Although the ordinance makes no specific mention of Africans, it was interpreted along those lines. Chroniclers during this period, such as Labat, reported that an official authorization for slaves in the colonies was granted in 1638 by Louis XIII with the intention of converting enslaved Africans to Christianity. There is no clear consensus among scholars on the authenticity of this report. (Miller, 2008).

Additionally, the use of indentured workers to work the land in the New World was already established. The Company of the Isles of America was considerably ahead of its contracted population growth of 4,000 Catholics in a 20-year period on all the islands (there were already 7,000 by 1642; Petitjean Roget, 1980). Prior to his death in December 1642, Richelieu had Louis XIII authorize more privileges and power for the company in a final show of fidelity for the venture that he founded and supported. The directors of the company could then offer better incentives to attract more colonists to the islands; anyone who developed land on the islands with at least 50 men for a period of two years would be granted nobility (Garraway, 2005).

Despite the change in the French ordinance discussed above or the incentives offered to the French to settle in the colonies, the need for more labor was a continual issue. Because of the planters' need for more land for cultivation, combined with labor-intensive requirements of the sugar economy, the colonies were pushed to consider using enslaved labor from Africa. So it was in the 1640s that the enslaved Africans gradually started to replace the engagés from France.

According to the 17th century missionary Father Pelleprat, enslaved Africans were brought from Angola, Cape Verde, Guinea, Senegal, and neighboring regions (Petitjean Roget, 1980). It must be noted that identification of specific countries by name in Africa by early chroniclers in most cases do not refer to present-day boundaries but to the general region from the western coast of Africa to West Central Africa. There is more agreement among recent scholars on specific ports of the slave trade. Geggus (2000) states that the port of Whydah, in Benin, and the West Central African ports of Malembo, Cabinda, and Loango were the most active in the French slave trade of the 1800s. Enslaved Africans were not from the same ethnic backgrounds, and they spoke about a dozen different languages. The influx of slave labor was great, and by the 1660 census in Martinique, there were 2,580 people of French or European descent, along with 2,683 Africans, gens de couleur and Caribs, a total of 5,263 individuals (Petitjean Roget, 1980).

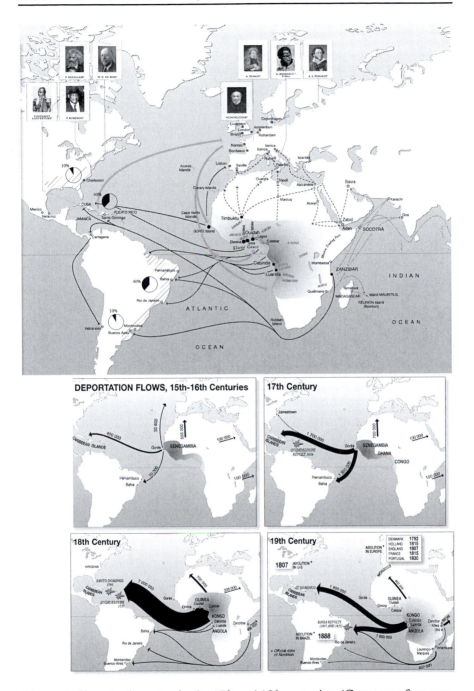

Figure 6. Slave trade routes in the 17th and 18th centuries. (Courtesy of unesco. org/culture.)

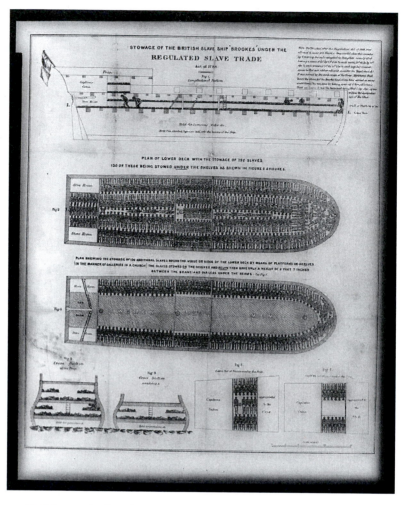

Figure 7. Schematic drawing of a British slave ship in the 1880s. (Courtesy of the Library of Congress, Washington, DC.)

The increased numbers of enslaved Africans and the brutality of the slave system contributed to increases in their escape or rebellion. In Simone Schwarz-Bart's novel *The Bridge of Beyond,* Ma Cia offers the following gut-wrenching analogy to describe a slave: "If you want to see a slave, you've only to go down to the market at Pointe-à-Pitre and look at the poultry in the cages, tied up, and at the terror in their eyes" (Schwarz-Bart, 2013, p. 54). Not surprisingly, some enslaved

Africans ran away the moment they disembarked, with the false hope of returning home; others ran away later to escape harsh treatment (Petitjean Roget, 1980).

Alliances between *marrons,* a term for runaway enslaved Africans, and Caribs were common and quite powerful in Martinique during the 1650s, with one uprising requiring help from the Dutch to prevent the seizing of du Parquet's compound and overrunning the colony (Boucher, 2008). The marrons were an important cultural force throughout slavery in Martinique and beyond. The art of drumming, for example, very evident in Martinique today, was not only a form of musical expression among the enslaved, but also of communication for marrons (Delphin and Roth, 2009). The expulsion of the Caribs by the end of the decade did not end slave escapes or revolts, which continued throughout the era of slavery (Savage, 2007), with ebbs and flows along the way.

Creole as a "Language of Compromise"[12]

Because the French language as we know it was not uniform across France in the 17th century, the flibustiers and French pioneers of the 1620s who settled in St. Christophe and later in Martinique and Guadeloupe spoke a variety of dialects. Those from Normandy spoke *Normand,* those from Vendée spoke *Vendéen,* those from Poitou spoke *Poitevin,* and those from the Paris region spoke *Francien* (Confiant, 2009). It was only after Cardinal Richelieu established the French Academy in 1635 (Tapie, 1975) that French began to be standardized. Similarly, enslaved Africans came from more than two dozen ethnic groups with distinct languages, including *Fons, Ibos, Haoussas, Aguas, Mina, Mesurade, Cangas, Bambaras, Senegalese,* and *Youlof,* to name a few (Delphin & Roth, 2009, p. 21).

---

[12] Confiant, personal communication, March 17, 2013.

The lack of uniformity in the French language may account for the early colonizers' failure to impose French on their slaves. The lack of mutual understanding underscored the need for a *lingua franca,* that is, Creole, given the disparity of African languages. Conversely, the uniformity of Spanish, which had a standard grammar and orthography by 1492, might account for the successful imposition of Spanish and the lack of a need to create a lingua franca in the Spanish colonies (Confiant, personal communication, March 17, 2014). As we have seen in Chapter 1, numerical superiority of a colonizing group also played a role in imposition of the colonizer's language and, by default, eliminated the need for a language of compromise. This was the case in almost all Spanish colonies.[13]

As Confiant notes, "Thus, Creole evolved out of an urgent need to communicate"[14]   (Confiant, 2009, p. 1) among distinct ethnolinguistic groups who had to coexist, an adaptation by both the French and Africans. In addition, the adaptations and contributions of the Caribs to Creole language before they were ousted from Martinique should not be overlooked. A precursor to Creole, *baragouin,* was observed to have been spoken around 1640 as noted in Chapter 2; this corresponds to the period of 1620-1670 (the initial settlement of slaves) that Raphaël Confiant assigns to the development of Creole. The development of a lingua franca in this relatively brief time suggests the press for communication felt among these three groups (Confiant, 2009). It is worth noting that Creole is a vital common bond between individuals of French and African descent in Martinique to this day.

With the arrival of larger numbers of Africans, thanks to the success of the sugar market in Europe, this baragouin would

---

[13] With the exception of palenquero, a Spanish-based Creole developed in a small, isolated community of runaway slaves in Palenque de San Basilio, Colombia (Bernabé, 2013).

[14] *Le Créole est donc né d'une urgence communicative.*

transform into a real language, Creole, which would become the principal language of the first generation of White and Black children born in the Antilles.[15] (Etienne, 2003, para. 4)

Thus contemporary Creole is considered a "White and Black" language. In fact, the first Creole literature, a poem, *"Lisette quitté la plaine,"* was written in 1754 by Duvivier de la Mahautiere, a White planter from **Saint Domingue**, now Haiti (Confiant, 2009, part 2, para. 1). Slaves were not allowed to be literate, and the first Black writers of Creole literature emerged in the 20th century (Confiant, personal communication, March 17, 2014). A closer examination of the circumstances of Creole's emergence sheds light on its sociolinguistic role.

The sugar economy and development of the plantation society significantly affected both French and Creole, with each language acquiring different connotations and functions for the French and the enslaved Africans over time because of their different roles in the social structure. As French settlers became more prosperous, moving from being engagés and pioneers to wealthy *colons* (colonizers) and *békés* (plantation owners), the value of Creole in their eyes diminished and the superiority of French language and culture grew. Békés even went to the trouble of importing tutors from France so that their children learned Parisian French. They denigrated Creole as the "patois" or "jargon" of slaves, even though it was initially developed by the French as well. The aversion of the békés to Creole seems hypocritical, given that they spoke it among themselves.

Conclusion

---

[15] *Avec l'arrivée de plus en plus massive d'Africains, suite au succès de la commercialisation du sucre en Europe, ce baragouin va se transformer en une véritable langue, le créole, qui sera la langue de la toute première génération d'enfants blancs et noirs né aux Antilles.*

French colonizers arrived in Martinique in 1635 and within 10 years became a small established community that derived its economic, political, and cultural strength from France, creating the dominant host community (albeit an inhospitable one). This period also witnessed the development of Creole as the bridge of communication among the French, Caribs, and Africans. To buttress their nascent sugar enterprise, French colonizers forcibly enslaved Africans and brought them to Martinique, making them the subordinate newcomers. This intermediate phase (1627-1660) of the French presence in the Caribbean is evidence of the growing pains of the fledgling French settlements in St. Christophe, Guadeloupe, and Martinique. This period was punctuated by several significant developments in France and the Caribbean, most notably the deaths of Cardinal Richelieu and Louis XIII, the expansion of the slave trade, and the displacement of the original host community, the Caribs. Henceforth, the French colonial enterprise was epitomized by the rising supremacy of sugar and slave labor.

The public and private partnerships of the Company of St. Christophe and the Company of the Isles of America under Louis XIII and Richelieu failed because of the expense of administering the colonies. Subsequently, each colony was sold to the governors and their associates, with the monarchy retaining control. Louis XIV and his Minister of Finance Jean-Baptiste Colbert then shepherded the transition to the next stage of royal involvement with colonization, of which more is said later.

The mid-17th century also witnessed dramatic changes in the intergroup dynamics of ethnic groups on these islands and the emergence of new cultural group identities. The French supplanting the Caribs as the dominant host community, with enslaved Africans forced into the role of subordinate newcomers, defined the sociocultural dynamics of Martinique for the next two centuries. Accordingly, the issue of how the French managed to maintain control for so long is extremely relevant. The following chapter delves into the development of plantations and laws to regulate the lives of the enslaved, which were the rudders that steered the colonial society of Martinique.

Glossary

Company of St. Christophe - (French, *"Compagnie de Saint-Christophe"*) Enterprise of French adventurers to exploit the island of St. Christophe, now St. Kitts and Nevis.

engagés - (French) Contracted or hired labor.

flibustier - (From Dutch *vrijbuiter*, "freebooter") French term for sea adventurers; the Dutch term was *zeerovers* ("sea rovers"); the Spanish was *corsarios* ("corsairs").

Dutch West Indies Company - Founded in 1621 to wage economic war against Spain and Portugal by competing with their colonies in the West Indies and South America and on the west coast of Africa.

matelotage - (From French *matelot*, "sailor") Bond between shipmates, sometimes developing into an informal agreement between indentured workers in Martinique to share the cost of buying land or a business and the profits.

Company of the Isles of America - (French, *"Compagnie des Îles de l'Amérique"*) French company that in 1635 assumed administration of the French portion of St. Christophe from the Compagnie de Saint-Christophe; also directed to colonize other islands.

Capesterre - (French) Term used by early French settlers to describe the Northeastern or Atlantic side of Martinique or any Caribbean island.

Colonial Council of Martinique - Locally elected governing body of

Martinique.

livre tournois - (French) A gold coin; a French unit of currency from the Middle Ages.

sucrerie - (French) Sugar refinery.

marrons - (French) Runaway slaves who banded together in remote areas of the tropical forest.

colon - (French) Individual who leaves his homeland to settle and exploit a colony.

békés - (French) White plantation owners, or descendants of White planters. The term may come from the word *"béquet"* in Normand dialect, meaning a young billy goat, or have a West African source meaning "red man," or be derived from the French command *"bechez"* ("dig!").

Saint Domingue - French name for their portion of the island the Spanish named Hispaniola; it was renamed Haiti following the slave revolution leading to independence in 1804.

Reflective Questions

1. How did the relationship between d'Esnambuc and Cardinal Richelieu shape French colonization efforts? Discuss the social conditions in the Caribbean and France that formed the context for their relationship.

2. How did the lessons learned in St. Christophe inform Martinique's successful colonization? Discuss the roles of the English settlers and Caribs in the framework of cultural reciprocity.

3. Discuss the development of the new social hierarchy in St. Christophe and Martinique and its impact on cultural narratives and group identities.

4. Discuss factors involved in the deterioration of French-Carib relations leading to the exile of the Caribs from Martinique.

5. Analyze the repercussions of the rise in importance of sugar in Martinique on relations with mainland France.

6. In what ways is Creole an example of reciprocal adaptation of cultural narratives among the Caribs, French, and Africans?

Chapter 4

The Architecture of Dominance
Systems of Social Control

They [slaves] worked in bondage, they sang to console themselves,
they discussed, they had disputes, they shared love, they had dreams,
in short they lived in creole and only in creole…
from an instrument of communication,
this language became an unavoidable identity support.[16]

—Jean Bernabé
Professor Emeritus of Linguistics and Creole
Director of GEREC-F, University of the French West Indies Martinique

By the end of the 17[th]century, with the Carib presence all but effaced, the number of enslaved Africans rising, and the sociocultural and economic dominance of the French established, Martinique witnessed a momentous development: creolization. To reiterate from Chapter 1, by creolization we mean cultural hybridization in the context of involuntary migration or slavery. Enslaved Africans may have outnumbered French colonists for most of Martinique's history, but social instruments such as the *Code Noir* and the *Habitation* system, in addition to 200 years of mostly uninterrupted presence in Martinique (Britain occupied the island for brief periods), allowed France to cultivate a landscape dominated by her cultural and political will. This extensive period of contact with the French, and

---

[16] *"…on travaillait sous le joug, on chantait pour se consoler, on discutait, on se disputait, on se révoltait, on aimait, on rêvait, bref, on vivait en créole et seulement en créole… d'instrument de communication, cette langue est devenue aussi pour eux [the slaves] un incontournable support identitaire"* (Bernabé, 2013, p. 31).

their deliberate suppression of African languages and customs, had a calamitous impact on the Africans' ability to preserve their cultures. Assimilation to French language, religion, and other aspects of culture by the African community was inescapable, thereby suppressing their ethnic identities. Scholars in contemporary Martinique describe the effects of this assimilation: "It is a terrible condition to perceive one's interior architecture, one's world, the instants of one's days, one's own values, with the eyes of the other" (Bernabè, Chamoiseau, Confiant, & Khyar, 1990; p. 886).

The formidable travails of enslaved Africans and the development of the dominant French social, economic, and political structures in Martinique from the latter part of the 17th century through the 18th century are the focus of this chapter. A brief examination of the roles of the French monarchy (Louis XIV, the Sun King) and Minister of Finance Colbert are a good starting point in understanding how colonial policies were reframed during this period. Aspects of sugar production that stimulated the brutal and complex system of the slave trade from West Africa are also investigated. The birth of a White **Plantocracy** with its forceful imposition of Catholicism and French ways of daily life on the enslaved created a stark hierarchy: an elite powerful minority and a subjugated majority in bondage.

From Private to State Control

Although the Company of the Isles of America learned from the mistakes of its predecessors, it apparently did not learn enough. The financial drain continued, and by 1649 the directors saw the need to liquidate their holdings in order to recover their investments. Each colony was offered for sale to its respective governors or anyone willing to buy it (usually associates or family members of the governors). Starting with the purchase of Martinique from the company in 1650 until his death in 1658, Jacques Dyel du Parquet was owner-governor of Martinique. Dissension among elite planters, which had been simmering for some time, came to a boil with du Parquet's passing. Combined with Carib conflicts and slave revolts and escapes, political infighting was making Martinique unstable as well as dimming its bright promise of profitability (Boucher, 2008).

The most successful of the French colonies thus far, Martinique's woes received the attention of Louis XIV and his Minister of Finance Jean-Baptiste Colbert. There was the further problem of Dutch traders in Martinique and elsewhere who siphoned profits away from France. To address these deficiencies and chaotic colonial administration in Martinique and the other Caribbean colonies, the **French West India Company** was created under the auspices of Louis XIV in 1664, which purchased all colonies back from their private proprietors (Crouse, 1940). This buyback program, not without resistance from the owners, was eventually completed. In 10 years, the company and its assets (i.e., the colonies as a whole) would be rendered unto the king. This change, though significant, seemed to merely add administrators to the colonies and reconfigure their authority (Munford, 1986). A noteworthy motif constant through this change of ownership was the Plantocracy's rebelliousness and attempts for independence from the mainland; it can be argued that this iconoclastic streak was and is a core element of Martinican planters' identity, with traces remaining to the present.

Expansion of the Slave Trade in the 17ᵗʰ Century

The West India Company of 1664 was also charged with supplying slaves to the French colonies. Over the next 20 years, the company went through several iterations to meet the growing demand for slaves in the colonies. Most company ships were outfitted and authorized to transport 1,000 slaves per year to the colonies. For example, in 1685 the shipping company *La Compagnie de Guinée* (managed by Colbert's son) had the sole right of transporting slaves from that region in Africa and, as Riddell (1925) states, the company was compensated "...thirty *livres*...for every Negro from Guinea" (... *pour chacune tête de Nègre de Guinée*, p. 322). Ultimately, the need for slaves was so great that these state-sponsored ventures in the slave trade were not sufficient for planters in Martinique. During this period, the consistent involvement of the Dutch West India Company and other illegal Dutch and French merchants proliferated to fill this need; the actual number of slaves transported to the colonies sometimes exceeded the official quota by 40%, demonstrating the robust illegal slave trade (Thomas, 1997). Below is a discussion of how the sugar industry facilitated this explosion in slave labor and the establishment of the plantation society.

The dynamics of sugar production, from growing cane to harvesting and processing, determined the design of the Habitation, or plantation system, in Martinique (of which more is said later) and expansion of the French slave trade. Cultivation of sugar cane required far more land than tobacco because cane, once harvested, begins to deteriorate quickly in no more than a few hours, providing a smaller yield. Thus plantings had to be staggered, requiring multiple fields in various stages of production (Tomich, 1990b; "Patrimoine de la Martinique," 2014). Besides, manufacturing sugar was labor intensive, requiring many people to coordinate their work precisely for a profitable outcome. This may partly explain why sugar production had a comparatively late start in Martinique.

When d'Esnambuc and his entourage of seasoned habitants from St. Christophe arrived in Martinique in 1635, they brought their experience with tobacco cultivation and trade and made it the primary cash crop until 1670. The advantage of tobacco as a cash crop was its scalability; both small and large farms could be profitable with minimal investment of capital other than labor (Singler, 1995), unlike sugar plantations, which must be large for profitability. There was nevertheless a major role for slave labor in tobacco production in Martinique. Petitjean Roget (1980) points out that between 1639 and 1640 there is evidence of 300 enslaved Africans and 700 Whites in Martinique. However, this proportion is quite substantial, considering that the slave trade was not fully established at this time. This was probably one of the only periods in Martinique's history when Whites outnumbered Africans.

During early colonization and before the start of the slave trade, the engagés, or contracted labor from France, were the only labor force, besides the Caribs. Estimates show that 15,000 to 20,000 engagés came to the Caribbean from France between 1620-1660; about 20% were skilled tradesmen, and the majority were laborers (Boucher, 2008). Despite their large numbers, they did not fare nearly as well as a labor force compared with enslaved Africans. The latter were a precious commodity at the start of the slave trade (prior to 1643), but became more obtainable and affordable. In his 1640 visit to Martinique, Jesuit Jacques Bouton is imputed to have remarked on the superior return on investment by enslaved Africans, compared with French indentured workers (Peabody, 2004). Hiring engagés from France became an expensive proposition. As noted in Chapter 3, many had difficulty coping with the unforgiving tropical environment and working conditions, perishing before the end of their contracted terms. Furthermore, the contracted term was not long enough to maintain enough workers experienced in sugar production, forcing planters to train each cohort of new engagés. The harsh working conditions, disregard of contractual obligations by the planters, and low social standing resembles the plight of the Indian indentured workers who arrived in Martinique after the abolition of slavery. (A comprehensive discussion of Indian indentured workers follows in Chapter 7.)

Employers had the right to transfer or trade their engagés' contracts to another employer. This pattern of trading, selling, and leasing of workers, whether engagés from France, slaves from Africa, or indentured workers from India, was an important feature of the French colonial enterprise. At the end of their contracted period, some engagés renewed their contracts and continued working because they could not pay the return fare, or were in debt to the landowners (this phenomenon would repeat itself with Indian indentured workers). Many chose to return to France and some became flibustiers to seek their fortune. Yet others engaged in island hopping, either to explore opportunities elsewhere or settle in Carib communities (Riddell, 1925; Boucher, 2008).

As the need increased for large numbers of cheap, experienced laborers to work the sugar plantations, so did concerted efforts to increase human trafficking from Africa to the French Caribbean for permanent resettlement. As early as 1643, merchant ships left the French port of La Rochelle to engage in the slave trade. Within a span of approximately 20 years starting in 1670, 45 such expeditions were launched from La Rochelle; several other ports, such as St. Malo, Bordeaux, and Dieppe, engaged in similar operations (Thomas, 1997).

In 1660, sugar-producing colonists in Martinique, including Governor Du Parquet (who owned 161 slaves) and the Jesuits (who owned 30 on one of the first sugar plantations), used slave labor (Butel, 2002). Growth in the slave population was slow at first, but increased dramatically. People of African, Carib, and mixed descent in Martinique reached almost 52 % of the population in 1660 and rose to 61 % by 1670, even without large-scale sugar production (Singler, 1995). Of all the French colonies, Martinique witnessed the largest growth in the number of slaves toward the end of the 17th century, increasing from 7,000 in 1670 to 15,000 in 1700 (Butel, 2002).

In the early phase of this human trade, enslaved Africans were brought as couples or families. In contrast, most French pioneer colonists and engagés who settled Martinique and other parts of the Caribbean were male. The shortage of women on these islands became counterproductive to populating and establishing a colony. Several letters were sent by the early French settlers (1635-1642) imploring Richelieu to send women. In an attempt to remedy this imbalance, Richelieu is said to have shipped prostitutes and orphaned young girls to the islands (Confiant, personal communication, March 17, 2014).

By the 1700s, with the surge of the sugar industry in Martinique, opening of the human trade from the Guinea coast in 1716, and the increasing demand for able-bodied men, the male-female ratio of enslaved Africans was unbalanced. There were about 120-130 male to 100 female Africans in Martinique; greater gender balance does not appear to have been achieved until the latter half of the 18th century (Riddell, 1925; Gautier, 2000).

The need loomed large to both prepare slaves for plantation work and exert the social control necessary to keep them working, especially as their numbers in relation to the French ballooned. Designing social, linguistic, and economic structures to address these needs was an urgent task for the colonists. The development of Creole (as discussed in Chapter 3), the obligatory imposition of Catholicism and the Code Noir, and the carefully skillfully planned Habitation system all played critical roles in these designs.

Salvation and Slavery
A Peculiar Relationship

It is difficult to disentangle the goal of promoting Catholicism in the French colonial enterprise from that of promoting the growth of a plantation economy based on slave labor. France's civilizing and evangelical missions (*mission civilisatrice*) were strongly expressed as early as 1615 by Antoine de Montchrétien in his *Traité de l'économie politique* (Confer, 1964). Missionaries played an important role in colonization from the outset. Three **Capuchin** Friars were a part of France's first mission to St. Christophe in 1627 (Crouse, 1940). Evangelism was presented to Louis XIII and the investors of the Company of St. Christophe as a rationale for its creation and continued to be a pillar of the colonial enterprise until the 1750s. With the explicit goal of communicating the gospel, French clergy, primarily from the Dominican order but also Jesuits, were among the first to develop linguistic proficiency by teaching French to the enslaved Africans and learning their African dialects (Boucher, 2008). These attempts to bridge language barriers were important factors in the emergence of the Creole language.

Evangelical Audiences: Caribs and Africans

However central proselytizing was to the colonial enterprise, the enthusiasm of French missionaries for converting enslaved Africans was not as initially strong as their desire to convert the Caribs. Although both groups were seen as needing salvation, the missionaries believed that enslaved Africans, perceived as more backward, might benefit more, but unfortunately there was also a sense that Africans had a limited capability to understand Catholicism. Sue Peabody (2004) captures this attitude, documenting that many missionaries, including the renowned Du Tertre, began their work with convictions about the Africans' innate inferiority, ignorance, and suitability for slavery. The Caribs, however, were seen as more intelligent and worthy of embracing the Catholic faith.

As noted in Chapter 2, this positive impression of the Caribs was ultimately not supported by experience. The Caribs may have shown great interest in the trappings of Catholicism, but very few practiced the religion; as Peabody recounts from Du Tertre's historical volume, "...they will agree to be baptized for a knife, a shot of brandy, or knickknacks and 'a quarter of an hour later, they will think of it no more'" (Du Tertre, 1671, as cited by Peabody, 2004, p. 118). Over a 30-year period from the beginning of French missionary work in the Caribbean, there were roughly 20 genuine Carib converts (Boucher, 2008).

How can their resistance to conversion for such an extended period of time be accounted for? To begin, the Caribs were the original host community in Martinique, and the French were the newcomers. It was readily apparent that the French needed the Caribs more than the Caribs needed the French; the Caribs' knowledge of hunting, navigating the environment, growing crops, etc. was critical for the French. Furthermore, the Caribs had a functioning society replete with language, religious beliefs, foods, traditions, spiritual rituals, family structures, and history. In short, they had a collective sense of their history and culture with social structures to maintain and transmit them. The same argument can explain why French Capuchin missionaries in the early 1600s had little success in converting Africans along the west coast of Africa in Guinea and Senegambia. Given these challenges, by 1639 missionary efforts were terminated in West Africa, and missionaries turned their attention to the Carib population of the Lesser Antilles. There is some evidence that a small number of enslaved Africans (mostly from the areas of Angola and Kongo) arrived in the Caribbean already converted to Christianity (Peabody, 2002).

In contrast to Caribs, Africans were forcibly uprooted from their homelands and cultural contexts, endured a long and horrific journey to an alien environment, only to suffer arduous labor under threat of severe brutalization. In this coerced assimilation to a new language, religion, and way of life, their original societal structures were profoundly disrupted (to say the least). Many saw conforming to Catholicism as a path to learning Creole and communicating with other slaves, as well as with Whites. There are also accounts indicating that enslaved Africans perceived conversion as conferring higher status and perhaps some spiritual parity between them and their masters (Peabody, 2002). It is therefore not unfathomable that Du Tertre observed that within the same 30-year period mentioned above, (1627-1657) several thousand enslaved Africans in the French colonies had been converted, and missionaries could communicate with 63% of their flock, partly in Creole and partly in French; some enslaved Africans learned enough French to interpret for the priests (Peabody, 2004; Boucher, 2008).

The French missionaries' perception of slave receptiveness to Christianity does not seem to have changed with the Code Noir in 1685, which made baptism of enslaved Africans mandatory. Toward the end of the 17th century, Père Labat's observations suggested that the enslaved Africans were more naturally inclined to become Christians than the Caribs (Butel, 2002). French attitudes toward non-Europeans seemed predicated on perceptions of how receptive they seemed to be to Catholicism. As Peabody (2004) puts it, "...religion was the crucial divider between the 'insider' and the 'outsider'" (p. 121). By this metric, enslaved Africans who were baptized, practiced the Catholic faith, and observed its rituals were perceived as superior to those who practiced African spiritual rituals, an attitude that slave owners also tried to inculcate in their slaves, as this quote from Father Labat indicates:

> These ways give the new Negroes an exalted idea of the
> position of Christians; and since they are naturally prideful
> they endlessly beg their masters and priests to baptize them;
> so that to satisfy them, one takes whole days to teach them

the doctrine and prayers.[17] (Labat, 1722, p. 454)

Enslaved Africans and French missionaries in Martinique and elsewhere in the French Caribbean seemed to have engaged in a mutually beneficial arrangement. French missionaries gained more converts to their faith and the enslaved Africans enhanced their social status in their community. To bring salvation through Christianity to the enslaved Africans, Jesuit priests intentionally spoke Creole, and they also made an effort to learn some African dialects to communicate with newly arrived Africans. Father Pelleprat describes some of these linguistic accommodations:

> We accommodate ourselves…to their manner of speaking, which is ordinarily by the infinitive form of the verb, as for example: 'me pray God; me go to church; me no eat,' to mean 'I prayed to God; I went to church; I haven't eaten anything.' And adding a word that marks the future or the past: 'Tomorrow me eat; yesterday me pray God,' and so on for the rest. (Peabody, 2002, p. 61)

Missionaries established parishes and priests, *"curés des nègres,"* exclusively for the enslaved Africans. Butel (2002) refers to two in the city of Saint-Pierre and discusses modifications by curés des nègres in Saint-Domingue to tailor their services and offer special masses to suit their African parishioners. With time, progress in the missionaries' evangelical goal no doubt contributed to more positive attitudes toward enslaved Africans, even advocating for more humane treatment in some instances.

---

[17] *Ces manieres font concevoir à ces Négres nouveaux une haute idée de la qualité de Chrétien; & comme ils font naturellement fort superbes, ils importunent sans cesse leurs Maîtres & leurs Curez, afin d'être batisez; de sorte que si on les vouloir satisfaire, on employeroit les jours entiers à leur enseigner la doctrine & leurs prieres.*

The clergy at times found themselves at odds with the Plantocracy over the treatment of enslaved Africans and even the fundamental issue of slavery. Over time, the Capuchin order evidenced the most conflict with the békés. In one instance, they were expelled from St. Christophe in 1646 for preaching that keeping Africans baptized into Catholicism enslaved was sinful. Tempering their rhetoric after this, they still took unpopular stands, as when a curé des nègres in Martinique sided with enslaved Africans he believed to be unjustly condemned to death. In a public display of defiance, he had them buried "… dressed in red, as though they were martyrs" (Peabody, 2002, p. 69).

The above accounts suggest that the French missionaries adapted their methods in order to win over as many African converts as possible. In the words of the Jesuit missionary Pelleprat in 1655, "We make use of every sort of means to win both [Indians and Africans] to God" (Peabody, 2002, p. 60). By the same token, the Africans appeared to reciprocate. Africans' receptiveness to Catholicism could have been fueled by any of the following:

- the legal requirement of religious indoctrination of all slaves (the Code Noir), or
- by displaying a "natural inclination" towards the faith as Père Labat asserted, or
- by accommodations made by the priests, or
- by sheer *"débrouillardisme"* (roughly speaking, hustling or cunning improvisation) to move up within the social ranks and learn Creole.

What is clear is that Catholicism was a platform for reciprocal influence and exchange between the French and the Africans that is a critical aspect of Martinican cultural identity today.

The Code Noir

The French government, represented by Minister of Finance Jean-Baptiste Colbert, shared the missionaries' interest in the religious education of enslaved Africans. This shared interest was a substantial part of the Code Noir, a set of edicts implemented for "The Discipline, the Administration and the trade of Negros to the Americas" (*la Discipline, l'Administration, et le commerce des Nègres aux isles de l'Amérique*; Delphin & Roth 2009, p. 24). A draft of the Code Noir was compiled by Colbert and ratified after his death by Louis XIV in 1685. Although written in mainland France, its provisions and structure were influenced by King Louis XIV's representatives on the islands, the *Intendant* Patoulet and Governor General De Blénac. They gathered information regarding the use of slave labor on plantations from councilmen in Martinique, most of whom owned slaves and some who also owned plantations (Palmer, 1996). The introductory paragraph of the Code Noir states explicitly that it is a response to a perceived need on the islands for the monarchy's help in imposing Catholicism and governing the daily lives of the enslaved Africans (Dubois & Garrigus, 2008).

The Code Noir was an instrument of social, economic, religious, and political control for the White Plantocracy, but some articles provided protections and legal recourse for slaves. One compelling case in point is of a planter in Guadeloupe convicted in 1743 of excessive mistreatment of his slaves who was banished for 5 years and prohibited from owning slaves (Butel, 2002)! The Code Noir included establishment of Catholicism as the only religion on the islands; requirements for food, clothing, and care of the sick and elderly enslaved (including penalties for not providing these); definition of slave status and conditions under which they may be freed; regulations concerning the legal, marital, and economic standing of enslaved Africans; and penalties for misconduct by enslaved Africans.

It is noteworthy that the Code Noir specifies policies and punishments for both slave owners and the enslaved. Article 11 for example, limits the right of slave masters to marry off enslaved Africans against their will, but it was also unlawful for the enslaved to marry without consent of their masters. Although there was no law against enslaved Africans marrying, owners were reluctant to allow this because they could no longer be sold separately. In some instances, owners banned enslaved Africans from marrying those owned by another master to limit the movement of enslaved Africans between the plantations and the risk of escaping, or *marronage,* and other schemes (Gautier, 2000).

Although the Code Noir was intended to efficiently regulate slavery for the benefit of the colonial enterprise, it is not hard to imagine why some colonists did not follow this document to the letter. The edict originated in France for enforcement in the Caribbean by colonists, who resented its limitations imposed on them in the islands. There appeared to be a pattern of lax implementation in Martinique, akin to that in frontier towns in the American West, with similar resentment of federal attempts at control (Schloss, 2007). The actual treatment of enslaved Africans was not always consistent, and some masters displayed a laissez-faire attitude toward some clauses of the Code Noir. Some masters provided time and land for the enslaved to produce their own food, sell their goods, and to own property, all of which were unlawful under the Code Noir. If they adhered strictly to these laws, slave masters ran the risk of marronage, and incurring sizeable costs to bring escapees back (Debien, 1996). More detail on the unintended consequences of how the Code Noir was (or was not) enforced is found in Chapter 5.

Nevertheless, some central features of the Code Noir were consistently upheld. Among those were imposition of Roman

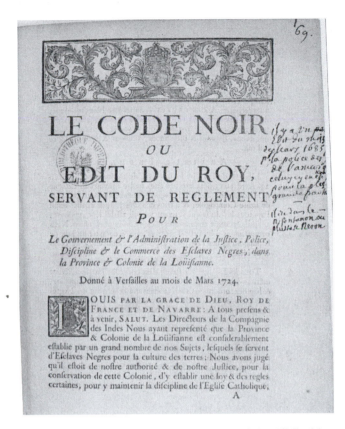

Figure 8. First page of the Code Noir. (Courtesy of the Bibliothèque national de France.)

Catholicism and suppression of all other religious expression, especially African traditions (Riddell, 1925). There is consensus among scholars that the strong and consistent emphasis of Catholicism in the Code Noir was a major factor in the loss of African spiritual traditions (Geggus, 1983; Trouillot, 1992; Yelvington, 2001; Savage, 2007).

Other less consistently enforced aspects were the minimum level of treatment, circumstances under which *manumission*, or freeing of the enslaved, was permitted, and penalties for not abiding by these laws (Schloss, 2007). However, there were many modifications to the Code Noir regarding manumission in Martinique and France (when enslaved Africans traveled to France), possibly because of the increase of gens de couleur (mixed-race individuals) and a perception that stricter oversight was needed (Palmer, 1996). In 1713, an amendment was passed prohibiting owners from manumitting enslaved Africans without the governor's consent. Following this, an edict passed in 1721 prevented slave owners under the age of 25 from freeing, trading, or selling their slaves. Because these laws were widely flouted, more stringent measures with harsher penalties were adopted in 1736 (Riddell, 1925).

The following two articles of the Code Noir relating to family structure likely affected the ability of enslaved Africans to preserve some original cultural elements, particularly folktales and culinary practices. One provision stated, "Husband and wife and infant children belonging to the same master are not to be sold separately..." (Riddell, 1925, p. 325). This is in stark contrast to the typical practice in American slavery of selling enslaved Africans without regard for family integrity (Yelvington, 2001). The other article defines slave status as matrilineal; the child of a female slave (regardless of the father) is a slave. Adherence to these articles in the Code Noir put unique pressure on gender roles and family dynamics in slave communities (Cook-Darzens & Brunod, 1999).

Within this family structure, many generations of women lived together with primary domestic and childrearing responsibilities (for their own children), attempting to provide some guidance and stability by continuing their oral histories and cultural practices. It is clear from our recent visit to Martinique (Spring 2014) that the tradition of oral history is still present, based on our lengthy discussions and casual conversations with Martinicans. Enslaved African women also had to care for their masters' children, which put them in the delicate position of nurturing and caring for their own survival as a people (*"donner à vivre,"* or "give life") and simultaneously caring for the oppressors' offspring (*"vivre pour vivre,"* or "live in order to exist"; Cook-Darzens & Brunod, 1999, p. 435). This situation was further compounded if the father of the slave child was the master, which was common for women who were household slaves.

In order to improve their family's future (and their own), women, who were considered the *"potomitan"* (central pillar in a *voudu* temple) of the slave family, were compelled to strategize and resort to adaptive measures or debrouillardism. Strategies ranged from acquiescing to all demands of the master, especially sexual, to aborting their unborn children, to poisoning the master's family. Conversely, enslaved African men faced pressures of obeying the master's demands for work and avoiding harsh punishments for poor performance; after the early slave trade, there was less emphasis on maintaining family units, and less opportunity for enslaved African fathers to assume traditional male roles as father and husband. For purposes of survival, their role was limited to yet another form of debrouillardism, *"vivre pour soi,"* or "living for oneself" (Cook-Darzens & Brunod, 1999, p. 435). The multilayered roles of enslaved women contributed to the modern **matrifocal society** (Cook-Darzens & Brunod, 1999) in Martinique, in which mothers and grandmothers are still the pillars of the family. Portrayals of matrifocal society in Guadeloupe and Martinique are exemplified in Schwarz-Bart's novel *The Bridge of Beyond*, and Euzhan Palcy's film "Rue Cases-Nègres," respectively.

To be sure, the Code Noir was first and foremost a blueprint for managing the large enslaved labor force the French needed to maintain and expand the sugar economy on the islands. It can be argued that any of its provisions for the wellbeing of slaves arose from the same sentiment as that of an entrepreneur wanting to maintain the equipment of his trade. Nevertheless, it is remarkable that the Code Noir provides explicit details of how much food and clothing the enslaved should get, the requirements for tending to their illnesses no matter the reason, as well as the penalty of prosecution for failing to do so (Riddell, 1925).

These examples indicate a serious double standard and a moral paradox. On the one hand, there is the staggering hubris of the exploitation of another individual's labor for one's own profit. On the other hand, there is a humane sentiment in acknowledging the need for fair treatment, however lopsided the definition of fairness might be, or how infrequently it may have been applied. Another quotation from Father Labat illustrates this double standard eloquently:

> When they [the slaves] are bought and brought to the *Habitation*, one must avoid at all costs the insatiable avarice and extreme brutality of certain planters who make them work upon arrival, without allowing them a chance to even catch their breath. To act in this manner displays neither charity nor prudence, and pays no heed to one's own interests. These poor people are exhausted from a long voyage, the entirety of which they were shackled two by two with an ankle iron. They are debilitated from hunger and thirst, which never relented during their passage, not to mention their discontentment at being detached from their country with no hope of ever returning there. Is this not a means of increasing their pain and suffering, to press them to work without giving them some days of rest and good food? ... These good practices, in addition to the clothes that we give them and other acts of kindness we show them renders them affectionate and helps them forget their country and the unfortunate state that their servitude has reduced them to.[18] (Labat, 1742, pp. 451-453)

---

[18] *Lorsqu'ils font achetez & conduits à l'Habitation, il faut éviter fur toutes choses l'insatiable avarice, & l'horrible dureté de certains Habitans, qui les font travailler tout en arrivant, sans presque leur donner le tems de prendre haleine. C'est n'avoir point du tout de charité ni de discretion, & n'entendre rien en ses propres interêts, que d'en agir en cette manière. Ces pauvres gens sont fatiguez d'un long voyage, pendant lequel*

This pattern appears to have been a consistent theme in French treatment of Africans in Martinique, and arguably played a role in both the loss and the preservation of African cultural elements, a theme discussed more fully in the next chapter.

The Habitation System

Large plantations, or *grandes habitations*, generally comprised smaller plots granted to French engagés, artisans, military personnel, etc. for their services early in colonization. Most of these plots of land had been used for tobacco, coffee, and food or other crops. As sugar prices rose, the value of land increased, and the owners of these small plots sold them at a great profit to discharge debts or purchase passage back to France. More successful plantations were found on the Caribbean side than the Atlantic side, because the latter had a late start in cultivation as they were under Carib control until 1658. In 1671, there were 70 sugar mills and 74 sugarcane plantations on the Caribbean side, but few on the Atlantic side (Butel, 2002). When Britain took over St. Christophe in 1691, pioneers left this island to join prominent plantation owners in Martinique. Their combined capital could only have assisted expansion of the sugar industry in Martinique (Butel, 2002).

Each plantation averaged close to 741 acres and functioned as a self-contained city-state governed by the plantation owners, or békés. The spatial and social structure of the Habitation was an architectural design par excellence for efficient sugar production and maintaining

---

ils ont toujours été attachez deux à deux avec une cheville de fer. Ils font extenuez de la faim & de la soif, qui ne manquent jamais de les faire souffrir beaucoup pendant la traversée, sans compter le déplaisir où ils font d'être éloignez de leur pais, sans esperance d'y jamais retourner. N'est-ce pas le moyen d'augmenter leurs maux & leur chagrin, que de les pousser au travail, sans leur donner quelques jours de repos & de bonne nourriture…. Ces bons traitements, joints aux habits qu'on leur témoigne, les rend affectionnez, & leur fait oublier leur pais, & l'état malheuruex où la servitude les réduit.

a dependent slave society. Augustin Cochin's poignant description of the Habitations gives clear insight into the operations of these self-contained entities: "Prisons without walls, using odious means of producing tobacco, coffee, sugar and consuming slaves"[19] ("Patrimoine de la Martinique," 2014, para. 1).

In the 30 years between 1660 and 1690, the sugar industry grew at an exponential rate, with tremendous investments of land and money. As the volume of production increased, so did the pressure of critical timing in manufacturing sugar once the cane was cut; this amplified the need to centralize all aspects of the process in close proximity ("Patrimoine de la Martinique," 2014). Thus, each Habitation was strategically laid out so that the master's house overlooked the slave quarters and cane fields to allow a clear view of the lives of the enslaved without direct involvement of the master. The sugar mills were near cane fields for speedy processing, and water sources to power the mills were usually not far. Habitations also had warehouses with port access for easy export of sugar and import of goods and machinery.

Some Habitations had hospitals and most had chapels. Vegetable gardens and pastures to raise food and livestock were interspersed between the master's home, slave quarters, and cane fields. *Mornes,* or small hills, formed protective boundaries for the Habitations but also became refuges for escaped Africans, which is discussed further in Chapter 5 (Delphin & Roth, 2009; Beuze, 1998). Apart from selling various sugar products and receiving shipments of manufactured goods and other supplies from abroad, each plantation was largely isolated from other plantations in Martinique. By 1685, "...everyone either owned a plantation or lived on one"[20] (Petitjean Roget , 1980, p. 1479).

---

[19] *Des prisons sans muraille, des manufactures odieuses produisant du tabac, du café, du sucre, et consommant des esclaves.*
[20] *...tout le monde a une habitation ou est sur une habitation.*

Figure 9. View of *mornes* (hills) behind the Plaisance Plantation in St. Pierre. (From Cicéri & Hartman [1851], *Album Martiniquais,* p. 5. Courtesy of the Beinecke Lesser Antilles Collection, Burke Library, Hamilton College, NY.)

Figure 10. View of the hospital on the Pécoul Plantation in St. Pierre. (From Cicéri & Hartman [1851], *Album Martiniquais*, p. 6. Courtesy of the Beinecke Lesser Antilles Collection, Burke Library, Hamilton College, NY.)

The Habitation was designed to keep enslaved Africans isolated from the outside world and from other enslaved Africans. A rigid hierarchy was inherent in the plantation system: from the plantation owner, to the manager, to the accountant, to the foremen, and then to the enslaved Africans (who had their own hierarchy), everyone had a specific role, with any deviation largely dictated from the top. Domestic slaves had the highest status, followed by skilled tradesmen and artisans in the sugar mills, fishermen and hunters, and then field slaves, who were further subdivided based on physical strength, health, and age (Delphin & Roth, 2009). As Père Labat (1742) notes, an additional layer of hierarchy among enslaved Africans, based on the fervor and length of their practice of Christianity, intensified existing social divisions. When new enslaved were lodged in the quarters of baptized enslaved Africans to be trained to work on the plantations, hospitality toward the newcomers did not include sharing meals or sleeping quarters with them. Enslaved Africans who were not Christian were considered inferior and unworthy of that level of personal engagement.

There was typically limited interaction among enslaved Africans from different plantations, except for those loading products from the sugar factories onto ships in the ports. The plantation owners deliberately tried to separate enslaved Africans from similar ethnolinguistic groups, placing them on different plantations so that they would not be able or have the opportunity to band together and rebel against slave owners and ruin their profitable sugar industry (Desroches, 1996). Furthermore, foremen constantly monitored interactions among enslaved Africans in public, and even in fields and factories (François Rosaz, personal communication, March 21, 2012). This made it difficult for enslaved Africans to communicate about anything not directly related to the work they were forced to do. The constant oversight of interactions with each other and the lack of ethnic homogeneity among them were major contributors to the loss of their original languages and customs (Yelvington, 2001).

Due to the insular nature of the plantation system, each owner or master had near-total control over his domain and his slaves, which led to the considerable variation in observance of the Code Noir. Some articles of the Code Noir that protected the rights of enslaved Africans, such as limiting the days and amount of time they worked or the severity of punishment, were not always observed by masters. Similarly, articles meant to restrict rights of the enslaved Africans were sometimes ignored by the masters as well. For example, enslaved Africans were not allowed to engage in trade such as selling surplus from their kitchen gardens, yet many masters did not enforce this provision (Riddell, 1925).

Conclusion

From the latter part of the 17th and throughout most of the 18th century until about the French Revolution in 1789, Martinique was considered "the jewel of the French Lesser Antilles" (Kelly, 2008, p. 396). There were more enslaved Africans in the French than in the English colonies, and the production of sugar and other commercial products (rum, molasses, coffee, indigo, and cotton) was superior to that of the English colonies (Kelly, 2008). The value of the enslaved Africans well surpassed that of the White engagés, and the White Plantocracy was fully cognizant that enslaved Africans, as Munford (1986, p. 61) noted, were "the sole agents of production" and the backbone of the entire colonial enterprise and its plantation society; without this labor force, the economic structure would have crumbled.

The extensive economic edifice of the French colonial enterprise that stretched from the Caribbean to mainland France accounted for the emigration of almost 100,000 French people to the Americas and 1.25 million enslaved Africans (Hodson & Rushforth, 2010; Geggus,

2001). This edifice required specific social structures to maintain and facilitate its operation. The Code Noir and the Habitation system were the foundations that supported the colonial enterprise and enforced French control over every aspect of the lives of enslaved Africans. Munford captures the sugar plantation societies and the institution of slavery in the following lines:

> In a constant and burdensome act of creation, slaves in the French West Indies produced the material values that sustained the life of the ruling class and all others on the island. It was a measure of the supreme inhumanity of the system that the only people whose lives were all too often *not* sustained by the productive efforts of the slaves were the slaves themselves. (Munford, 1986, p. 65)

By extension, the impact of the loss of the slave trade on the French economy would have been dramatic; it is imputed that around 20 French seaports engaged in the Atlantic slave trade during the 18th century. From 1669 to 1864 there were 4,033 French slave expeditions and, as a testament to the importance of the slave trade, France even lifted the ban on slave trade with other nations (a practice hitherto illegal, yet robust) to Martinique and Guadeloupe in 1783 (Geggus, 2001). In addition to the well-known ports of Nantes, Le Havre, Honfleur, La Rochelle, St. Malo, and Bordeaux, smaller ports engaged in this trade. Nantes alone accounted for 1,708 voyages that set sail to buy, sell, and exchange enslaved Africans (Geggus, 2001, p. 122). In aggregate, these seaport towns became prosperous largely due to Atlantic imports and exports. During the reign of Louis XIV, the livelihoods of approximately 400,000 people in France depended on the slave trade and colonial economy ("Patrimoine de la Martinique," 2014).

Figure 11. Map of France indicating major ports of slave expeditions. (Courtesy of the Bibliothèque nationale de France.)

Notwithstanding the oppressive colonial system in Martinique, enslaved Africans were the engines that propelled the "sugar train," and the White Plantocracy and French monarchy were the conductors. The entire society revolved around how to best exploit the labor of enslaved Africans for the Plantocracy's profit. With this objective, a language for mutual communication, Creole, evolved from French and African contributions. Enslaved Africans were forced to cut, crush, boil, refine, and pack sugar cane under brutal working conditions for maximum production. To prevent enslaved Africans from running away or rebelling, the Plantocracy devised severe punishments, and laws were manipulated by them to justify and better enable all these practices. So, Martinique's history from 1660 through the French Revolution, and even until 1848 and the abolition of slavery, belongs to neither France nor Africa but to the lives and struggles of the enslaved; it is *their* history (Munford, 1986). The next chapter explores the multifaceted nature of the struggles of enslaved Africans and their relentless attempts to wrest control of whatever aspects of their lives they could.

Glossary

Code Noir - (French, "Black Code") Decree initiated by Jean-Baptiste Colbert and mandated by King Louis XIV of France in 1685 after Colbert's death that regulated the conditions of slavery in the French colonial empire and forbade the exercise of any religion other than Roman Catholicism.

habitation - (French) Self-contained group of people, animals, and buildings forming the estate of a planter for growing sugar cane and other crops and the production of sugar.

Plantocracy - White proprietors of sugar plantations who exerted total political and economic control of the colonies.

French West India Company - Trading company founded in 1664 by Jean-Baptiste Colbert and dissolved in 1674. The company received the monopoly from the French monarchy for 40 years for trade with French possessions on the Atlantic coasts of Africa and America.

La Compagnie de Guinée - (French, "Company of Guinea") Founded in 1684 by Louis XIV; important in the slave trade and the triangular trade between Nantes and the island of Saint Domingue (Haiti).

Mission civilisatrice - (French, "civilizing mission") Term referring to France's goal to impose its culture on other cultural groups in its colonial empire. France's colonial and missionary motivations and its justification of the enslavement of Africans are also closely associated with this term.

Capuchin Friars - Members of Order of Friars Minor Capuchin (O.F.M. Cap.), an autonomous branch of the Franciscan Order of religious men, begun in 1525.

curés des nègres - (French) "Priests for the slaves."

débrouillardisme - (French) Literally "resourcefulness," by legal or illegal means.

Intendant - (French) Representative of the king in the colonies who had considerable power.

marronage - (French , "running away") Referring to enslaved Africans escaping from plantations.

manumission - Formally or informally freeing an enslaved African.
potomitan - (Creole, "center pillar supporting the [Vodou] temple") Term referring to women as the main support and focal point of the family.

matrifocal society - Society in which mothers are the heads of families and fathers play a less important role in the home and in bringing up children.

mornes - (French, "hills") Term in the Antilles referring to small isolated hills.

Reflective Questions

1. What factors contributed to the desire of colonists in Martinique to resist French control? To what extent can the proposition that this rebelliousness is a defining feature of Martinican plantation society be supported?

2. Describe at least three factors influencing expansion of the slave trade in Martinique from 1640 to the early 1700s and how these factors might be interrelated.

3. What were the effects of teaching enslaved Africans Catholicism on their sense of community among themselves and with the French? Discuss the effects of this religious education on French and African cultural narratives.

4. Discuss the paradoxical role of missionaries in relation to the system of slavery and implementation of the Code Noir.

5. The Habitation or plantation system was a business strategy for producing sugar; how did its spatial, logistical, and work arrangements help create plantation society?

Chapter 5

Adaptive Responses to the System of Slavery

Antillean identity or creole identity is suffering because it has been discounted and questioned by the colonial powers. With the beginning of slavery, in the 15ᵗʰ and the 16ᵗʰ centuries, they [the colonial powers] hesitated to acknowledge the human status of these populations....¹

—Édouard Glissant
Martinican novelist, poet, and essayist
1928-2011

A century and a half of the Code Noir and Habitation system, and the changing sociopolitical climate in Martinique, France, and neighboring Haiti, saw the emergence of new layers in the social hierarchy of Martinique. The bottommost layer consisted of the Africans, the gens de couleur occupied the middle layer, and the uppermost echelon was held by the French.

This social hierarchy also contained substrata. Within the African community, the enslaved held the lowest status, followed by *patronnés* (Africans who were not officially free but whose masters allowed them to act as if they were), and finally, the manumitted (those freed by their masters). As for the gens de couleur, a majority of them were not free and held the same status as the enslaved Africans or the patronnés, but some were free. The French in Martinique also had their own hierarchy. The *petits blancs* (tradesmen) held the lowest position,

---

¹ *Quant à elle, l'identité antillaise "identité créole" est souffrante parce qu'elle a toujours été mise en doute et en interrogation par les puissances coloniales. Au commencement de l'esclavage, aux XVe et XVIe siècles, on hésite à reconnaître à ces populations le statut d'homme....* (Glissant, 2002, para. 6)

followed by the Catholic missionaries and the king's appointed officials. The békés, or the wealthy plantation owners, constituted the topmost layer of Martinican society.

Political divisions in mainland French society appeared as well. Notable political factions in France included the abolitionists, those who opposed slavery, and the anti-abolitionists, those who supported slavery. It goes without saying that the White plantocracy in Martinique threw their support behind the anti-abolitionists in France and sought to influence colonial policies in their favor. The gens de couleur, who enjoyed a certain degree of freedom of movement, often acted as liasons between enslaved Africans and abolitionists.

How did the social ecology of Martinique affect the adaptive responses of groups who were willingly or unwillingly part of the colonial enterprise? What were some of the unintended consequences of these responses? First and foremost, we consider the spectrum of adaptive responses of these groups to the evolving social climate. When the structure of social institutions and interactions is deliberately developed to the detriment of a particular group, interactions are oppressive (García-Ramírez, de la Mata, Paloma, & Hernandez-Plata, 2011). This structure is the stage on which the mutual adaptation and acculturation of groups unfolded, as described in Chapter 4. Despite the Plantocracy's architecture of social dominance to regulate colonial society in ways conducive to its profitable sugar economy, not everyone assigned to the bottom of the hierarchy was quietly resigned to staying there. The challenges to accessing resources and the abilities to cope with inequities of a slave-holding society were ever present, but even in bondage, individuals struggle for self-definition and autonomy. Changing adaptations to the system of slavery over a century and a half, as well as inter- and intra-group dynamics (expanded on in the following chapter) constitute the heart of this phase of creolization in Martinique.

Adaptive responses by enslaved Africans to the institution of slavery in Martinique were varied and frequent, though subject to many factors. Gender, age, relationship with masters, how long they had been enslaved, and their position in the plantation hierarchy are some of the most relevant. Adaptive responses ranged from subtle and compliant to defiant and violent. Avoiding or minimizing work through short-term absenteeism (*petit marronage*) or planned inefficiency was a classic form of subtle resistance that affected productivity. Discreet (and sometimes indiscreet) artistic expressions, such as drumming, dancing, singing, and storytelling, became tools of coded communication, self-preservation, and self-expression. Many of these cultural elements functioned as covert resistance to oppressive circumstances, and can be placed under the conceptual umbrella of debrouillardism.

Direct resistance to the plantation regime of the French host community did occur, however, and must be understood as another form of adaptation to subjugation. From the beginning of the colonial process, more defiant and sometimes violent methods were employed by enslaved Africans to oppose the system of slavery, and by the White Plantocracy to uphold it. However, the frequency and intensity of methods used by both groups amplified after the French and Haitian revolutions: petitions, nascent labor movements, escape from plantations (*grand marronage*), poisonings, armed uprisings, arson, brandings, and executions are some of the examples discussed.

Subtle Forms of Adaptive Response

The most common subversive adaptations by the enslaved Africans directly affected the overall profits of the masters through limiting their labor. Work slowdowns, petit marronage (Delphin & Roth, 2009), feigning illness or a lack of understanding, and self-inflicted injuries were all ways of undermining the plantation regime by lowering productivity. The free movement of enslaved Africans around the plantations, ranging from a few hours to an entire day or two (sometimes outside the plantation as well) had become so common by the 1820s that the masters came to accept petit marronage as a cost of doing business. They feared the repercussions of enslaved Africans running away permanently or organizing strikes if they cracked down on this practice (Savage, 2006). Other subversive actions included stealing food, tools, and sundry daily necessities for survival from the masters. Destruction of agricultural implements, animals, and crops were also common acts of overt resistance; abortions and infanticide were less common, more desperate protests (Munford, 1986).

Debrouillardism

The concept of feedback loops, in which responses to an environment trigger changes in that environment that spur modifications to further responses and so on, is applicable to the meaning of debrouillardism in Martinique. "A *debrouillard* is someone who is always looking for solutions for personal profit on every plane.... In the end, *débrouiller* means to be selfish..." (Browne, 2002, p. 382). Debrouillardism is a form of shrewd adaptiveness that can be extended to linguistics, social norms, and other behavioral aspects, not only of slaves but of the French colonizers and Indian indentured workers who arrived after the abolition of slavery as well. The literal translation of debrouillard however, refers to a resourceful person. The different interpretation and value of debrouillardism in France as opposed to Martinique is essentially the distinction between being clever enough to work within the system to get the best deal, and being clever enough to beat the system without getting caught.

This Martinican perspective on an initially French term is an example of creolization shaped by the hardships of slavery. The term implies not simply an improvisational strategy for physical survival, but also a form of covert resistance to oppression, or improvisation for psychological survival. For example, Black women sometimes maintained relationships with their White masters as a way to protect their mulatto children from the hardships of slavery, often elevating their own position in slave society in the process (Cook-Darzens & Brunod, 1999). Ironically, features of the French model of slavery may have encouraged both covert resistance and improvisations for survival.

Following the logic of Frantz Fanon, the 20th century psychiatrist and anti-colonial theorist (Julien, 2000), the insistence on rule-breaking as a fundamental characteristic of a debrouillard is an example of sublimation as a defense against the need for violent catharsis against the colonizer. Given the context of a Martinican creole society in which supplementing one's income through illicit activities is viewed as an act of bravery, intelligence, resourcefulness, independence, ambition, etc., "it is not a sin to be a débroulliard" (*"débouya pa péché"*; Browne, 2002, p. 381). Although several examples stress the outlaw aspect of debrouillardism for enslaved Africans, a case can be made that the Plantocracy was quite ready to display such traits regarding French regulations when it suited them (which was often). In the final analysis, there seems to be a difference between mainland France and Martinique in the perception of how shameful debrouillard behavior might be. As an illustration of creolization (or cultural hybridization in the case of the Indian indentured workers), Martinican connotations of a debrouillard are an interesting morph of the French cultural value of individualism.

Artistic Expression

Evidence from archaeological exploration of a plantation in

Creve Coeur in Martinique shows pottery in African styles crafted and used by enslaved Africans despite efforts by their masters to denigrate and efface African culture (Kelly, 2008). Other art forms with links to African culture that were used as tools of indirect resistance to slave society were music, storytelling, and dance. Music, particularly drumming, remained an important component of African culture that survived the experience of enslavement and played a significant role in uprisings, a phenomenon observed in many other sites of the African diaspora. Drumming was not only a form of musical expression, but also of communication; this made it a vital part of most African resistance movements, including marronage, or running away from the plantation (Delphin & Roth, 2009). Drumming was used to signal the best times to escape, where the patrols were, and when an uprising would occur. Parallels can be found in the traditions of Negro spirituals in the United States and *capoeira* in Brazil (cf. Geggus, 1983; also, Trouillot, 1992).

Storytelling and other forms of oral history, often accompanied by music, were shared and performed in the evenings and on Sundays as a means of passing on traditions, rituals, wisdom, and as an avenue of clever covert self-preservation. This oral tradition was certainly related to drumming, but had less connection to marronage and uprisings than to debrouillardism (Browne, 2002). As an illustration of the process of cultural creolization, African folktales often thematically relate to the good of a group or community as a whole, whereas Martinican forms of these tales have more individualistic outcomes. Perhaps part of the psychological trauma of being enslaved lies in the situational need to transform and co-opt collective goals and values to individual expressions. Many of these stories used African folktales and the animal world as a backdrop, representing plantation life and hierarchy in allegory. A theme repeated in these stories is the value of not meeting force with force, but outwitting those who have power (Browne, 2002). Similar sentiments endorsing and encouraging trickery in the face of injustice are found in compilations of traditional Creole folktales by prominent Martinican writers such as Chamoiseau and Confiant (Chamoiseau, 1995; Confiant, 1995).

The formation of slave associations (*associations serviles)* in cities, with regular gatherings for funerals, weddings, and dances, was an example of carving out spheres of autonomy for the cultural and social purposes of enslaved Africans. These associations had elected leaders and provided various kinds of support for the paid membership (Savage, 2006, p. 38). Dancing to traditional African rhythms in the evenings and Sundays in slave quarters was an essential way to build some sense of community and share common cultural connections to Africa. A dance known as the *calenda* was very popular, as noted by the colonists and Father Labat:

> In order to prevent the *calendas,* ordinances were made on the islands, not only because of the indecent and completely lascivious postures that this dance contains, but also not to allow the opportunity for too many Negroes to gather, who find themselves overly joyous, and most often under the influence of brandy, can incite revolts, uprisings, and robberies. However, despite these ordinances and all the precautions that the masters can take, it is almost impossible to prevent them from doing it, because of all their diversions, this is the one that pleases more than any other....[2] (Labat, 1742, pp. 466-467)

[2] *On a fait des Ordonnances dans les Iles, pour empêcher les calendas non-seulement à cause des postures indécentes, & tout à-fait lascives, dont cette danse est composé, mais encore pour ne pas donner lieu aux trop nombreuses assemblées des Nègres, qui se trouvent ainsi ramassez dans la joye, & le plus souvent avec de l'eau-de vie dans la tête, peuvent faire des révoltes, des soulevemens, ou des parties pour aller voler. Cependant malgré ces Ordonnances, & toutes les precautions que les Maîtres peuvent prendre, il est presque impossible de les en empêcher, parceque c'est de tous leurs diverstissemens celui qui leur plaît davantage....*

In time, slave associations moved these dances and other gatherings to public squares in cities such as St. Pierre. However, the focus of these gatherings especially in city squares was more toward political expression than recreation. A case in point, discussed by Dale Tomich (1990a, p. 88), was the appropriation of some lyrics of French revolutionary songs to fit the context of their struggles:

> From *La Parisienne* the line *en avant marchons contre les canons* (march against the cannons) was reported to have been changed to *en avant marchons contre les colons* (march against the colonists) while a line from *La Marseillaise* was changed from *abreuvons nos sillons d'un sang impur* (water our furrows with unclean blood) to *abreuvons nos sillons du sang des colons* (water our furrows with the colonists' blood).

In an effort to quell these subtle yet powerful ways of fanning the flames of resistance and revolution among the enslaved Africans, colonial authorities imposed limitations on and militiary oversight of these gatherings (Tomich 1990a). The French also introduced social dances such as the minuet, *courante*, and *passe-pied* (Labat, 1742) to replace the African dances they perceived as promoting unrest and group solidarity among enslaved Africans.

Defiant Forms of Adaptive Response

The brutal coercive nature of plantation society in Martinique made covert resistance attractive to anyone who was not French. Pretending to go along with the White Plantocracy, but in ways that either sabotaged it, furthered one's own goals, or both, was an effective strategy, whether for enslaved Africans or gens de couleur. For some, however, the daily indignities of discrimination were unendurable, and they sought more direct means of achieving their freedom. The following quotation from an anonymous letter dated September 1789, signed by enslaved Africans and addressed to the Intendant in St. Pierre, Martinique reveals that a breaking point had been reached:

> But in the end, it is in vain that we seek to convince you by invoking sentiments and humanity, for you have none; but by using blows, we will have it, for we see that this is the only way to get anywhere. It will start soon if this prejudice is not entirely annihilated...there will be torrents of blood flowing as powerful as the gutters that flow along our streets. (Dubois & Garrigus, 2006, pp. 65-66)

Petitioning

The anonymous letter above is an example of demanding one's rights by threatening violent retaliation. There were also petitions demanding better treatment and rights; the appeal to "sentiments and humanity" referenced in the quotation. Petitioning authorities, often in France, was primarily a tactic of gens de couleur to address discrimination. Some békés actually joined gens de couleur in 1727 to protest the poll tax in Martinique. However, by 1789-1790, as the number of gens de couleur increased dramatically (the ratio of gens de couleur to Whites was one to two) the White Plantocracy became more antagonistic to their petitions. Planters hung and assaulted other Whites for supporting gens de couleur and their petitions and also terrorized gens de couleur by mass executions of petitioners, as in St. Pierre (Elisabeth, 1972; Peabody, 2002).

Figure 12. Petition of free gens de couleur in 1829 in Martinique and Guadeloupe. (Courtesy of the Bibliothèque nationale de France.)

When some gens de couleur of Fort de France attempted to submit a petition in 1820 for judicial reform, they were met with anger and violence by the White Plantocracy. Haunted by the powerful role of gens de couleur in Haiti's independence in 1804, Martinique's White Plantocracy perceived all acts, especially petitions, by gens de couleur as plots to overthrow the colonial system, as our discussion of the Bissette Affair in Chapter 6 illustrates. In this incident, manipulation of the colonial legal system by the White Plantocracy was so apparent that it even caught the attention of the mainland French.

Demands for Labor Rights and Free Time

Prior to the Code Noir, slave masters frequently allotted small parcels of land and free time (on Saturdays) for enslaved Africans to grow their own food. Labat (1742) describes this practice by some Martinican planters in his *Nouveaux Voyages aux Iles de l' Amérique*: "... to give Saturdays to the slaves for them to work and provide food and clothing for themselves and their families with the profits"[3] (p. 201). This helped slave-owners to economize on feeding enslaved Africans and allowed them some freedom. This system did not always work efficiently, with both parties often shirking their responsibilities resulting in malnutrition and unrest of the enslaved Africans. As discussed, the Code Noir established mandates for feeding, housing, and clothing enslaved Africans by their owners, which not only regulated the lives of the enslaved on the plantations, but also ensured that slave owners were responsible for them. Although the tradition of free Saturdays was disallowed by the Code Noir, it was a popular way for masters to circumvent the letter of the law while hewing to its spirit. Furthermore, many enslaved Africans and masters found free Saturdays to be a convenient arrangement and did not renounce the practice, especially during food shortages and economic downturns. It was not until the Mackau Law of 1845 that provision plots for enslaved Africans to grow their own food were accepted in lieu of planters' responsibility for providing required rations (Tomich, 1990b).

The unfairness of having to exert themselves to grow their own food in addition to toiling all week to enrich the plantation owners did not hinder enslaved Africans from taking advantage of this individual farming provision as a platform for entrepreneurship and autonomy. Enslaved Africans grew enough food for their own

---

[3] ...*donner le Samedi aux Nègres pour travailler pour eux, & s'entretenir de vêtements & de nourritures eux & leurs familles par le travail & le gain qu'ils font pendant ce jour-là.*

consumption and sometimes had surplus to sell at markets for a profit. The economics of free Saturdays affected the hierarchy of the slave community, to the extent that some enslaved Africans made enough profit to hire other Africans to work for them. In addition to material prosperity, free Saturdays offered the psychological benefits of human dignity, independence, and expression of some personal style (e.g., by purchasing fine clothing). This window of opportunity for enslaved Africans to earn income readily expanded into hustling, including stealing commodities such as sugar, food, or tools (Browne, 2002), none of which was seen as wrong, as they perceived it as merely expropriating from the expropriators. Thus, the free Saturday tradition clearly had the unintended consequence of stimulating debrouillardism.

Revisions to the Code Noir in 1784 and 1786 acknowledged the prevalence of free Saturdays but did not legalize them. More important, these revisions affirmed the obligations of slave owners to provide food for the enslaved, and to only use the free Saturdays to supplement their nourishment. These changes in the law altered the dependent relationship between enslaved Africans and masters, creating mutually understood distinctions between the rights of masters to the time and labor of enslaved Africans and their rights to free time. The very fact that if slave owners wanted enslaved Africans to work on Saturday they had to compensate them (if not in payment, then in additional time off), shows the evolution of slave labor into something akin to an employer-employee relationship (Tomich, 1990b).

Beginning in 1789, with revolutionary refrains of liberty resounding throughout the French empire, free Saturdays were formally instituted in several parishes in Martinique and soon took on a life of their own in terms of labor relations between enslaved Africans and masters. Demands by enslaved Africans for three days off per week began during this time and persisted after emancipation in 1848. A rumor on the plantations was that the "three days off" reform was a royal concession to which enslaved Africans were entitled but that masters were unwilling to grant. According to Pierre Dessalles, a planter from Martinique, "All of the slave poisoners that we arrest say that they are only attacking their masters because their masters did not want to grant them their 3 days"[4] (Elisabeth, 2009, p. 57).

Between 1789 and 1831, enslaved Africans on several plantations, including Le Carbet, Lamentin, and Fort Royale, insisted on having three days off to spend more time with their families and cultivate their personal plots. Although the continuing demand for three days off does not seem to have been the immediate cause of a particular incident, the protracted grievance was an underlying catalyst for several violent uprisings, including the slave revolt of 1822 in Le Carbet, and numerous incidents of slave-initiated poisonings, especially of livestock, throughout this period (Elisabeth, 2009). "Here is one of the most vile and strange results of slavery. Poison! It is the organized poisonings of livestock by the slaves"[5] (Schoelcher, 1842, p. 121).

Poisonings and Quimboiserie

"Poison is to the slave as the whip is to his master, a moral force. If the master has the right to beat, the slave has the right to poison"[6] (Schoelcher, 1842, p. 121). Poisoning was perceived as a widespread and effective form of asymmetrical warfare against the colonial enterprise in Martinique. Yet, there is uncertainty as to whether all alleged instances of slave poisonings were organized and well-executed acts of resistance. Or, were accounts exaggerated because of ignorance

[4] *Tous les nègres empoisonneurs, qu'on arrête, déclarent qu'ils ne faisaient du mal à leurs maîtres que parce que les maîtres n'avaient pas voulu donner 3 jours.*

[5] *Voici un des plus horribles et des plus étranges produits de l'esclavage. Le poison! C'est à dire l'empoisonnement organisé des bestiaux par les esclaves.*

[6] *Le poison est à l'esclave ce que le fouet est au maître, une force morale. Si le maître a droit de battre, l'esclave a droit d'empoissoner.*

and fear of herbal medicines that the paranoid White Plantocracy saw as planned schemes of revolt? Or were poisonings evidence of random pockets of unrest? What is evident is that incidents of slave poisoning did affect productivity and profit as well as spread terror and confusion among the White Plantocracy. Poisonings also provided enslaved Africans with an effective riposte to the master's oppression and a way to preserve African herbal knowledge.

Initially, poisonings were often directed toward livestock and fellow enslaved Africans, but as the institution of slavery wore on, poisonings were directed at the masters by trustworthy enslaved Africans who worked in the plantation house (Schloss, 2007). Enslaved Africans would rarely testify against poisoners. This may have had to do with the increase in targeting slave owners. In general, it seemed to the Plantocracy that the enslaved Africans were "all in it together." In the words of a **Provostial Court** judge, "neither the fear of torture, nor the threat of punishment as accomplices to the crime will bring slaves to denounce their comrades" (Savage, 2007, p. 637).

Savage (2006) notes a fascinating correlation between the challenges of making a profit in the sugar industry, tighter controls on the slave trade, relentless pressure on the enslaved African workforce, and the increase in reported cases of poisoning. In effect, the pressure on sugar plantations for increased production prompted more intense workloads that were enforced with greater brutality; given that it was hard to replace enslaved Africans, the existing ones were forced to work at a ferocious pace in a dangerous job with less rest and nourishment. The death rate among enslaved Africans, imputed to poisoning by the Plantocracy, may well reflect their being worked to death. Rumors of poisoning often led to tighter security and increasing intensity of punishments, which led to higher mortality from suicide and infanticide and could well have incited overt and covert rebellion through poisonings: "If the master demands more of him or something that he is not accustomed to doing, he fights back with inertia; when the master insists that he do it, he retaliates with poison"[7] (Lavollée, 1841, p. 124).

Poisoning as a form of resistance appears to have facilitated survival of the African cultural tradition of herbalism or *quimboiserie*, introduced in Chapter 1. Quimboiserie involves the use of roots, herbs, and rituals for healing, shamanic practices, divination, and sorcery, and was important in the lives of many enslaved Africans as well as in poisoning their masters (not to mention fellow enslaved Africans; Savage, 2007). Though the practice had to be adapted to the available flora and conditions of Martinique, it seems that there were sufficient commonalities because most of the knowledge of the *quimboiseurs* was applicable then and is still being used for healings, divination, ensuring good luck, guarding against ills, and wishing fortune or misfortune on others. "To fight against daily challenges, Martinicans voluntarily reach out to healers and their traditional beliefs, which does not hinder them from being devout Catholics"[8] (Corteggiani, 1994, p. 6). Given that these traditions were passed from parents to children, provisions in the Code Noir that kept families intact were likely instrumental in maintaining these practices.

As an example of reciprocal cultural influence, the West African roots of quimboiserie hold that its power is determined by family networks, that is, without close blood ties or other committed relationship, rituals are less effective. This may account for why the initial poisoning attacks were directed toward fellow enslaved Africans, but later attacks targeted masters, whose connections with at least some enslaved Africans became increasingly intimate. Furthermore, immersion in the Catholic religion could certainly have influenced

---

[7] *... si le maître lui demande plus ou autre chose que ce qu'il est accoutumé à faire, il le combat par la force d'inertie; lorsqu'on insiste, il répond par le poison.*

[8] *Pour lutter contre les angoisses quotidiennes, les Martiniquais se tournent volontiers vers les guérisseurs et leurs croyances ancestrales, ce qui ne les empêchent pas d'être de fervents catholiques.*

enslaved Africans to share the French view of African spiritual traditions as malign witchcraft (Savage, 2007).

Grand Marronage and Uprisings

As shown previously, the Code Noir and Habitation system provided societal structures for interactions between French colonists and enslaved Africans. Although such structures existed primarily to force Africans to work involuntarily in the colonial sugar economy, they also allowed enslaved Africans to protest mistreatment. In the 1800s enslaved Africans even appealed for equal treatment under the law despite the unlikelihood of censure of the master and the likelihood of reprisals (Butel, 2002). Active participation by enslaved Africans in the legal redefinition of their status by the French is an important development in Martinican cultural narratives (Savage, 2007). Fierce resistance to the system of slavery through grand marronage and slave uprisings were other frequently observed outcomes.

Desperation led some enslaved Africans to grand marronage (Delphin & Roth, 2009), which was organized flight into the hills (*mornes*) surrounding the plantation with no intent of return to slave labor. Less discussed is marronage by leaving the island altogether. This occurred when ship captains returning to France were in need of able-bodied hands for the journey. They allowed enslaved Africans to flee the island for France and elsewhere in return for their labor during the voyage. Laws and penalties were established to punish captains who engaged in this, which attests to its frequency (Boucher, 2008).

Inhumane treatment and lack of food were the main reasons enslaved Africans ran away. Absenteeism among some plantation owners who spent long periods of time in France, leaving subordinates in charge, was also a contributing factor (this was especially the case in Saint-Domingue). Plantation borders with forested hills made convenient hideouts for marrons (Butel, 2002). From the early days of slavery in 1665, planters waged war on marrons, who were assisted by the Caribs; high bounties were paid for their capture (Meslien, 2009, pp. 6-8).

Figure 13. Pursuit of a runaway slave, or marron Negro (date unknown). From Schmidt, N. (2012), *Slavery and Its Abolition, French Colonies, Research and Transmission of Knowledge* (p. 10). Courtesy of UNESCO.

Slave catchers were often recruited from the gens de couleur community, which did not improve relations between them and enslaved Africans. This was another way to manage the unrest of enslaved Africans: pitting two disenfranchised groups against each other (Savage, 2006). Often, French planters also responded with harsher punishments and by extending the workday of grueling labor (Munford, 1986). With time, it became abundantly clear to the White Plantocracy that grand marronage was an effective tool for the enslaved to threaten Martinique's plantation society. Governor Vioménil conveyed the gravity of the situation in 1789: "If we do not remedy the problem promptly, this small band of *nègres marrons* will be the nucleus that will produce the miseries that this colony fears so" (Dubois & Garrigus, 2006, pp. 64-65).

Uprisings by enslaved Africans were a recurring phenomenon, with significant rebellions in 1717, 1789, 1811, 1822, 1831, and

1844 (Schloss, 2007). An epic example of a rebellion escalating from grand marronage involved Francisque Fabulé in 1665. Fabulé led a troop of marrons who were not simply content with escape, but also staged periodic raids on plantations, sometimes aided by the few remaining Caribs. Fabulé was so adept at eluding capture that to end his harassment of planters, the governor was forced to grudgingly negotiate his surrender by paying him a tidy sum in tobacco, freeing him and giving amnesty to his followers who returned from the hills (Debien, 1996). Continuing this tradition of resistance, a sizeable uprising occurred in 1678 in which many died and 10 or so were condemned to be burned to death. The condemned exhibited steely resolve by smoking tobacco while being burned at the stake. A gesture equally as defiant, if not as dramatic, was that of an enslaved African woman who repudiated marriage, unwilling to welcome new life into a world of oppression (Boucher, 2008).

The slave revolt of 1789 was similar in origin to uprisings triggered by the rumor that the king had granted enslaved Africans three days off, with békés refusing to honor the proclamation. No news of the beginning of the French Revolution had even reached Martinique, but another rumor spread, purportedly initiated by a Capuchin priest in St. Pierre, Father Jean-Baptiste. This rumor stated that the king had granted liberty to the enslaved, but the local authorities and White Plantocracy were unwilling to execute the king's wishes. A letter by Governor Vioménil to the Minister of the Marine and the Colonies details the uprisings that ensued. Enslaved Africans from two plantations joined forces, seized weapons, and escaped to the mornes above St. Pierre, probably to unite with other marron communities to form a large resistance force. This uprising was quelled when the leaders were captured and publicly executed as a deterrent to future insurrections (Dubois & Garrigus, 2006).

Comparatively small in terms of the number involved and the

ease with which it was suppressed, the 1822 uprising in Le Carbet occurred shortly after installation of the Provostial Court, and shared features of poisonings of their masters by those trusted enslaved Africans (Savage, 2007, p. 639). It was also reported that a slave-owner's widow was nearly killed by an enslaved African she had raised after his mother's death (Schloss, 2009). The fact that there were other White fatalities during this uprising, which was unheard of during this period, exacerbated the Plantocracy's outrage.

Contravening the limited size of this revolt, its influential impact echoed throughout Martinican society, reinforcing the apprehensions of the Plantocracy over the rebelliousness of slaves and the problematic justice system in place to punish their behavior and maintain social control. In fact, despite the expeditious and brutal sentences of the Provostial Court (including 21 executions, 10 life sentences at hard labor, and 17 floggings; Schloss, 2009, p. 94), many békés denounced the governor, other colonial administrators from France, and the mainland French as creating a climate in which this revolt and others like it would be inevitable. The defensiveness generated by the Carbet revolt no doubt triggered the raids leading to the Bissette Affair in 1823 (Kennedy, 1960; Baber, 1985), discussed in Chapter 6.

The 1831 revolt in St. Pierre was organized by enslaved Africans with more freedom from masters and plantation life. Some were hired for day labor in the port of Saint-Pierre and were known as *nègres de journée* (African day laborers) or *nègres à loyer* (Africans for hire). Their numbers increased considerably and by 1822 approximately 12,143 resided in St. Pierre (Schloss, 2007). The 1831 revolt unfolded over a few days from February 5-10, starting with vandalism of a gallows in the middle of the city. Barge pilots, craftsmen, longshoremen, and other enslaved Africans for hire were instrumental in organizing this revolt. Sugar cane fields outside the city were burned a couple of evenings after the gallows incident, which fanned speculation that St. Pierre itself was next. Commerce ground to a halt as fearful businessmen shut their shops. Their apprehensions were justified, as two days later arsonists targeted 11 plantations around St. Pierre and in the city. Only the fortuitous arrival of Governor Dupotet on February 9 in response to pleas from captains and ship owners disrupted this uprising. Dupotet's troops, crews of cargo ships, police, and militia (many of whom were gens de couleur) were able to evacuate most of the White women and children from the town, secure it, and quell the revolt (Tomich, 1990a).

Conclusion

Changes in any social system generate a complex array of adaptive responses from its members. These adaptations can be incidental or comprehensive, passive or active, cooperative or hostile, gradual or abrupt, and visible or invisible. The adaptive responses of Martinican society to the system of slavery over the course of two centuries ran the gamut of all these. As is so often the case in human interactions, unanticipated repercussions occurred, as they have throughout Martinique's history. Granting free Saturdays and de-facto manumissions by planters of enslaved Africans as cost-saving measures are examples of strategies with outcomes counter to the Plantocracy's overall interests. Often slave uprisings were instigated and coordinated by enslaved Africans who were given discretionary time to work for themselves in the cities (Schloss, 2007). Likewise, it was enslaved Africans with the closest ties to plantation owners who perpetrated poisonings. Further, changes in the Code Noir that tightened requirements for manumission and travel to France seem directly connected to concerns of poisonings and uprisings. Enslaved Africans who accompanied their masters to France and free gens de couleur who traveled there for education experienced a freer society and developed a desire for more equal treatment. Upon returning to

Martinique, members of both groups often collaborated with other gens de couleur and enslaved Africans to petition for more rights and organize revolts against the White Plantocracy.

Prior to the French Revolution and the independence of Haiti, responses by enslaved Africans to the system were usually subtly defiant and evasive, with pockets of more violent uprisings. Similarly, the White Plantocracy imposed harsh and brutal dominance to maintain the system of slavery and all its trappings. Planters frequently resorted to manipulating legislation and the colonial judicial system to undermine the progress, freedom, and social mobility of enslaved Africans, gens de couleur and other groups that threatened their elite status. In some instances, planters manumitted enslaved Africans or showed humanity by allowing some latitude and freedom of movement.

However, with the waves of the French and Haitian revolutions crashing on the shores of Martinique, visible, defiant, and violent responses escalated among the enslaved Africans, gens de couleur, and the White Plantocracy. Uprisings, poisonings, marronage, and executions and deportations of enslaved Africans became more commonplace, with social tensions reaching a breaking point. The end to slavery was inevitable.

As we have seen throughout this chapter, enslaved Africans and other less-oppressed groups were forced to adapt to the system of slavery. However, it is equally clear that such adaptations elicited diverse responses from plantation owners and the mainland French. Thus, social groups in Martinique and France, with their varying vested interests and objectives, defined a complex set of inter- and intra-group dynamics. The intricate network of reciprocal exchanges is the main focus of the next chapter.

Glossary

Patronnés - (French) Enslaved Africans who were not officially free but enjoyed most of the liberties as those formally manumitted.

Petits blancs - (French) French merchants and tradesmen who were not part of the elite Plantocracy.

Petit marronage - (French) Short-term absenteeism by enslaved Africans (usually for a few hours, days, or a couple of weeks) followed by return to the plantation.

Grand marronage - (French) Permanent escape from the plantation by enslaved African individuals or small groups.

Capoeira - (Indigenous Brazilian term adopted by Portuguese) Dance-like martial art of Brazil accompanied by call-and-response singing and percussive music, associated with slave resistance.

Associations serviles - (French) Mutual aid associations of enslaved Africans with elected leadership that held celebrations, weddings, and burials for members and their families; similar to social clubs.

Calenda - (Spanish) Dance of West African origin, characterized by the French as sexually provocative.

Intendant - (French) Agent of the King of France with unlimited authority in one or more provinces.

free Saturdays - Practice of plantation owners of providing land and time for enslaved Africans to grow their own crops.

Provostial Court - judicial body functioning as a military tribunal in response to the many poisonings and revolts by enslaved Africans in the early 19th century; sentences by the court were typically severe.

Nègres de journée / Nègres à loyer - (French, "slave for a day"/"slave for hire") Enslaved Africans allowed by their masters to work for hire, usually in cities.

Reflective Questions

1. From your reading of this chapter, do you think that marronage in all its forms was an effective method of resistance? Provide examples to support your argument.

2. Discuss the idea that debrouillardism in Martinique originated in the oppressive system of slavery. Would you say that debrouillardism is simply being "street smart" or a form of covert resistance? Provide examples.

3. Gospel music and jazz are often associated with slavery in the United States. What artistic forms seem rooted in the experience of slavery in Martinique?

4. Describe resistance by enslaved Africans in the context of the French and Haitian revolutions. How did these events affect resistance movements?

5. From your readings, were poisonings by enslaved Africans mere rumors perpetrated by the paranoid planters or clever strategies? What social and economic factors seem connected to the rumored and actual incidents of poisonings?

6. "Even in bondage, human beings struggle for self-definition and autonomy in whatever ways are available." Although this statement is specifically about slavery, how do struggles for self-definition and autonomy relate to your experiences and the experiences of people around you?

7. Creolization involves cultural groups adapting to each other, resulting in the loss, preservation, and evolution of aspects of their original cultures and the creation of hybrid forms. In what ways did adaptive responses to slavery (both covert and overt) punctuate the process of creolization in Martinique?

Chapter 6

Inter-Group and Intra-Group Dynamics from Slavery to Abolition

> *Transmitting cultural traits happens according to
> conditions and situations in which groups get placed.
> Cultural transmission operates where there is
> a foundation and a context that allows it to exist.
> It is a tributary of history, sociology, and politics.
> It is not a mechanical reflex.[9]*
>
> —Gerry L'Etang
> Professor of Anthropology
> University of the French West Indies, Martinique

Subgroups that developed in the framework of White colonial society and enslaved African society of Martinique from 1640 to 1789 are important to the discussion of cultural identities and creolization. By the beginning of the 19th century, Martinican White society consisted of békés, (descendants of pioneers and original landowners of the 17th century), petits-blancs (mostly descendants of the engagés), Catholic missionaries, government officials from France, and artisans, merchants, and tradesmen who settled in Martinique (Schloss, 2007). Developing a clear hierarchy among the White population had been ongoing for quite some time.

African slave society comprised those who were enslaved,

---

[9] *... la transmission des traits culturels s'établit en fonction des conditions, des situations, dans lesquelles se trouvent placés les groupes qui portent ces traits. La transmission culturelle s'opère quand qu'il existe des bases objectives et un contexte qui la permettent. Elle est tributaire de l'histoire, de la sociologie, de la politique. Elle n'est pas une reconduction mécanique* (L'Etang, 2003, para. 54).

patronnés (slaves given more mobility and freedom), and manumitted ex-slaves. Gens de couleur became a group to reckon with and, as we have seen, played a powerful role in Martinique's politics, culture, and history. Their motives and interests were many, making their interactions with other groups in Martinican society complex. Interactions between French colonists of Martinique and the French from mainland France, especially government representatives and the pro- and anti-abolitionist groups lobbying them, are investigated in this chapter.

The following pages explore the complexity of the inter- and intra-group dynamics between these groups and how each group's perceptions and behaviors affected their cultural narratives. Chapter 5 focused on the responses of enslaved Africans to the system of slavery; this chapter focuses on the responses of other groups to that system and to each other. The proliferation of social groups and increasing differentiation within each group generated a synergy that put Martinique on an irreversible path to end the system of slavery. The central marker on this path was the decree of emancipation, which resulted in cultural reverberations in Martinican society that are felt to this day. This chapter also briefly delineates the immediate aftermath of abolition, how it set the stage for the arrival of indentured workers, and the transition from creolization to cultural hybridization.

Gens de Couleur

There is a direct correlation between the role of this group in colonial affairs and their increase in numbers, especially in relation to Whites, from the late 1600s. In 1687 (after the Caribs had been ousted and slavery had begun in earnest), there were 433 gens de couleur and 4,976 Whites in Martinique. However, by 1789, the number of gens de couleur had risen to 5,236 (more than a 12-fold increase) and Whites to 10,634 (a little over a 2-fold increase; Peabody, 2002).

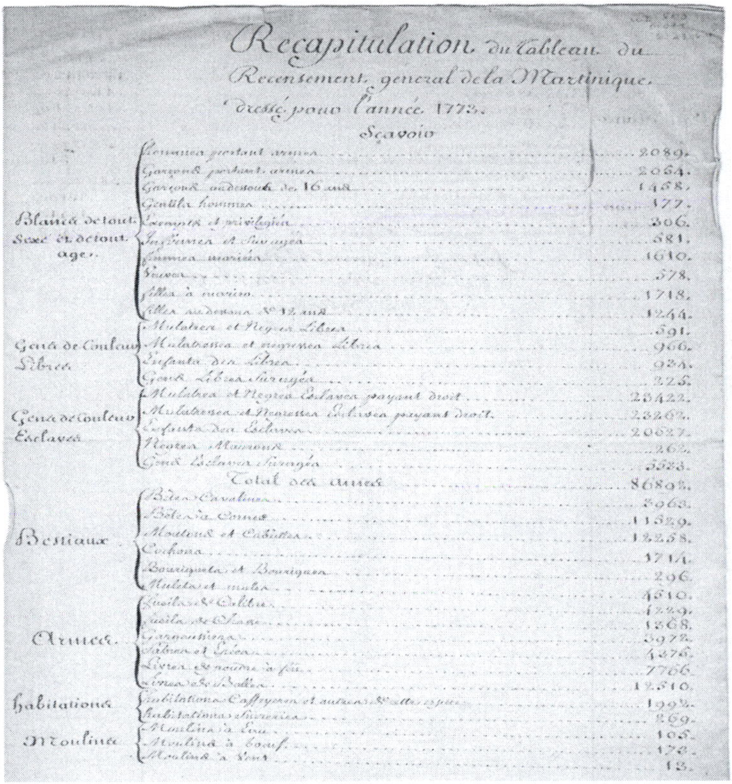

Recapitulation du tableau du Recensement general de la Martinique dressé pour l'année 1773.

Sçavoir

Blancs de tout Sexe et de tout age.	Hommes portant armes	2089.
	Garçons portant armes	2064.
	Garçons au dessous de 16 ans	1468.
	Gentils hommes	177.
	Exempts et privilegiés	306.
	Infirmes et Surangés	581.
	Femmes mariées	1610.
	Veuves	578.
	filles à marier	1718.
	filles au dessous de 12 ans	1244.
Gens de Couleur Libres	Mulatres et Negres Libres	591.
	Mulatresses et negresses Libres	966.
	Enfants des Libres	924.
	Gens Libres surangés	325.
Gens de Couleur Esclaves	Mulatres et Negres Esclaves payant droit	23422.
	Mulatresses et Negresses Esclaves payant droit.	23262.
	Enfants des Esclaves	20627.
	Negres Marons	262.
	Gens Esclaves Surangés	5523.
	Total des ames	86802.
Bestiaux	Bêtes Cavalines	3063.
	Bêtes à Cornes	11329.
	Moutons et Cabrittes	12258.
	Cochons	1714.
	Bouriquets et Bouriques	206.
	Mulets et mules	4510.
Armes.	Fusils de Calibre	4229.
	fusils de Chasse	1368.
	Gargoutières	3972.
	Sabres et Epées	4376.
	Livres de poudre à feu	7766.
	Livres de Balles	12510.
habitations	habitations Cafféyeres et autres de d'autres especes	1998.
	habitations Sucreries	269.
Moulins	Moulins à Eau	105.
	Moulins à boeuf	178.
	Moulins à Vent	13.

Figure 14. Martinique census of 1773 listing the number of whites, gens de couleur, enslaved Africans, livestock, arms, plantations, and sugar mills. (Courtesy of the Beinecke Lesser Antilles Collection, Burke Library, Hamilton College, NY.)

By the slave uprising of 1831 (discussed in Chapter 5), the enslaved African population was 86,289, the number of gens de couleur had almost tripled to 14,055 and the number of Whites had dropped to 9,362, making their minority status in Martinique pronounced (Savage 2007; Schloss 2007). As Confiant pointed out in an interview, the increased number of gens de couleur resulted not only from the growth in illegitimate offspring of White fathers and enslaved African mothers, but also from free gens de couleur engaging in endogamy, or marrying within their group (personal communication, March 17, 2014).

During this volatile period in Martinique, many White fathers were in the habit of sending their (illegitimate) sons to France for education. On their return to Martinique, these gens de couleur were appalled by the social, economic, and educational backwardness of enslaved Africans; their disgust prompted them to join with the resistance in their demands for more rights. The gens de couleur tried to carve out a niche, largely in business, legal, and medical fields in Martinique. Schloss (2009) also discusses the increasingly empowered social and economic status of gens de couleur with respect to the White Plantocracy, especially in their roles as Commissionaires, or liaisons, who facilitated marketing the island's cash crops in France and also supplied Martinique's Plantocracy with materials for sugar production.

This pattern is consistent with Confiant's remarks (personal communication, March 17, 2014) about the historically strong political presence of gens de couleur as representatives to the Colonial Council, the French Assembly, and as local officials, such as mayors. Given this pattern of seeking opportunities within the French system, it is understandable that this form of debrouillardism often put them at odds with the population of enslaved Africans (Browne, 2002). From the early 1700s through the early 1800s, gens de couleur rarely sought common cause with enslaved Africans, but rather with the Plantocracy. Only after the Bissette Affair of 1823 (discussed below) did the free population of color seem to grasp that the architecture of dominance of slavery maintained their own inequality in relation to the White Plantocracy, which motivated them to support the cause of abolition (Elisabeth, 1972). There are also examples of gens de couleur feigning allegiance to colonial or French interests to support the causes of enslaved Africans, seen with some poisonings and rebellion plots.

Uneasy with the rise of gens de couleur in the social hierarchy, the White Plantocracy tried to contain their influence. They accused the gens de couleur of poisonings, sedition, and helping to overthrow the colonial elite, and accused the French government of supporting the rise of the gens de couleur. The powerful planter Dessalles described the gens de couleur as follows: "They have but one thing in mind... the destruction of [w]hites and the overthrow of the government" (Schloss, 2009, p. 93). As a case in point, in 1823 well-to-do gens de couleur were charged the week following their confirmation into the Catholic faith with poisoning members of the White Plantocracy (Savage, 2007). This case bolstered the Plantocracy's increasing resentment of clergy who supported the aspirations of enslaved Africans and gens de couleur, and may have been connected to the eventual ouster of Jesuits from Martinique.

Various laws limited the legal recognition of gens de couleur; for example, they could not be referred to as *"sieur"* or *"dame"* in official documents (Schloss, 2009). Louis-Hilaire Lasserre, a planter in Grand'Anse, refused to use these titles in addressing gens de couleur, including his own brother-in-law. Lasserre was notorious for altercations with many gens de couleur; one resulted in exile of a gens de couleur from Martinique for eight years for fighting with Lasserre. However, when Lasserre set fire to the home of a manumitted African, causing his death, he received only a fine (Flandrina, 2009).

Many békés took judicial matters into their own hands and meted out punishments too severe for the alleged crimes committed by gens de couleur. In the Bissette Affair of 1823-1827, a gens de couleur, Cyrille Charles Auguste Bissette, and six others were accused of spreading negative propaganda about the future of gens de couleur under the Plantocracy in Martinique. They were tried (under questionable circumstances) by a béké, filling in for an official from France. The trial was not public and the accused were sentenced to be banished from Martinique and have their property seized. Dissatisfied with the lack of severity of this sentence, planters appealed for a second trial, after which additional sentences were imposed. Some of the seven defendants were branded and imprisoned and others were deported with no hope of return. The defendants responded by appealing to the **Court of Cassation** but their appeal was deliberately delayed for two years. This manipulation by the Plantocracy of the colonial legal system was not viewed favorably in France. The Court of Cassation found Bissette guilty, but imposed a lighter sentence; Bissette's second appeal to the court was denied. The Bissette affair revealed three things: the level of frustration among the gens de couleur; increasing paranoia of the Plantocracy, with ensuing manipulation of the colonial legal system; and mainland France's displeasure with such manipulation (Kennedy, 1960).

In 1833, the French government passed a law giving full political rights to gens de couleur, raising resentment and anger among Whites. From Grand'Anse in the northeast to St. Pierre in the northwest, rumors of impending offensives by the gens de couleur proliferated, aggravating the climate of fear and confusion. Because this law of full citizenship stipulated the requirement of property ownership, it limited the number of gens de couleur who qualified (one in eight); thus frustrating them in their quest for citizenship (Flandrina, 2009).

The Martinican French

Petits Blancs

Not all Whites in Martinique owned land or slaves. The *petits blancs* (about 4,000-7,000 in 1830-1848) comprised low-income skilled and unskilled laborers, shopkeepers, and merchants, as well as artisans and professionals who provided the workforce, merchandise, and businesses underlying the successful functioning of the colonial economy. Mostly descended from engagés, petits blancs had complex relations with the békés; at times supported by them in paternalistic ways, at times treated as partners in the colonial enterprise, but frequently blamed for perpetrating miscegenation and other social ills. The White Plantocracy saw them as responsible for the decline of their elite way of life and for undermining the architecture of dominance. In an effort to prevent poor French islanders or petits blancs from aiding and forming alliances with gens de couleur against the békés, plantation owners increased their contributions to charities run by parishes to help these lower-class Whites (Schloss, 2009).

Public interaction between petits blancs and gens de couleur (and enslaved Africans) were perceived by békés as a threat to the very definition of Whiteness. Many interactions with gens de couleur were a matter of necessity in conducting business, but raised suspicions nonetheless, especially the activities of female petits blancs. Female petits blancs in business and trades seemed dangerous to plantation society, given that citizenship was determined by one's mother. Social interactions between White women and non-White men created profound anxiety in the békés, who were bent on limiting the leverage of gens de couleur and preserving White advantage (Schloss, 2009).

For example, unrest on February 9, 1831 in St. Pierre, discussed in Chapter 5, was evidence of the feared banding together of supposedly disparate groups on the island: two petits blancs joined gens de couleur in this uprising, widening divisions among colonial Whites (Schloss, 2007). One of the petits blancs was in a relationship with an African woman, which brought to the forefront the issue of defining who was White. Essentially, if poor Whites contributed to the spread of "**sangmélé,**" or mixed blood, only the elite planters could be considered White. Following this uprising, attempts were made to preserve the "pure" White lineage by imposing rigid protocols for the mobility, education, and behavior of elite White women on the island.

White Plantocracy

"Long ago, a nest of ants that bite peopled the earth, and called themselves men..." (Schwarz-Bart, 2013, p. 54). This is how Ma Cia in *The Bridge of Beyond* presents Guadeloupean planters, who were not appreciably different from their counterparts in Martinique. Maximizing sugar production in an efficient manner with cheap slave labor was the primary objective of the White Plantocracy in Martinique and elsewhere in the French colonies. The wealthy plantation owners largely determined the economic, political, and social affairs of Martinique. This Plantocracy consisted of descendants and relatives of the following: French pioneers and early settlers (including flibustiers), the French royalty's entourage, those who were given land and titles of nobility from the French monarch for settling the island, and successful entrepreneurs and tradesmen. Their independent entrepreneurial bent, combined with their strong ties to wealthy investors, businessmen, and politicians in mainland France, were instrumental in the development of the plantation economy. An equally instrumental component in the maintenance of the plantation economy was the ruthless and inhumane treatment of enslaved Africans by the Plantocracy as an essential part of their business model, hence, Ma Cia's charaterization of them.

Martinique's slave-based economy fattened the coffers of France, allowing the Plantocracy's abusive power to go largely unchecked, which generated mixed reactions in mainland France. Although planters began as the numerically dominant group in the early part of the 17th century (1627-1640), by the time of the French Revolution, approximately 150 years since the arrival of enslaved Africans in Martinique, there were 83,000 enslaved Africans, 10,600 Whites, and 5,000 gens de couleur (Browne, 2002, p. 384). By 1831, the number of Whites had dropped to about 10,000, with the self-

Figure 15. Mural of plantation life found at Hotel La Bateliere, Fort de France. (Photo by authors, 2014; artist and date of mural unknown.)

identified White Plantocracy numbering about 2,000. This drop in population may help explain their fear of losing power reflected in the Plantocracy's more brutal actions.

The Plantocracy thus became preoccupied with controlling enslaved Africans through discipline, preventing marronage, and limiting the conditions of manumission, or freeing enslaved Africans, especially after the Haitian Revolution.[10] Paradoxically, in an effort to limit expenses associated with freeing enslaved Africans (the manumission tax), some slave-masters gave enslaved Africans freedom without adhering to bureaucratic procedures. This practice was so widespread that, by the 1830s, the number of informally manumitted enslaved Africans, or *esclaves patronnés,* was comparable to that of the legally freed (Schloss, 2009). To avoid the supervisory and disciplinary

[10] The large population of gens de couleur, marrons, and recently arrived enslaved Africans were vital to Haiti's revolution and eventual independence in 1804 (Bernabé, personal communication, March 18, 2014; Confiant, personal communication, March 17, 2014).

difficulties of the undefined legal status of the patronnés, who were neither enslaved nor exactly free but had great latitude of movement, some colonial authorities recommended their legal manumission. It should be noted that some slaveholders allowed enslaved Africans free time as an incentive for loyalty and good work, particularly when they didn't have resources to compensate them in other ways (land, livestock, extra food, etc.), or when they developed a bond (not always sexual) with certain enslaved Africans (Savage, 2006). In a further example of accommodation to avoid disrupting productivity, some planters overlooked polygamy, a customary practice in some African societies (Boucher, 2008).

An unintended consequence of free Saturdays, discussed in Chapter 5, was that enslaved Africans left the plantation to sell their goods, recruit other enslaved Africans for labor, or otherwise conduct business. This made it difficult for owners to know who was enslaved and who was a marron, a paradoxical situation arising from a cost-cutting measure instituted by planters (Savage, 2006).

Deportation by the Colonial Council was another tool of control, which removed the offending enslaved African as an influence, saved the expense of imprisonment, and basically made taking care of the individual someone else's problem. Enslaved Africans were deported to other Antillean islands and parts of North America. Some were sent back to Africa as a form of punishment, which is ironic because being brought to Martinique against their will was certainly not a reward. France, however, saw this as an evasion of justice (Savage 2006). Despite such efforts by the Colonial Council and Provostial Court to quell slave uprisings and other crimes, they were not effective in reducing unrest; on the contrary, they seemed to incite more. Discipline and punishment was sometimes handed over to slave-owners to carry out on the privacy of their plantations, avoiding oversight and providing much room for abuse.

However, the gross negligence of the Provostial Court in Martinique and its severe punishments of enslaved Africans became evident to the mainland French. In 1823, a group of enslaved Africans appealed judgments by the Provostial Court, whose decisions heretofore had been final. The fact that the Court of Cassation (highest court in France) was willing to hear their appeals and reduce the sentence of one appellant was a blow to the colonists' autonomy, and their sense of betrayal by their *"Mère Patrie"* ("mother country") was a natural result (Geggus, 1983; Savage, 2007).

The rising influence of the gens de couleur was another force to be reckoned with by the Plantocracy. They took a number of actions to limit suffrage of newly freed people and gens de couleur. Article 59 of the Code Noir granted enslaved Africans who had been freed the same rights and privileges as those born free, but it was not always carried out in practice (Butel, 2002). As noted earlier in this chapter, by 1833, gens de couleur had the same voting rights as the White Plantocracy, but eligible voters were required to pay a tax. The Plantocracy increased this tax in the 1834 elections for the Colonial Council well above what France mandated. To add insult to injury, property of the gens de couleur was deliberately devalued so they would not have resources to pay the poll tax; this was the situation that one Auguste Havre faced, whose assets were depreciated by a planter named Eyma in Grande-Anse. Subsequently, Auguste Havre's name was removed from the roll of eligible voters. Previously, he had been denied a promotion in the militia to which he was entitled. The following phrase summarizes the feelings of planters who did not see freedom (Liberty) as the same thing as equal rights (Equality): "... that they [the planters] would never vote with the gens de couleur in the electoral colleges, and that they would

never recognize them [the gens de couleur] as officers of the militia"[11]

[11] *... qu'ils ne voteraiant jamais avec des mulâtres dans les colleges électoraux et qu'ils*

(Flandrina, 2009, p. 41).

To the planters' dismay, even the French Catholic missionaries generally were to some degree against slavery, particularly after enslaved Africans had been baptized and confirmed. However, missionaries showed their ambivalence to slavery in numerous ways, permitting some enslaved Africans to be church officials, pressing authorities to allow freedmen and enslaved Africans to marry, and advocating better nourishment for enslaved Africans. Although many missionaries owned plantations and enslaved Africans, they were not consistently supporters of slavery (Peabody, 2002). The gradually waning influence of formal religious instruction was also a factor in generating fear and paranoia among the Plantocracy. As the number of enslaved Africans swelled almost exponentially, the clergy could not maintain the pace of their mission because of the challenge of finding clerics willing to brave the hazards of the Caribbean and gradually dwindling support from plantation owners. To compound the Catholic Church's recruitment difficulties, French society in general was less inclined to support efforts at evangelism, as more secular and rationalist Enlightenment ideals began to take hold in the decades preceding the French Revolution (Peabody, 2002). With the ratio of priests to enslaved Africans going from about 3 for every 1,000 in the 1680s to 1 for every 10,000 in the 1780s (Peabody, 2004, p. 122), instruction in Christianity was reduced to a cursory and hasty affair.

Over time, this dilution of Catholic religious education opened the door for more widespread practice of spiritual traditions from West Africa among the enslaved Africans. With the now-overwhelming number of newly arrived Africans interacting with those already enslaved who practiced Catholicism, syncretism of Catholicism and African spiritual practices became more visible (and alarming) to the colonists. Quimboiserie is one such tradition that became well known during this period. Because of limited training and insufficient access

ne les reconnaîtraient jamais pour officiers dans les milices.

to European medicine in the 18th century, the White Plantocracy was quite willing to adopt quimboiserie as alternative medicine. However, as the reputations of the quimboiseurs grew, slave-owners feared the possibility of being poisoned: "The terror of poison is widespread on the island; the slave uses this to dominate his master"[12] (Lavollée, 1841, p. 124).

Because poisoners attacked livestock and fellow enslaved people (even family members) as well as slave-owners, a climate of suspicion and uncertainty developed in Martinique. The slave-owners saw threats from enslaved Africans, freed Africans, gens de couleur, and even petit-blancs at every turn, as each group had at some point aided and abetted the poisonings and at other points were the target (Savage, 2007). This uncoordinated, widespread targeting of victims made it difficult to organize a resistance movement, as occurred during the Haitian Revolution. But the unpredictability of such attacks still had a destabilizing effect on plantation society because incidents of poisoning increased, especially by the enslaved closest to their masters. Governor Donzelot expressed some of the betrayal the planters seemed to feel from the trend of poisoners being some of the most-trusted and best-treated enslaved Africans (Savage, 2007). Slave-owners responded fiercely to their suspicions by increasing the severity of punishment for suspected poisoners. Like the fabled Hydra, who sprouted two heads for every one cut off, this relentless cycle of suspected poisonings followed by savage punishments seemed only to result in more poisonings.

The Plantocracy's lack of familiarity with African herbalism and spiritual practices, often perceived as sorcery, led to significant misinterpretation of what constituted "poisoning" rather than "healing." This quickly fanned colonists' fears of disruption of the social order (Savage, 2007). It is interesting that herbalism is mentioned by the early missionaries, but not in the context of poisoning; the Code

---

[12] *La terreur du poison est grande dans le pays; par elle l'esclave domine le maître.*

Noir makes no reference to the crime of poisoning either. Given that the earliest policies about poisoning did not appear until the 1720s, planters' deep-seated mistrust of slaves' use of herbal lore evidently began in the 18th century (Boucher, 2008).

Unrest combined with ongoing debate in the French National Assembly concerning the abolition of slavery alienated the White Plantocracy, which perceived the situation as a well-planned scheme on the part of the enslaved Africans, gens de couleur, and abolitionists in France to destroy the colonial system. The Plantocracy retaliated aggressively toward enslaved Africans and the other groups perceived as threatening their way of life, and the planters were even willing to cut their ties with motherland France. When France abolished slavery in 1794, the Martinican Plantocracy wholeheartedly embraced the British colonial empire in order to perpetuate slavery, and Martinique remained under British control for eight years (Ferguson, 2008).

This was not, however, the case in Guadeloupe, where slavery was abolished in 1794 and reestablished by Napoleon Bonaparte in 1802. During this brief period of abolition, several plantation owners in Guadeloupe were killed and many fled the colony, opening the door for Martinican plantation owners to buy their land. Guadeloupeans still resent that Martinicans assisted in re-colonizing them. Because most of these Martinican plantation owners were absentee landlords, enslaved Africans in Guadeloupe enjoyed greater freedom than their Martinican counterparts. Some Guadeloupeans (particularly gens de couleur) held positions of authority that had been traditionally reserved for Whites in Guadeloupe and France. Commandant Camille Mortenol (1859-1930), son of an enslaved Guadeloupean, who held a prominent military post in France, is a noteworthy example. Such upward movement of descendants of enslaved Africans was much less common in Martinique where plantation owners had tighter control over society (Bernabé, personal communication, March 18, 2014).

The threats posed by Haitian independence in 1804, the end of the slave trade in 1815 (agreed to by France in the Congress of Vienna[13]) and the growing abolitionist movement in France convinced the Martinican Plantocracy that all were against them, and they saw insurrection at every corner. The Plantocracy's responses grew ever more frantic with their increasing sense of isolation in Martinique. In their efforts to retain as many people enslaved as possible, as well as maintain power, they became more stringent with slave manumissions in general, but specifically of females of child-bearing age so that the planters would continue to own children born into slavery (Schloss, 2009). Fines for transporting enslaved Africans without payment and authorization became steep and routine. The obligations of slave-owners to ensure the safety of the enslaved and account for their whereabouts and activities (particularly when traveling to France) became more burdensome (Savage, 2006).

To reinforce the békés' feelings of racial and moral superiority, marriages between Blacks and Whites were banned. The great literary minds of the Enlightenment, along with the abolitionist movement in mainland France that advanced the notion of liberty and racial equality, were vehemently opposed to these desperate measures and sentiments of the Martinican Plantocracy (Confer, 1964).

The Mainland French

The 1315 Royal Ordinance of Louis X, mentioned in Chapter 3, may be considered an early precursor to anti-slavery sentiments in France throughout colonial history. Nevertheless, neither the French monarchy nor populace had a unified voice or perspective on plantation society, especially the matter of slavery, until abolition in 1848. The profitability of the colonial enterprise was rarely in question, which

---

[13] Though the slave trade formally ended in 1815, the last known slaving expedition from France, *La Virginie*, set sail from Nantes in 1830 (Icart, 2007).

explains approximately 350 years of colonization. The moral question surrounding slavery among the mainland French was a constant thorn in their sides. This ambivalence became starkly evident as enslaved Africans became more visible in Paris and major port cities. A number of enslaved Africans were manumitted upon entering France as early as 1571 and 1691 and through the French Revolution (Riddell, 1925; Chatman, 2000). But the presence of enslaved Africans, and issues concerning their rights in mainland France, continued to occupy the monarchy, politicians, religious leaders, intellectuals, and the general public.

By the mid 1700s, enslaved Africans traveling to France with their masters as domestics, cooks, or nannies had become fairly routine. Slave masters did not want to lose their property through forced manumission, and tried to circumvent the ordinance of 1315. The loose interpretation of this ordinance compounded by inconsistent implementation prompted modifications to the Code Noir of 1685 so that it was applicable to mainland France as well. Some of the more noteworthy restrictions imposed on slave-owners required paying deposits to ensure enslaved Africans' return to the colonies, registering the enslaved in France, limiting their length of stay there, and constraining marriages between enslaved Africans. There were also penalties, including forfeiture of enslaved Africans, for violating these policies (Riddell, 1925; Chatman, 2000).

The hefty manumission tax imposed by colonial authorities was intended to curtail slave manumissions in Martinique and the other French colonies. However, some slave- owners ignored the tax and freed their enslaved Africans, others sent them to France to be manumitted; many manumitted women were or had been in relationships with their White masters or supervisors. In addition to limiting manumission, other social, political, and economic measures were implemented in 1764, 1765, 1773, and 1781 to considerably restrict and oppress gens de couleur and manumitted slaves (Schloss, 2009). However, after the Bissette Affair of 1823 (discussed earlier), slave manumissions were completely halted.

Prior to the French Revolution, anti-slavery and anti-colonial sentiments were expressed by great French writers and philosophers. Eighteenth-century intellectuals such as Rousseau, Montesquieu, and Voltaire all advocated liberty and equality; however they were less vocal about abolishing slavery in the colonies. Some were willing to overlook slavery for economic reasons, others for religious reasons, and others believed that enslaved Africans were ill-suited for freedom. For example, Voltaire had a financial stake in the island colonies, and Montesquieu did not oppose business with the colonies because they provided goods not otherwise available in Europe. Montesquieu, however, was especially opposed to the religious objectives of slavery. There was nevertheless consensus among the intelligentsia regarding humanitarian arguments against slavery, which served as a rallying point for the cause of abolition (Confer, 1964; Geggus, 1989).

The abolition movement in France gained momentum with a group in Paris, *La Société des amis des noirs,* founded in 1788. This organization consisted mostly of French philosophers and intelligentsia, including the Marquis de Condorcet, Abbé Grégoire Brissot, and Lafayette. The society focused on humanitarian grounds for emancipation and was opposed by another group, the **Club Massiac**, whose members had major economic interests in the Caribbean and who were primarily plantations owners who lived in France, entrepreneurs, and businessmen who directly profited from the colonial sugar trade (Ferguson, 2008).

Figure 16. Abolitionist medallion with the translated inscription "Am I not a man: a brother?" (1789, Adrien Dubouché National Museum, Limoges). From Schmidt, N. [2012]. Slavery and Its Abolition, French Colonies, Research and Transmission of Knowledge, p. 10. Courtesy of UNESCO.)

The political path to abolition was just as circuitous and equivocal as the philosophical path. The Constituent Assembly (a representative body formed after the French Revolution to draft a constitution) did not elect abolitionists to its Colonial Committee, and provided the colonists cover for continuing slavery with a decree in 1790 that essentially promised a non-interference policy, allowing the colonies to determine their own laws. The Club Massaic was instrumental in lobbying for this decree. The effectiveness of the Club Massaic and its allies in politically outmaneuvering the abolitionists slowed progress toward granting freedom to enslaved Africans and gens de couleur. However, the Haitian revolt in 1791 brought the issue back to the Constituent Assembly with renewed purpose. Stalled efforts to recognize the rights of non-Whites were at last being debated openly, with the abolitionist cause gradually gaining momentum (Geggus, 1989).

On February 6, 1794 the Montagnard Convention abolished slavery in French colonies and bestowed citizenship rights on all persons in the French empire. Under this decree, slave-owners would be forced to free 700,000 people, without financial compensation. However, just weeks prior to this convention, seeing the writing on the wall, the White Plantocracy in Martinique allowed the colony to be occupied by the English to avoid abolition and continue to profit from the institution of slavery and the sugar economy. Martinique did not see the emancipation of slaves on the island until 1848, at which time the slave owners were compensated for the loss of their enslaved workforce (Butel, 2002; Geggus, 1989).

The harsh responses of White elites to poisonings by enslaved Africans, and the February, 1831 slave uprising in Martinique, further fueled anti-colonial sentiment in France (Confer, 1964). Several documents from independent sources and government appointees hinted at the brutalization of enslaved Africans by paranoid elites trying to cling to power. The reports contributed to the sense among the mainland French that the colonists were inhumane and uncivilized (Schloss, 2007). Despite the growing public animosity toward slavery, there were still pockets of resistance in France to its abolition. The editors of the *Journal du Havre* in France in the May 1831 edition described the crisis in Martinique as not of "political economy but French blood" (Schloss, 2007, p. 232) suggesting unquestioning support for their colonial brethren.

Thus, with waning enthusiasm in France for the colonial enterprise, the abolition movement took a slightly different form in 1834, pursuing a strategy of gradual expansion of rights. The *Société pour l'abolition de l'esclavage* worked to ease the severity of punishments, increase access to education, and make freeing enslaved people easier (especially if they came to France; Ferguson, 2008). Victor Schoelcher, who had seen the effects of slavery in his travels in the the Caribbean, took over leadership of the Société in 1840 and advocated a quicker end to slavery. It became glaringly apparent, as Alexis de Tocqueville, the famous French historian and writer, and a founder of the Société pour l'abolition de l'esclavage, declared, "It is no longer a question of whether slavery is bad or if it must end, but when and how must it end"[14] (Beuze, 1998, p. 44).

A major step toward full emancipation was the passage of the Mackau Law of 1845, which curtailed the length of workdays for enslaved Africans and, most important, eased conditions for manumission, allowing enslaved Africans to buy freedom for themselves and their families as long as they committed to five years of salaried work for their former owners (Butel, 2002). This law was a classic example of a compromise that left no one satisfied: the planters objected strenuously that it went too far, and the abolitionists chafed that it didn't go far enough. It is fair to state that the primary legacy of the Mackau Law was that it made the inexorable momentum toward full emancipation for enslaved Africans felt by the White Plantocracy, French abolitionists, and the enslaved themselves.

Emancipation Decree of 1848

Swept along by this momentum, as Undersecretary of State to the Minister of the Navy, Schoelcher gained the power to champion legislation abolishing slavery. He stated clearly that "… no French territory can be home to slaves"[15] (Beuze, 1998, p. 47) and formed a commission on March 4, 1848 for immediate emancipation. Though he tried to obtain reparations for enslaved Africans, that clause was defeated in favor of compensating slave-owners, in contrast to the Montagnard Convention 1794 abolition decree discussed above

---

[14] *Il ne s'agit plus de savoir si l'esclavage est mauvais et s'il doit finir, mais quand et comment il doit cesser.*
[15] *… nulle terre française ne peut plus porter d'esclaves.*

(Ferguson, 2008). Subsequently, the French government established the Bank of Martinique to help the White Plantocracy pay wages to the formerly enslaved, who would no longer work without pay. By the same token, the White Plantocracy was no longer legally bound to provide housing, food, clothing, or any care for the newly freed people, leaving them with their freedom but not much else (Confiant, personal communication, March 17, 2014).

Before its work was complete, news of Schoelcher's commission reached Martinique by April 12, 1848; enslaved Africans and gens de couleur were eager for the formal decree of emancipation, which caused unrest in Martinique (Beuze, 1998). Many enslaved Africans stopped working, which made planters nervous because the harvest season was upon them. Faced with increasing agitation, Director of the Interior in Martinique Husson implored the enslaved Africans for patience, because "Liberty is coming…. The good masters have requested that for you… thus, nothing has changed yet. You will remain slaves until the law is proclaimed"[16] (Butel, 2002, p. 292).

On April 27, 1848, the Emancipation Decree was signed in Paris, ending slavery in Martinique. Although the actual piece of legislation would have arrived in Martinique to be proclaimed on June 3 by Commisioner Perrinon, a Martinican gens de couleur, news of the Emancipation Decree reached Martinique much sooner. Frustration grew everywhere as Martinicans awaited the impending decree, spurring violent altercations between planters, the militia, and enslaved Africans. Tens of thousands of the enslaved cast off the physical chains of slavery, reclaiming freedom by their own initiative. This momentous event is succinctly described in Creole as *"Nèg pété chenn"* ("the slaves broke off their chains"; Héber-Suffrin, 2014, p. 22). They refused to cut cane, walked out of factories and off plantations, and crowded town

---

[16] *La liberté va venir… Ce sont de bons maîtres qui l'ont demandée pour vous… Ainsi, rien n'est change jusqu'à présent. Vous demeurez esclaves jusqu'à la proclamation de la loi.*

squares; 16,000 gathered in St. Pierre alone. Several enslaved Africans, gens de couleur, and planters were killed in the ensuing riots on May 22, and fires set to plantations and homes of planters. The gens de couleur were fully engaged in the protests and petitioned in major towns of Martinique for the immediate return of Bissette (Beuze, 1998). Many of the Plantocracy sought safety in the ships docked in the port of St. Pierre. Having had enough of this tumult, Governor Rostoland of Martinique proclaimed on May 23, 1848, "Slavery is abolished as of today in Martinique..."[17] (Butel, 2002, p. 294). This proclamation only triggered more destruction and pillaging of plantations in Morne Rouge, St. Pierre, and Fort de France, but it also unleashed shouts of exultation from the now-free people.

Immediate Aftermath of Abolition

Freedom for enslaved Africans came with many challenges and conditions, largely because of the colonial interest in maintaining a large, low-cost labor force to operate their sugar plantations. The decree of April 1848 did institute "... the rights and freedoms of association, expression and press publication, as well as male universal suffrage to designate representatives to the national assembly, freedom of employment and access to education for all. "They [these rights and freedoms] were also potentially self-nullifying" (Schmidt, 2012, p. 16-17). Several laws and decrees soon after (within a few weeks) systematically impinged on the rights of newly freed people to participate and flourish in a free society.

Access to education for the children of the newly emancipated (after the age of 12) and free public assembly and self-expression in the press were curtailed either by the colonial authorities or hefty

---

[17] *L'esclavage est aboli à partir de ce jour à la Martinique....*

taxes. Even the ability of these now-free people to farm as they saw fit was limited by punitive tariffs on what were deemed non-essential crops. Their freedom of movement was carefully limited by vagrancy regulations that required newly free individuals to provide documentation of their employment to justify movement between plantations and towns or face arrest as criminals. The exorbitant tax on children's education kept many from attending school, and thus the application of these vagrancy laws to children was particularly tragic. The French government's position that children "must be prevented from becoming vagabonds and thieves" (Chilcoat, 2004, p. 59) provided enough of a justification for plantation owners to use child labor in exchange for food and shelter under the guise of rehabilitating these children through plantation work, replicating the system of slavery (Schmidt, 2012).

Africans continued to constitute the majority of the population on Martinique after abolition as they had since the mid-17th century. Once freed, many left plantations for cities (primarily St. Pierre and Fort de France), but many also stayed on plantations in their houses or *cases*, worked as hired farmhands, and continued to cultivate their own plots of land. They saved their income to buy land so that they could become independent agriculturalists. Thus, a new class of small farmers developed; these now-free people were landowners who aspired to the same life their former masters enjoyed. Some bought additional plots of land, hired other freed Africans to work their land, and started to develop a neo-plantation economy.

Figure 18. "The Abolition of Slavery in the French Colonies in 1848," by Francois-Auguste Biard, 1849. (From Schmidt, N. (2012), Slavery and Its Abolition, French Colonies, Research and Transmission of Knowledge, p.18. Courtesy of UNESCO.)

Conclusion

By the 19th century, the sociopolitical climate in Martinique, France, and Haiti was the major factor driving the inter- and intra-group dynamics of the colonial enterprise. Important events fueled resistance among Martinique's oppressed groups, such as:

- the French Revolution of 1789,
- the Declaration of the Rights of Man and the abolition of slavery in the French colonies in 1794,
- the reinstatement of slavery by Napoleon in 1802,[18] and finally
- Haitian independence in 1804.

A sense of hope among Africans and gens de couleur, and speculation

---

[18] *This reinstatement did not apply to Saint Domingue (Haiti), which was embroiled in its revolutionary war.*

that the principles of liberty and equality that toppled Louis XVI's regime and ended France's colonial empire in Haiti could apply to them, became tangible. It is in this environment that the inter- and intra-group dynamics among the various groups discussed in this chapter coalesced in the abolition of slavery in 1848.

The grave economic consequences of abolition dreaded by the Plantocracy were in fact short-lived. Sugar exports from Martinique sharply fell from 39,337 tons in 1847 to 15, 065 in 1850. However, by 1851 Governor Vaillant anticipated sugar exports to reach 22,500 tons (Butel, 2002). The societal upheaval was far more significant, however, with new social divisions emerging in old settings and the arrival of groups of laborers from India, Africa, and China who would transform the social hierarchy. With the end of slavery and the arrival of new immigrant groups, Martinique's cultural evolution transitioned from creolization to hybridization.

Glossary

Sieur - (French, "Mister") Term of respect and courtesy used as a prefix to a man's surname or by itself.

Dame - (French, "Lady") Term of respect and courtesy used as a prefix to a woman's surname or by itself.

Court of Cassation - Highest court of appeal for criminal and civil cases in the French judicial system.

sangmélé - (French, "mixed blood") Refers particularly to individuals with both White and Black parentage.

Mère Patrie - (French, "Mother Country") Patriotic synonym for France.

La Société des amis des noirs - (French, "The Society of the Friends of Blacks") Abolitionist organization founded in 1788 in Paris by French intellectuals.

Club Massiac - Organization supporting colonialism and slavery, largely of plantation owners and those who profited from the sugar trade.

Société pour l'abolition de l'esclavage - (French, "The Society for the Abolition of Slavery") Organization founded in 1830, of which Victor Schoelcher assumed leadership in 1840.

Mackau Law - Legislation enacted in 1845 that improved working conditions for enslaved people and expanded the conditions by which they could be freed, including purchasing freedom for themselves and families.

Reflective Questions

1. Gens de couleur played a critical role in resistance movements against slavery, both in Martinique and Haiti. How did their relationships with enslaved Africans and the White Plantocracy change over time, and how did they leverage their unique status to effect change in Martinique?

2. Not all the French in Martinique saw eye-to-eye on all matters. Analyze the intra-group dynamics of the Martinican French in terms of the interests of each subgroup.

3. Provide examples to discuss the ways in which the White Plantocracy manipulated articles of the Code Noir and the colonial judicial system to their advantage. What were some unintended consequences of these attempts, and how did they ultimately empower enslaved Africans?

4. It is apparent that anti-slavery sentiments in France existed as early as the 1300s. Discuss the ambivalence of the mainland French toward slavery and the colonial enterprise.

5. By the 1830s, the White Plantocracy in Martinique felt besieged and interpreted everyone and everything as conspiring against them. Give three examples that illustrate their perception of persecution.

Chapter 7

The Era of Indentured Workers
Coolies and Dual Host Communities

The entire indianité movement is structured around the painful process of deconstructing the wretched image of the Indo-Martinican. This work has been so active that in just a few years, the image of the Indian has improved significantly....[1]

-Juliette Sméralda
Professor of Sociology
University of the French West Indies, Martinique

When Commissioner Perrinon arrived in Martinique on June 3, 1848 with the Emancipation Decree in hand, he had two principal aims. The first was ensuring voting rights for the newly freed people and the second was to ensure the availability of work for them (Butel, 2002). The second goal seems to have been more challenging because many now-free people fervently desired to be no longer associated with the plantation economy that was closely connected to slavery.

The newly freed people left the plantations to either farm for themselves or find opportunities in more urban areas, creating an acute labor shortage on the plantations and threatening the lucrative sugar industry to its core, with anticipated financial ruin for the French Plantocracy (Pillai, 2005). Governor of Martinique Auguste Vaillant described the labor vacuum on the plantations as dire and

---

[1] *Tout le mouvement de l'Indianité s'est structuré autour du souci de déconstruire cette image misérabiliste de l'Indo-Martiniquais. Ce travail a été si actif que, en quelques années, l'image de l'Indien s'est fortement améliorée...* (Sméralda-Amon, n.d., para. 26).

requiring immediate attention (Thaniyayagam, 1968). As for the planters, emigration to neighboring islands and to the United States was a promising option (Butel, 2002). Those who chose to remain in Martinique faced the challenge of resolving the immediate economic crisis that loomed large over the plantation economy.

One way to address the desperate need for labor and to continue the huge profits they had become accustomed to was to saturate the market by importing **indentured workers,** or a contractual labor force, similar to the *engagés* from France during the early phase of colonization. The larger the labor pool and the fewer the available jobs, the less the plantation owners needed to pay laborers. This simple, yet effective, application of the supply and demand concept was set in motion by plantation owners. For his part, Napoleon III issued a decree in 1852 allowing the recruitment of "foreigners" to work on plantations, supporting the planters' strategy. Subsequently, 37,008 indentured workers; 10,521 from Africa (Congo-Kinshasa, Sierra Leone, and Gabon), 25,509 from India, and 978 from China were brought to work on sugar plantations (L'Etang, 2003). However, because of abolitionist protests in mainland France and Martinique and opposition from Britain, which accused France of continuing a camouflaged form of slave trade, importing African indentured workers lasted only five years (1857-1862; Desroches, 1996). Chinese immigration lasted only one year from 1859 to 1860.

This chapter is dedicated to the journeys and narratives of a forgotten and often overlooked group in Martinican history, Indians from South Asia. Of the 25,509 Indians who arrived in Martinique starting in 1853, 16,000 perished by 1900. In the first years following their arrival in Martinique (1856-1860), the mortality rate was 58%. Today, Indians from South Asia account for less than three per cent of the population of Martinique, and most are of mixed heritage (Sméralda-Amon, 2004). Their contributions to Martinican history and culture are rich and evident in art, cuisine, and fashion, but awareness of the people who made these contributions has come to the forefront only in the last 10-15 years. Research from Martinique on Indian indentured workers is still not prolific but excellent in quality. Raphaël Confiant, Patrice Domoison, Yves and Roselyne Gamess, Gerry L'Etang, and Juliette Smeralda, among others, are leading scholars in this field.

The first vessel, *L'Aurélie,* bringing 314 Indian indentured workers or *coolies* (a term referring to hired manual labor in India) reached the shores of Martinique on May 6, 1853 (Ramassamy, 2012), and Indian immigration continued for 30 more years, until 1885. The majority of these indentured workers hailed from the French enclaves of Pondicherry, Karaikal, and Mahé (mostly *Tamil*-speaking regions in southern India). A smaller minority came from Chandernagore in the Bengal region of northeastern India. Following an agreement by the British and the French on July 1, 1861, France was allowed to recruit indentured workers from British India, which France formerly had done surreptitiously. A much smaller number of indentured workers (926) arrived later in Martinique from the regions of Uttar Pradesh and Bihar, which were under British rule (L'Étang & Permal, 1994; Desroches, 1996). Major restructuring of the Martinican social hierarchy was on the horizon.

For the freed people unburdened from the cruel institution of slavery after almost 200 years, the future was full of hope. Conversely, French colonists, who feared collapse of the sugar industry and loss of their economic success, viewed the abolition of slavery as nothing less than calamitous. The majority of Indian indentured workers were illiterate, poor, and came from lower castes. They had little or no knowledge of French or geography to understand the implications of their contracts or even the distance they were to travel. Thousands boarded ships with the belief that leaving India was their only chance for breaking the cycle of poverty. To them, Martinique represented the

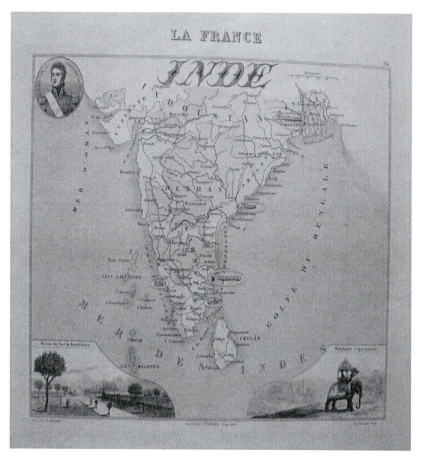

Figure 19. Map of India highlighting French enclaves c.1768. (Courtesy www.themaritimegallery.co.uk)

promised land. While the Plantocracy and the Indians embraced the indentured worker program, the newly free people were disillusioned by it. Very simply put, one man's food was the other man's poison. As Sméralda-Amon points out, "But one's optimism feeds the pessimism of others"[2] (2004, sec. 1). Anti-colonial revolts and pro-abolitionist movements in Martinique, in France, and in Haiti that heralded the emancipation of enslaved Africans and saw the renaissance of the indentured worker system in Martinique are reviewed first in this

---

[2] *Mais l'optimisme des uns nourrit le pessimisme des autres.*

chapter as a prelude to Indian emigration to the island. Unlike the French settlers, whose emigration to Martinique was voluntary, or the enslaved Africans, whose emigration was involuntary, emigration of the Indians was somewhat peculiar in that it was largely voluntary, but under demanding conditions. The next section of this chapter explores the social ecology of India that precipitated emigration to Martinique, as well as the demographic characteristics of these emigrants. A brief review of some narratives of the challenges they faced during the arduous three-month journey to Martinique is also included. The power asymmetry created by dual host communities (French and the newly freed) in relation to the newly arrived indentured workers, and the challenging three-way group dynamics that followed are explored in the fourth section of the chapter. A discussion of how factors of social ecology and group dynamics among these three ethnic groups affected Indians' original language and culture concludes this chapter.

Social Ecology of Martinique, France, and Haiti

Shifts in the demographic, political, and economic climates in Martinique in the early 1800s, referred to earlier, were catalyzed by several internal factors such as slave uprisings, slave poisonings, and a dramatic rise in the number of free people of color. Slave poisonings in 1820s (Savage, 2007) and the slave uprising of 1831 (Schloss, 2007) were both highly revelatory of three major phenomena, all interconnected—an intense fervor on the part of the enslaved to end slavery, the fragmentation of Martinican society (among both enslaved and White populations), and France's increasingly debilitated colonial presence in Martinique.

Several major political and sociocultural dynamics in Haiti also had a considerable influence on Martinique's resistance movement and fanned anti-colonial sentiments in mainland France. As reviewed in Chapter 6, even prior to the French revolution, anti-colonial sentiments had been spreading through various segments of French society; famous literary figures, philosophers, and government officials played an important role in shedding light on the immorality and iniquity of slavery (Confer 1964). These sentiments gradually grew worse with the start of slave uprisings in *Saint Domingue* (Haiti) in the 1750s and especially after the massive slave revolt of 1791 that culminated in the creation of the independent state of Haiti in 1804.

Just prior to its independence, Haiti was the most profitable of the French colonies, producing the largest share of the world's sugar. It also boasted some of the wealthiest and well-armed *grands blancs* (French plantation owners) of the French colonial system. Despite their well-established position, the French minority in Haiti was outnumbered and their elite status eventually succumbed to the uprising of the large number of enslaved African and gens de couleur populations. There are indications that large numbers of *petits blancs* (vestiges of the French indentured workers from the earlier phases of colonialism) also backed the efforts of enslaved Africans' resistance that eventually led to Haitian independence.

Social Ecology of India

Circumstances Of Emigration

India's social ecology and its effects on the emigration of Indian indentured workers is critical to understanding shifting social hierarchies and cultural narratives in Martinique from 1848-1884. For thousands of Indians, immigrating to Martinique was an appealing opportunity, and for many others, a necessity. As a direct result of administrative restructuring by British colonial policies, many rural village communities in India were experiencing economic hardships and social displacement (Carter & Torabully, 2002). Drought and famine were widespread, forcing desperate people in the rural areas to leave their homes in search of food and better opportunities.

The real fear of death from starvation has been metaphorically depicted in Confiant's historical fiction *La Panse du Chacal* (*The Belly of the Jackal*), in which people fear being eaten alive and ending up in the bellies of jackals: "It was necessary! Ever since the English had dispossessed the farmers of their land and took over to plant cotton and only cotton, overwhelming hunger had begun to torment us .... It was necessary to leave!"[3] (2004, p. 216).

Unlike slavery, which was entirely involuntary, in the indentured worker system Indians signed a contract in the presence of a magistrate. Although this appeared as a reasonable proposition on the surface, information about their journey and working conditions at the destination was provided by recruiters, or *mestris*, who frequently coerced the villagers or used tawdry means to dupe them into these contracts. These engagés (indentured workers) were unaware that their work was only a cut above slavery, although advertised as high paying and easy (Jayawardena, 1968; Thaniyayagam, 1968). It is fair to state that although the immigration of indentured workers to Martinique was considered voluntary, it was under circumstances that were dubious for some and compelling for many others. For these Indians— poor, hungry, rural, illiterate, and bearing the social limitations and stigma of being low caste—Martinique represented a beacon of hope for social advancement and a better life. They soon came to find out that they would live and die unrecognized on sugar plantations in Martinique.

---

[3] *Il le fallait! Depuis que les Anglais avaient exproprié les fermiers de notre région et s'y étaient installés pour y planter le coton et seulement le coton, une faim terrible avait commencé à nous tarauder... Il fallait partir!*

Demographic Characteristics of the Indian Emigrants

Most of the Indian emigrants had no idea what they were about to undertake. Because of the nature of the Indian caste system, they lacked the resources and social standing to question the authority of the mestris and other French representatives in India; the mestris undoubtedly took advantage of this. This pattern of passive and submissive behavior of indentured workers appears to have continued with their resettlement in Martinique, especially as newcomers in a foreign environment who did not speak French or Creole.

The plantation masters and their handlers also used the vulnerability of the newcomers as a tool to pit them against the newly freed to discourage them from banding together against the elite French Plantocracy. Confiant's fictional character Sosthène, an overseer on a plantation, addressed a group of Indian indentured workers as follows: "Strikes are for the Negros! [...] You Indians stay away from all that! It is not for you. You are good workers, you take good care of your families and you don't waste your time drinking rum and playing dice"[4] (Confiant, 2004, p. 195).

Records indicate that almost 90 % of the names of the people who boarded ships for Martinique were of Tamil origin (from the Indian state of Madras, now referred to as Tamil Nadu), and they were socially diverse. Most were rural farmers or craftsmen, and some identified themselves as people without specific jobs, *"gens sans profession"* (Desroches, 1996). In the social mix were also former prisoners and those who had rebelled against British rule in India. Then there was also the young couple (daughter of wealthy Indian royalty and her low-caste lover) fleeing the caste system that would not allow them to be together (Lecture by Gerry L'Etang at the University

---

[4] *La grève, c'est une histoire de Nègres! [...] Vous, les Indiens, restez à l'écart de tout ça! Ce n'est pas pour vous. Vous êtes de bons travailleurs, vous vous occupez bien de vos familles et ne gaspillez pas votre temps à boire du rhum ou à jouer aux dés.*

of the French West Indies, March 14, 2012). Given the general ethnic diversity in India, inherent variations of castes, dialects, traditions, customs, religious rituals, etc. among the indentured workers cannot be overlooked. For all, Martinique offered the opportunity for new beginnings. Because the Indian indentured workers did not have an ethnolinguistically and culturally homogenous critical mass, maintaining their original cultural identity was challenging.

Their Journey

An examination of the challenges the indentured workers faced once they left India presents a paradoxical picture of their responses to hardships they faced during their approximately three-month journey. In addition to the horrific conditions on the boats, psychological and emotional trauma stemming from a sense of betrayal for leaving their homeland, fear of the sea, and uncertain future made the journey all the more strenuous: "A great sense of loss and displacement, both physical and psychological, experienced by these Indian indentured workers leaving their homeland characterize this Diaspora" (Bannerjee, 2009, p. 2).

Notwithstanding the suffering these indentured workers faced on their journey to Martinique, some of the first attempts to preserve linguistic and cultural identity were made during the voyage. Most on board had no common familial or village connection, and yet they tried to maintain cohesiveness and hope during the most difficult phases of their journey. Hunger strikes were organized as a means of empowerment and to demand improvement in their conditions. The sick and elderly were cared for with no regard to caste or religion. Recitation of Hindu religious texts and singing religious songs were ways they managed to keep themselves emotionally strong (Bannerjee, 2009).

Antoine Tangamen, a Hindu priest and the last Tamil speaker

in Martinique who died in 1992, shared his grandmother's stories of her voyage to Martinique from India: "Therefore, sometimes to forget their misery they would gather on the deck to sing through the night"[5] (L'Étang & Permal, 1994, sec. "L'autre bord"). These narratives indicate striving to create a shared identity to cope with the harsh realities on the ship. Glissant's views on the effect of the journey on enslaved Africans, which was on one hand a total negativity or *"une négativité totale"* and on the other, an absolute positivity or *"une positivité absolue,"*[6] may also be applicable to the journey of the Indians. Admittedly, the journey of enslaved Africans was far more horrific, but the idea that the seeds of collective resilience can sprout from total despair is relevant to the Indians' journey as well.

Confronted with tumultuous high seas, however, the Indians resorted to a unique coping strategy. Many believed that they were no longer under the protection of the Hindu gods because crossing the ocean was sacrilegious. So they took solace in praying to an Islamic saint, *Nagour Mira*, who was deified in the coastal town of Nagore (near Karaikal in India) for his miraculous nautical powers (Confiant, 2004). Of the 25,509 Indian indentured workers who came to Martinique, there were approximately 3,700 Tamil Muslims. There were bound to have been Muslims on most ships leaving India, which would explain their reaching out to a Muslim saint. Nagour Mira's miracles were believed to have protected the lives of several people from harm on the high seas. In Martinique today, Hindu temples include, among many Hindu symbols, Islamic symbols such as the crescent moon, the star, the hand of Fatima, and a boat representing their journey from India. This unusual Islamic twist to the practice of the Hindu religion, a form of religious syncretism, is one of the few elements of Indian culture that still prevails in Martinique and in many other parts of the Tamil diaspora today (L'Etang, 2011b).

---

[5] *Alors parfois, pour oublier, ils se réunissaient sur le pont et chantaient jusqu'à la nuit.*
[6] As quoted in L'Étang, 2011a, para. 18.

Power Asymmetry between the Two Host Communities and the Newcomers

Arrival of the Indians set the stage for a critical battle of cultural, social, economic, and political power in Martinique between 1853 and 1884, resulting in major hierarchical shifts. Demographics, economic strength, and cultural dominance dictated the structure of this hierarchy.

As discussed, involuntary settlement began in the 1640s with the African slave trade initiated by French colonizers for workers on their sugar plantations. By 1831, there were approximately 86,200 enslaved Africans in Martinique, and an overall population of almost 110,000; the remainder comprised the French Plantocracy and gens de couleur (Schloss, 2007). The first vessels carrying Indian indentured laborers arrived in Martinique between 1852 and 1853, and by January 1885, the number of Indians who had immigrated to Martinique was approximately 25,000 (Sméralda-Amon, 2004).

The social structure in Martinique at that time comprised two major host communities: the numerically dominant Africans and the economically and culturally dominant French colonists. And in the mix were also gens de couleur, whose population and influence were clearly on the ascent (Schloss, 2007). Thus the new subordinate group, Indian indentured workers, found themselves in a deliberately crafted position in the Martinican social hierarchy, which was not significantly different from what they had left in India (as noted earlier, the indentured workers hailed mostly from lower castes). One of the characters in Confiant's *La panse du chacal* compares the Martinican hierarchy to the Indian caste system: "Fundamentally, the Creole world was similar to ours with its caste system and interdictions. Up top were the white plantation owner—*Brahmins*, in the middle were the mulatto—*Vaishyas*, in the bottom were the negro—*Sudras* and we, the Indian—*Pariahs* were beneath them"[7] (2004, p. 202).

Caught between a Rock and a Hard Place

Having heard how well the system of Indian indentured workers was functioning in the colonies of Mauritius, Trinidad, Guyana, Reunion, and Jamaica, the arrival of Indian indentured workers in Martinique largely quelled the fears and anxieties of the French Plantocracy. They saw the Indians as perfect replacements for enslaved Africans, thus assuring the continuity of their profitable sugar industry and the economic future of Martinique. With the arrival of the Indians, they clamored loudly that "Indian immigration is the future of Martinique"[8] (Sméralda-Amon, 2004, p. 1).

The planters might have celebrated the arrival of the first Indian indentured workers in Martinique in 1852 and 1853, but the newly freed saw the arrival of Indians from an entirely different angle. For the most part, they considered indentured labor a form of slavery, against which they had fought a long, painful battle. They also expressed resentment of Indian indentured workers, whom they saw as rivals for economic and social position (Thaniyayagam, 1968; Pillai, 2005). Their sentiments are conveyed by Desroches: "...the *coolie* had come to obstruct a wish [to end a camouflaged form of slavery] expressed by the majority of the population in 1848"[9] (1996, p. 33). Being targets of stigmatization and xenophobia made the integration of Indians into Martinican society extremely challenging (Sméralda, personal communication, March 19, 2014).

---

[7] *Au fond, le monde creole était pareil au nôtre avec ses castes et ses interdits, c'est à dire tout en haut, les Békés-brahmanes, au milieu les mulâtres-vaishya, en bas les Nègres-shudra et encore plus bas, nous autres les Indiens-parias.*

[8] *l'immigration indienne c'est l'avenir de la Martinique.*

[9] *...le kouli venait contrecarrer une volonté exprimée par la majorité de la population en 1848.*

The term *"kouli"* has always been pejorative to Martinicans of Indian descent, but originally (in Tamil) the term simply referred to wages received by day laborers, or to the laborers themselves. Bernabé recalls as a young boy that the term *"kouli"* was used to belittle and humiliate Indians (personal communication, March 18, 2014). A common insult that most Martinicans of Indian descent have heard is the Creole phrase *"Kouli manjé chyen,"* or "dog-eating coolie." This is particularly hurtful considering that the majority of Indian indentured workers did not eat meat. Antoine Thangamen recounts the fistfights and stones thrown between the African children and those of Indian indentured workers on some plantations; he adds that this was, however, not the case on all plantations, including Gradis where he grew up. Such conflicts, he recalls, were more common in town markets (L'Etang & Permal, 1994).

In an attempt to be accepted by the majority community, a common narrative began among Indian indentured workers regarding the circumstances of their emigration. Generally the story involved indentured workers duped into boarding ships to join a celebration involving alcohol. When they regained consciousness some time later, they found themselves at sea heading for Martinique, with the only explanation that they must have been drugged and kidnapped. Research does not support this story in its entirety, and certainly not for the vast majority of indentured workers from India who voluntarily signed work contracts. We do know that similar kidnapping narratives (with varying details) are found throughout the Caribbean where Indian indentured workers emigrated, even though they came from different parts of India and were unlikely to have been in communication with one another. This leads to the hypothesis that this largely imaginary narrative served as an effective tool for Indians to deflect some of the animosity felt toward them. This attempt to shift the context of their emigration from voluntary to involuntary was perhaps intended to create common cause with the descendants of slaves and make their own situation worthy of sympathy rather than antagonism (Lecture by Gerry L'Etang at the University of the French West Indies, March 14, 2012).

Guadeloupe's history of Indian indentured workers is somewhat different. Twice as many Indian indentured workers came to Guadeloupe as Martinique. In contemporary Guadeloupean society, descendents of Indian indentured workers have established themselves as an economically thriving community. The term *"kouli"* has been out of favor for some time and is practically nonexistent today (Bernabé, personal communication, March 18, 2014).

Although both Africans and Indians were brought to Martinique by the French for the same purpose there was not only little intermingling between these communities, but considerable resentment and hostility. A brief recap of salient aspects of slavery in Martinique is a good starting point for understanding the complex nature of this challenging inter-group relationship. The institution of slavery and implementation of the Code Noir as detailed in Chapter 4, with its forceful imposition of Catholicism, French language, and French ways of life on enslaved Africans for over 200 years, systematically marginalized and suppressed most African linguistic, religious, and cultural practices. The Habitation system, with its hierarchical society, exerted social, cultural, and economic dominance over enslaved Africans. The more favorable terms for Indian indentured workers were in contrast to the harsh imposition of the Code Noir and the Habitation system.

First, Indian indentured workers in principle signed contracts (usually of between three and five years) to work on plantations for stipulated wages. At the end of their term, as outlined in their contracts, they had the option of returning to India or renewing their contracts. Available research suggests that approximately 4,260 returned to India

(Desroches 1996, p. 32), although the exact number may never be known. Enslaved Africans, who were brought involuntarily, had no hope of return to their homeland.

In contrast to enslaved Africans, who had to practice their rituals (like quimboiserie) clandestinely for fear of accusations of witchcraft and poisoning, Indians were allowed to continue exercising some of their religious and cultural practices in Martinique. Some plantation owners supported building *petites chapelles* or small Hindu temples in consideration of their religious practices (Desroches, 1996). The story behind the construction of the temple in Galion, located in the Canton of La Trinité,[10] echoes similar reciprocity seen earlier with plantation owners' adoption of quimboiserie. Indians were sometimes permitted to build places of worship close to water (rivers and streams) because most religious rituals involved fresh water (Benoist, Desroches, L'Étang, & Ponaman, 2004). In addition, as pointed out by Thaniyayagam (1968), some concessions were spelled out in their contracts acknowledging important Tamil cultural celebrations such as the harvest festival of Pongal; celebrations of this festival with the traditional killing of lambs took place on plantations.

Some flexibility was shown by the békés regarding housing arrangements of indentured workers. Indian families were allowed to live in the same *case* or shack and preserve their family structure. These houses were close to their place of worship, and also close to their work to keep families united (Desroches, 1996). Even though

---

[10] Local lore has it that after a severe drought in the 1850s, Indians performed an animal sacrifice to plead to the Hindu gods for rain in return for building a temple. When rain came after the sacrifice, the Hindu temple at Galion was constructed (Patrice Domoison, personal communication, March 19, 2014).

Figure 20. Exterior of the Hindu temple in Sainte-Marie, Trinité. (Photo by authors, March 2014.)

Figure 21. Interior of the Hindu temple in Sainte-Marie, Trinité. (Photo by authors, March 2014.)

in the Caribbean were not ethnically homogenous, most came from southeastern coastal regions of India, and there were some cultural, linguistic, and social commonalities. Coupled with concessions by the békés and the relative leniency of the terms of their contracts, the Indians appear to have been able to recreate a fragile micro-Indian community on the plantation.

A Cut above Slavery

Even with evidence indicating that Indians were treated slightly better than enslaved Africans, life on the plantations for them was far from easy and can be considered as only a cut above slavery. The following lines offer a glimpse of their daily life on the plantations and the physical toll it took on these newcomers:

> The reality was quite different. The contract was not respected. The immigrants were in horrible conditions on the Plantations. They were literally placed in the shacks where the former slaves previously lived.... There are no doctors, no infirmaries as stipulated in the contract....[11] (Gamess & Gamess, 2003, p. 54)

Very few, if any, modifications had been done by plantation owners to the living quarters for the new immigrants. The medical care and attention stipulated in their contracts was not always provided. Food provisions were limited and brutal punishments were given by békés for the smallest infractions. The living quarters of the Indians

---

[11] *La réalité est tout autre. Le contrat n'est pas respecté. Les immigrés sont logésmisérablement sur l'habitation. Ils sont littéralement parqués dans les cases des anciens esclaves, [...] Il n'y a pas de médecin, pas d'infirmerie comme le prévoyait le contrat....*

were nothing more than a small dark room of nine or ten square meters (Pillai, 2005). Because their shack was "miniscule," Antoine Tangamen recalls his family using it only for sleeping (L'Etang & Permal, 1994). Though their contracts called for a nine-hour workday, they invariably exceeded 13 hours. Of the approximately 25,500 Indian immigrants to Martinique, mistreatment and malnutrition resulted in the deaths of 14,809 (Desroches, 1996). The greedy objective of the French colonists is described vividly by Confiant (2004): "We became prisoners of this land without a God, of this brutal, cynical, dirty, fatalistic Martinique dominated by Whites who only worshipped money"[12] (p. 364).

The emotional and psychological toll of resettlement appears to have been as great as the physical toll. The cultural and religious practices (animal sacrifices and ritual trances) of these indentured workers were shunned as "barbaric" by the békés and the newly freed, who had largely assimilated to French culture (Thaniyayagam, 1968; Pillai, 2005). This new subordinate group also perceived assimilation to the dominant French culture as a means of climbing the social ladder. Sméralda-Amon notes in this regard, "Interestingly, several Indian parents, convinced that their salvation was in total assimilation, abandoned their efforts to transmit their ethnic culture and, more importantly, the Tamil language"[13] (2004, sec. 5).

On December 17, 1884, the General Council of Martinique terminated the indentured worker program for Indians in order to "… reestablish equality between the Black worker and the Indian worker, to stop contrived competition between the two groups"[14] (Curtius, 2010, p. 114). However positive a step toward social equity this may

---

[12] *Nous étions devenus prisoniers de cette terre sans dieux, de cette Martinique brutale, cynique, paillarde, fataliste, peuplée de Blancs qui ne vénéraient que l'argent*

[13] *Curieusement, en effet, de nombreux parents, convaincus que leur salut résidait dans l'assimilation, renoncèrent à leur transmettre leur patrimoine culturel, la langue tamoule en tout premier lieu.*

[14] *… rétablir l'égalité du travailleur noir et du travailleur indien, cesser de faire de l'un le concurrent déloyal de l'autre.*

have been, the system of indentured workers from India was ended, disconnecting those workers in Martinique from direct cultural influence from India. This only accentuated the difficulty of preserving their original languages (primarily Tamil) and cultures.

Tamil Language and Culture in Martinique

With the development of Creole language as a communicative tool of compromise and necessity among the Africans, French, and (to a lesser degree) Caribs, Africans, as the subordinate group of newcomers, were unable to preserve their languages. As discussed, when Indian indentured workers arrived in Martinique, like enslaved Africans, they too occupied the lowest rung of the social hierarchy. Indians were caught in a quagmire between two inhospitable host communities, the békés and the Africans. On one hand, they faced intense pressures of assimilation to French language and culture, which discouraged them from identifying with and practicing their original languages and cultures. On the other hand, they were ostracized by the majority population of freed Africans, which forced them into social isolation. The idea that this ostracism from larger Martinican society may have helped to preserve various Indian religious rituals and customs is widely accepted among Martinican scholars (Lecture by Gerry L'Etang at the University of the French West Indies, March 14, 2012).

Tamil, one of the most ancient languages of the world, spoken predominantly in South India, was brought to Martinique by these indentured workers. Today, after more than 160 years, Tamil is practically extinct in Martinique for everyday communication. Nevertheless, diluted forms of certain Tamil cultural and religious practices, and gallicized Tamil last names, are still alive in Martinique. They remain *le fil d'Ariane* (Ariadne's thread) that connects them to their history and homeland, thus permanently altering Tamil from a predominantly **"spoken language"** to a **"declared language"** (Golovko, 2005), and a means of social and cultural identification for Martinicans of Indian descent. In his book *How Language Works* (2007, p. 336), David Crystal states, "A language dies when the last person who speaks it dies. Or perhaps it dies when the second-last person who speaks it dies, for then there is no one left to talk to." This quotation succinctly captures the last gasps of a dying language and the demise of spoken Tamil in Martinique. What caused the Tamil language to become nearly extinct in Martinique, yet left behind traces of original religious and cultural practices?

The question of how well informed this emigrant group was about the journey they were undertaking is important to consider. It sheds light on the lack of preparation and support that ultimately led to the loss of most of their language and culture. The desire of the indentured worker industry to fabricate and sensationalize the journey to and life in the French Antilles was dictated by three major factors: first, White plantation owners' desperate need for cheap plentiful manual labor in Martinique; second, the greed of the *Compagnie Générale Transatlantique* (CGT), which was paid per adult recruit transported from India arriving alive on the island; and third, the greed of the coyote-like mestris, or intermediaries, who, like their bosses, the subagents, were compensated for each qualified worker that they brought (Jayawardena, 1968).

Article 4 of the agreement between the Compagnie Générale Transatlantique and the Martinican government guaranteed the CGT 415 francs and 45 cents for each living adult who landed in Martinique— no payment was made for the transportation of children younger than 10 (Thaniyayagam, 1968). The lack of incentive for the CGT to bring families with children posed another challenge for indentured workers, most of whom lacked a family structure to effectively preserve and transmit their original culture to the next generation. The main criteria for hiring were good physical condition and farming experience. This meant that people were contracted as individuals and not as families.

Although it seems the criteria for hire were not very stringent, in actuality stipulations in the agreement between the government of Martinique and CGT imposed several limitations. Adult female workers had to be between the age of 14 and 30 and male workers between 16 and 36. All children over the age of 10 were considered adults and earned the company the same 415 francs and 45 cents each as adults. Because the company was not paid for children under the age of 10, this population was restricted to no more than 10% on board each vessel (Thaniyayagam, 1968). As a consequence, most of the people who signed up for indentured work were young men; in the initial phase of emigration, very few women and children contracted for indentured work. Many years later the requirement that 40 % of the workers on each ship had to be female was instituted (Jayawardena, 1968). Thus, the lack of female emigrants during early resettlement severely impeded the preservation of Tamil culture and may also explain the high rate of miscegenation in the Indian community.

The variation in the social makeup of indentured workers was another determinant in their ability to practice their customs and traditions. There is a striking difference in comparing the indentured labor system in Martinique with the *Kangani* system (1839-1950) that involved emigration of South Indians to Ceylon (now Sri Lanka) and Malaysia. In the Kangani labor system, consideration was given to each group's village, caste, and family affiliations, which appear to have facilitated preservation of their original language and culture. However, in Martinique, the mestris scouted for vulnerable farmers in many villages in rural areas, and thus workers seldom hailed from the same village or even the same caste (Jayawardena, 1968).

Just as enslaved Africans, who against all odds preserved

elements of their languages and cultures, Indian emigrants succeeded in preserving historical narratives and cultural identities in a few but significant forms: religion, last names, food, and clothing. These act as a connection with their ancestral land. Although there is no critical mass of Martinicans with purely Indian lineage that form an identifiable community (Sméralda, personal communication, March 19, 2014), anyone with some familiarity with Indian culture who visits Martinique will find living vestiges of it apparent there. Many Tamil words, créolized and gallicized, are used among Martinicans of Indian descent, especially during religious ceremonies. Some of these terms include *koilou* (Hindu temple), *velkou* (oil lamp), *katti* (machete), *vépélé* (sacred leaves), *pousali* (Hindu priest), *vatialou* (teacher of Tamil language), *Maliémin* (goddess Mariamman), *mandja tani* (holy water), *kandji* (rice milk), *paniaram* (sweet fritters), *nèl kutchi* (drum sticks), etc. (Desroches, 1996). Words such as *"madras"* (a type of cloth worn by early Indian settlers) and *"colombo"* (a concoction of spices used in South Indian cuisine) have become an integral part of Martinican culture and vernacular. In addition, several family names of Tamil or Indian origin have been preserved, although they too have been gallicized. Names such as *Nayaradou, Moutammalle, Moutoussamy, Moutou, Ramassamy, Sacarabany*, and *Kamatchy* are a few common examples (Thaniyayagam, 1968), which are still evident in business signs and surnames in Martinique.

It is extraordinary that *"Le sèvis zendyen"* or the religious service involving animal sacrifices and ritual trances, identical to the original version found in a remote part of southern India today, is still practiced in small Martinican Hindu temples (Lecture by Gerry L'Etang at the University of the French West Indies, March 14, 2012). We had the honor of visiting the temple of Sainte-Marie in Trinité during a visit to Martinique (March 2014), where we viewed statues and other

Figure 22. Ramassamy Driving School in Fort de France. (Photo by authors, March 2014.)

prayer items from the 1850s. This supports Clothey's insight (as cited in Naidoo, 2007, p. 55) that temples are "a world psychic space in which the community lives and acts out its identity."

History imposed upon indentured workers from India a fragmented identity and eroded most of their original language and culture. However, observations from our visits to Martinique confirm that buried deep within the crevasse of this fragmented identity lie the narratives that validate and acknowledge the experiences of these people. These stories and symbols reconnect them with their homeland and emblematize the collective heritage of this displaced group. In the words of one woman of Indian descent at the market in St. Pierre who is using her surname to trace her ancestry back to India, "I am searching for my ancestors (*Je cherche mes ancêtres*)."

Conclusion

Examining the intersection of cultural contexts in Martinique and India is an important dynamic for interpreting the experiences of Indian indentured workers. The perennial issue of inexpensive labor in Martinique was addressed by locating a population desperate to escape economic strangulation and social marginalization: engagés from India. The work contracts offered opportunities that were not available for Indians in their native land, though the benefits of these opportunities were exaggerated and the costs severely minimized. The harsh reality of just what they had gotten themselves into was revealed in the grueling journey across the high seas; there are notable similarities to the experiences of French engagés crossing the Atlantic as detailed in Chapter 3. These factors prior to their arrival in Martinique, along with the three-way group dynamics and the implementation of their contracts upon resettlement, were critical to both the loss and retention of their original cultures.

The shifting cultural narratives of Indian indentured workers, coupled with shifts in Martinican social hierarchy, form a major punctuation point for hybridization in Martinique. Chapter 8 discusses the narratives and contributions of the Congolese, Chinese, and Syro-Lebanese immigrants, whose histories are even less studied than those of the Indians. Their interactions with each other and the larger Martinican society should not be overlooked, however small their numbers.

As the 20th century approached, plantation owners found it difficult to profit as they had under the system of slavery. This was in spite of the influx of thousands of indentured workers from India, the Congo region, and China, not to mention advances in industrial technology. Some plantations shut down, and some plantation owners looked to producing rum as an alternative export ("Patrimoine de la

Martinique," 2014). Chapter 8 also addresses two major geopolitical conflicts (World War I and II) and their economic and social reverberations felt in Martinique.

The singular intellectual and political leadership of Aimé Césaire and his extraordinary role in Martinique's Departmentalization and becoming an integral part of France was another momentous inflection point for Martinique's cultural evolution. Martinique continues to be a part of France, their former colonial ruler. Delineating the factors that led Martinique away from the path most Caribbean nations took, that is, independence from European powers, is the major subject of the following chapter.

Glossary

indentured workers - Foreign laborers brought overseas to work for a specific length of time.

coolies - Nineteenth and 20th century term for contracted laborers primarily from South Asia and China, usually pejorative; possibly derived from a Tamil word for payment (*kuli*).

Tamil - South Indian language spoken by many of the indentured workers from the area of India then known as Madras (currently the state of Tamil Nadu); also spoken in parts of Sri Lanka.

mestris - (Tamil) Recruiters of indentured worker crews from India with supervisory roles.

Nagour Mira - (Tamil/Sanskrit) Muslim saint known for his nautical powers who is revered in the Martinican Indian community for safeguarding the passage of their ancestors over the tumultuous seas from India to Martinique.

petites chapelles - (French) Small place of worship; in this context for Hindu rituals.

case - (French) Meager cabin or hut housing slaves and indentured workers in Martinique.

le fil d'Ariane - (French) Expression derived from the Greek myth of Ariadne to describe navigating one's way out of a complex, maze-like situation.

spoken language - Language used on a daily basis for communication.

declared language - Language that is a signifier of cultural identity, but not used in daily spoken communication.

Compagnie Générale Transatlantique - French shipping company established in 1861 that contracted with the Martinican government to transport Indian indentured workers to Martinique starting in 1864.

kangani system - (Tamil origin) Indian system of labor recruitment (distinct from the indentured worker system) that involved an individual, a *"kangani,"* responsible for gathering workers (usually from the same village), accompanying them to the overseas workplace, supervising them, and serving as a liason with the plantation owner, with whom he shared the profits from their labor.

madras - (Tamil/Portuguese) Headdress of cotton fabric with a brightly colored plaid design worn by women in Martinique; word originates from the former name of the city of Chennai in South India.

colombo - (Tamil) National dish of Martinique, based on South Indian spices combined with meat or fish and vegetables; probably derived from the Tamil word *"kuzhambu."*

le sèvis zendyen - (French/Creole, "the Indian service") Tamil religious ceremony still practiced in Martinique involving animal sacrifices and trances. This practice appears to have been preserved intact by indentured workers and is identical to rituals in remote parts of rural South India, from which most indentured workers came.

176 Ramakrishnan and Smith

Reflective Questions

1. What precipitated the arrival of Indian indentured workers to Martinique?

2. Discuss circumstances that led to the departure of thousands of emigrants from India.

3. Compare key elements of the Indians' labor contracts to those of the Code Noir.

4. Compare the position of enslaved Africans to that of Indian indentured workers in the social hierarchy of Martinique. In what ways were they similar and in what ways did they differ?

5. After nearly 150 years after leaving their country of origin, Martinicans of Indian descent have successfully preserved a few significant aspects of their original culture. What factors might account for this?

6. Explain how the arrival of Indian indentured workers in Martinique and the subsequent group dynamics affected the process of cultural hybridization in Martinique.

Chapter 8

Sociocultural Assimilation to Political Assimilation

From Abolition to Césaire and Departmentalization

> ... in the darkness of the great silence,
> a voice was raising up, with no interpreter,
> no alteration, and no complacency,
> a violent and staccato voice, and it said for the first time:
> "I, Nègre." A voice of revolt. A voice of resentment.
> No doubt. But also of fidelity, a voice of freedom,
> and first and foremost,
> a voice for the retrieved identity. [1]

> —Aimé Césaire, 1913-2008
> Founder of the Négritude movement

April 27 and May 23, 1848 are probably the most significant dates in Martinique's history (in addition to March 19, 1946, the date of **Departmentalization**): these dates mark the ratification in France of the decree abolishing slavery, and the day the decree was implemented in Martinique. However, Martinicans and the residents of all of France's Overseas Departments commemorate the abolition of slavery on May 22, an official holiday. Almost two weeks before the actual decree arrived in Martinique, the arrest of a defiant enslaved African, Romain, from the Duchamp Plantation in Prêcheur, inflamed protests all over the region (Beuze, 1998). Thousands of enslaved Africans cast off their chains of bondage on May 22 (*Nèg pété chenn*, referred to in

---

[1] Diagne, 2014, "Négritude as revolt/Négritude as philosophy," para. 2.

Chapter 6), beginning the annual celebrations on this day.

With the Emancipation Decree of May 23, 1848 came French citizenship (for adult males, at least). In contrast, the right to vote was not granted to former enslaved Africans in British colonies when slavery was abolished throughout the British Caribbean in 1838. The connection of suffrage to emancipation may have been key to greater identification of Martinicans with France. Given that enslaved Africans were subjected to an anthropological rupture (Bernabé, 2013) from their homelands, their enfranchisement gave them a greater sense of identification with French culture, which had been imposed on them for two centuries. Besides, an alliance with France appeared the most straightforward path away from the nightmare of human bondage and toward the dream of better lives (Burton, 1995a).

Although they won the right to vote, legislation guaranteeing the formerly enslaved legal, political, and economic parity with the mainland French took almost a century beyond emancipation in the form of Departmentalization. As many scholars in Martinique readily point out, however, liberation from psychological and cultural vestiges of slavery is an ongoing struggle. As Telumee in *The Bridge of Beyond* reflects on post-slavery Guadeloupe, "… I think of the injustice in the world, and of all of us still suffering and dying silently of slavery after it is finished and forgotten" (Schwarz-Bart, 2013, p. 241).

This chapter continues to outline the ramifications of the abolition of slavery on societal, cultural, and economic fronts seen in Chapter 7, beginning with the demographic changes brought about by the arrival of lesser-known indentured workers, the Chinese and Congolese. The gradual movement from creolization to hybridization becomes increasingly apparent with the end of slavery and the infusion of new emigrant groups into the Martinican cultural matrix.

This chapter also surveys evolution of the sugar and rum economies at the turn of the 20th century. In addition, we explore how 4,000 miles of ocean between Martinique and France did not insulate the island from the socioeconomic and political effects of two world wars. Since its founding in 1635, Martinique witnessed its first home-grown identity movement, Aimé Césaire's *Négritude,* during this period. Equally significant was the first popular movement (also led by Aimé Césaire) toward Martinique's political and legal integration with France, or Departmentalization.

Post-Abolition Martinican Society, Continued

Congolese and Chinese Indentured Workers

The short-term labor challenges that followed the end of slavery were assuaged by contracted workers from India, the Congo/Niger River Basin,[2] and China. Chapter 7 focused on Indian indentured workers, their role in transformation of the post-slavery society and economy, and their contributions to modern Martinican culture. Less is known about integration of the Congolese and the Chinese into post-slavery Martinican society than about Indian indentured workers, but we would be remiss not to discuss their narratives and contributions to Martinique. These groups tried, under suboptimal circumstances, to maintain their cultural heritage in a plantation society still reeling from the end of slavery.

Here, in an unpleasant room with a low ceiling, is a small pedestal erected for Buddha by eight to ten Chinese; further away is a Hindu temple erected for Brahma, and what a

---

[2] All indentured Africans belonged to the Bantu ethnolinguistic group, which is spread throughout western, central, and southern Africa. There are hundreds of tribes and a rich cultural diversity among them. A generic label used by the French to designate this vast, diverse group was "le Congo" for the area and "les Congos" for its people.

temple! Even further beyond one can see African idols.[3]
(Meignan, 1878, as cited in L'Etang, 2003, para. 7)

The influence of Chinese immigrants on Martinican culture is minimal (Bernabé, personal communication, March 18, 2014), and their legacy is primarily the economic niche they carved out for themselves as the plantation economy began to wane. Most Chinese gravitated to the grocer's trade, becoming shopkeepers in urban areas such as Fort de France and St. Pierre. These first Chinese immigrants were not able to preserve as many of their religious practices as the Indians. This may have been largely due to the relatively small size of their community (978 immigrants). It is interesting to note that later waves of Chinese immigration (1925-1940) took a similar economic path, also opening restaurants, but they reinvigorated traditional Buddhist, Confucian, and Taoist beliefs and customs (L'Etang, 2003).

There are equally few traces of the Congolese footprint in Martinique, mostly found in the south of the island. Linguistic (including vocabulary and family names), culinary, and spiritual/ magical traditions from their heritage are all that remain. Although the African indentured group was much larger (10,521), they were a younger group overall (10-24 years of age) than their Indian or Chinese counterparts, resulting in greater assimilation to the dominant French culture. These demographics may help explicate the lack of a stronger Congolese cultural presence in Martinique (L'Etang, 2003).

As L'Etang observes, several factors are associated with the Indians' preservation of more of their original culture. Indians were not only significantly more numerous, but, more important, their 30-year period of immigration (1853-1883) and additional 17 years of connection with India through **repatriation** (1883-1900) helped

---

[3] *Ici, dans une chambre sale et basse, se trouve un petit autel élevé à Bouddha par huit ou dix Chinois; plus loin est un temple hindou, et quel temple! élevé à Brahma; puis, plus loin encore, on aperçoit des idoles africaines.*

with cultural preservation. Of the 25,509 Indians who immigrated to Martinique, 11,951 repatriated. In contrast, the Congolese and the Chinese experiences with immigration (five years for the former, from 1857-1862, and one year for the latter, 1859-1860; Desroches, 1996) were much shorter. Only two of 10,521 Congolese immigrants and one of 978 Chinese immigrants were known to have repatriated, leaving no further direct connections to their homelands (L'Etang, 2003).

Less cultural homogeneity of the Congolese and the Chinese groups may also have been significant in their difficulties in preserving elements of their original cultures. Based on their ports of embarkation, 56 % of the Chinese came from the Shanghai area and 44 % from the Canton area, regions with markedly different dialects, namely Wu and Hakka (Cantonese). Similarly, African indentured workers belonged to various ethnic groups, with a variety of languages and dialects. Ninety-four percent of them were from Congo-Brazzaville and Congo-Kinshasa, two percent from the Sierra-Leone region, one and one-half percent from the Gabon area, and the remainder from other unspecified regions of Africa (L'Etang, 2003).

Considering the challenging economic, political, and social climate of post-abolition Martinique, it is remarkable that these three groups of indentured workers, often viewed as inconsequential, nevertheless left their mark in Martinique's history. Their sweat and blood contributed greatly to the wealth of the békés and French investors because they were paid a fraction of what freed Africans were; for example, Indian indentured workers were routinely paid anywhere from one-third to one-half (depending on the plantation) of what freed Africans earned for the same work (Nicolas, 2009). Of these three groups of indentured workers, Indians retained the most of their original culture, reinforcing our premise that the contexts of emigration and resettlement operate as mediators in the preservation and loss of culture.

Elements of a Shared Identity

As noted in Chapter 6, the ideals of the French Revolution struck a sympathetic chord among enslaved Africans in the colonies but were vehemently opposed by the White Plantocracy. Similarly, socialist ideas emanating from mainland France resonated among Blacks but were resisted by the White Plantocracy and local authorities in Martinique. Strong political groups dominated by Blacks advocating better wages and working conditions were influential in Martinique and Guadeloupe by the 1880s (Butel, 2002). Their demands echoed those of socialist ideologies gaining popularity in mainland France during this period.

Regardless of the fact that labor strikes were illegal, Martinican workers, primarily Blacks, with help from gens de couleur, frequently organized strikes to protest salary inequalities and falling sugar prices. Gens de couleur were often perceived by planters as instigators and accomplices of these strikes by interfering with contracts between the planters and Blacks working on plantations as paid laborers (Butel, 2002; Nicolas, 2009). With the end of slavery, many gens de couleur, with no inheritance or wealth, felt estranged from their land of birth. Some wandered the countryside, seeking to reestablish themselves by seizing land and plantations abandoned by the békés, and some looted. As we see later in this chapter, free Africans and gens de couleur allied with France as the most expedient way to protect their interests from the békés.

Békés, who had the most to lose from the drastic shift in the socioeconomic order, coped with abolition in various ways. Some sold their plantations at reduced prices and left for other islands, to the United States, or back to France to start their lives anew. Others formed conglomerates to diversify their investments and industrialize sugar production. Rental real estate and retail businesses were popular investments. Because many gens de couleur acquired powerful positions in local legal affairs, civil service, and politics, békés focused on representing their political interests in France by serving on the General Council in Martinique. In the words of Gaston Gerville-Réache, an elite French Guadeloupean politician, "I leave for the negroes local public functions and political representation, but I reserve for myself the *Conseil Général*"[4] (Butel, 2002, p. 320).

Thus, each major social group in Martinique and the French Antilles strategically jockeyed for political influence locally and in France. The social climate in Guadeloupe during this time was probably similar to Martinique's. The discrimination that persisted in areas such as education and class distinctions was described in the Guadeloupean newspaper *Le Peuple* in 1891, "The Whites on top of the social ladder, the mixed race at about the same height, and the Negro at the opposite extreme, in other words, at the absolute bottom"[5] (Butel, 2002, p. 321). As discussed earlier, immigration of indentured workers had stopped by this point (1891), with some repatriated, but most resettling in the French Antilles. What, then, accounts for the lack of mention of any of these people in the Guadeloupe newspaper cited above? This omission is a testament to both their lack of numerical strength and their disenfranchisement as newcomers (they were considered foreigners) in comparison with the two dominant host communities, Whites and Africans. The political voices of the descendants of these indentured workers, especially the Indians, were not heard until well into the 20th century.

Granting that competition and enmity between groups persisted, as they often found their interests in conflict, by the end of the 19th century it seems that Martinicans found commonality in

---

[4] *Je laisse aux Nègres de la colonie la representation politique et les fonctions publiques, mais je me reserve le conseil général.*
[5] *Le Blanc en haut de l'échelle sociale, le mulâtre à égale hauteur, et le nègre à l'extrémité opposée, c'est à dire en bas tout à fait.*

shared historical and cultural narratives. The Creole language, Carnival and other cultural celebrations, and wariness of the French (despite lobbying them for support) were some common threads that connected them. As good debrouillards, they occasionally transcended their differences and came together to celebrate their shared creole identity and culture. A telling example of this is that these groups agreed to celebrate the raising of a statue of Josephine in 1851 in Fort de France. The Whites were thrilled that she was empress of France, and the gens de couleur claimed her as their own because she was raised by a *mulâtresse* or a woman of mixed race (Butel, 2002). Celebrations and festivities were temporary distractions for each group from the hardships of Martinican life, whether hurricanes and earthquakes, tropical diseases, unemployment, or labor unrest. We cannot, however, forget that French language and culture was the dominant matrix, then and now, within which the unique creole identity crystallized.

From Sugar Buzz to Rum High

> I do not know if coffee and sugar are necessary for Europe's happiness, but I know that these two crops have caused unhappiness to two regions of the world. America has been depopulated for planting these crops and Africa has been depopulated for cultivating them.[6] ("Patrimoine de la Martinique," 2014, para. 14)

The labor disruptions that immediately followed abolition, as critical as they seemed at the time, did not cripple the sugar industry for long. This was because many newly freed continued to work on plantations (they had few other options), and the labor vacuum created

---

[6] *Je ne sais pas si le café et le sucre sont necessaires au Bonheur de l'Europe, mais je sais bien que ces deux végétaux ont fait le malheur de deux parties du monde. On a dépeuplé l'Amérique afin d'avoir une terre pour les planter et on a dépeuplé l'Afrique afin d'avoir une nation pour les cultiver.*

by those who did leave was filled by indentured workers. Thus, the initial slowdown in sugar production was soon reversed. Production was so strong by 1869 that the number of sugar mills had increased from 495 in 1839 to 564. In 1845 a British entrepreneur constructed the first large-scale *usine,* or sugar factory, in Fort de France (Delphin & Roth, 2009). With the industrialization of sugar production peaking in the 1880s, changes in the world market for sugar, competition from beet sugar, and a continual shortage of manual labor saw the number of sugar mills in Martinique drop to 423 by 1882.

Not only were sugar factories producing more sugar than the old sugar mills or *sucreries* (e.g., 34,000 vs. 5,000 tons in 1887), the quality of the sugar was vastly superior. The sugar factories also created a new socioeconomic system, reflecting the change from a primarily agricultural plantation society to a primarily factory-based industrial society; the Plantocracy and field workers were overtaken by *usiniers* (sugar factory owners), factory workers, and skilled technicians. The large profits of the usiniers were revelatory of a fledgling capitalist paradigm (Butel, 2002; Delphin & Roth, 2009; Nicolas, 2009).

These advances were not without their own challenges that made it difficult for the Martinican sugar industry to maintain profitability. High production elsewhere drove prices down; for example, by 1913 Cuba had become one of the world's main sugar producers, outpacing Martinique by 2.6 million to 41 thousand tons (Butel, 2002, p. 324). Because of low prices and the high production costs associated with importing and maintaining factory machinery, planters resorted to lowering wages to preserve their profit margins; strikes and other forms of labor unrest spread. As noted earlier, even though local authorities banned collective labor activity, significant strikes in St. Pierre in 1881 and St. Marie in 1882 reflected "the dawn of the labor movement," and the epiphany that "…only solidarity will strengthen us"[7] (Nicolas, 2009, p. 69).

Just as tobacco was gradually superseded by sugar during the mid- to late 17th century, Martinique's sugar economy faced its first competition after two centuries of uninterrupted reign: the rum industry. Sugar mills gradually morphed into rum distilleries; as rum is made from fermented sugar cane juice, the extension is quite logical. From 1850 to 1898, rum production in Martinique increased 150%, and there were 19 distilleries in the city of St. Pierre alone. St. Pierre, with 26,000 inhabitants, was the cultural and commercial hub of Martinique and the most populous of the major cities of Fort de France, St. Marie, Rivière-Pilote, and Trinité (one in seven Martinicans lived in St. Pierre). Two thirds of all commercial imports and exports in Martinique went through St. Pierre. Ships from the United States, Canada, England, as well as France graced this important international port (Butel, 2002).

As with tobacco and sugar production, natural disasters and shifting Martinican and international political climates often affected rum production. The promising rum industry in Martinique was soon destroyed by the eruption of Mt. Pelée in 1902 because 16 industrial distilleries and several smaller agricultural distilleries in St. Pierre were leveled. The distilleries were largely owned by the oldest béké families, but some gens de couleur also bought discounted plantations to convert into distilleries (Butel, 2002). Before the eruption of Mt. Pelée in 1902, Martinique was the world's leading producer of rum ("Patrimoine de la Martinique," 2014).

Because of World War I and the demand for rum, the industry rebounded somewhat. Beet-growing regions of France were under enemy attack, dramatically reducing production of beet sugar, which was the major competitor to sugar from Martinique since its introduction in 1812 by Benjamin Delessert from Passy, France (Delphin & Roth, 2009). Prices for sugar cane thus rose again, making

---

[7] *l' éveil du mouvement ouvrier... seule l'union fait la force.*

Figure 23. Mount Pele (Photo by Jessica Pearce, 2015.)

Figure 24. Ruins of old St. Pierre (Photo by authors, 2014.)

the distilling of rum profitable. Rum was not only comforting to soldiers in dank perilous trenches, but also as an antiseptic for soldiers' wounds and used to make explosives. International interest in rum grew as well, inspiring a flurry of production in Martinique. The boom continued until after **Armistice** (November 11, 1918), when a surplus from overproduction led to a drop in prices. The competition this price drop posed for French brandy and other alcoholic beverages inspired vintners in France to lobby for taxes on colonial rum, which were implemented in 1922.

As "rum fever" broke, production dropped and, consequently, so did the labor force that was needed, resurrecting the labor unrest of the 1880s. Capitalists in Martinique and Guadeloupe (which faced the same challenges) diversified their income with banana cultivation as their cash crop of choice. They did this fairly successfully, and by the beginning of World War II they were exporting 200,000 tons of bananas on 26 refrigerated freighters (Butel, 2002). Sugar was no longer the only commodity in the Martinican economy.

March toward Political Integration

Martinique's economic struggles going into World War II were accompanied by arguably the most important developments in Martinique's history since abolition: Négritude and Departmentalization. Initiated by Black intellectuals, these two powerful movements, one social and one political, resonated in the Americas, Europe, and Africa. Aime Césaire, Martinique's most esteemed political and literary figure, sought to center the identity of Black Martinicans in their history and perspective through his Négritude movement of 1939. He also spearheaded the related political move toward Departmentalization, which aimed to bring Martinique into the political and legal framework of mainland France.

"...A Voice for the Retrieved Identity"[8]

Aimé Césaire, born in Basse-Pointe, Martinique in 1913, arrived

---

[8] From Aimé Césaire's 1978 lecture on Négritude in Geneva, Switzerland (cited in Diagne, 2014, "Négritude as Revolt/Négritude as Philosophy," para. 2).

in Paris from Fort de France in 1931 at the age of 18 to pursue higher education. Cesaire served as mayor of Fort de France from 1945-2001 and as a deputy to the French National Assembly from 1945-1993, the longest-serving mayor and deputy to date. In Paris, he befriended two young Black intellectuals, Leopold Senghor from Senegal and Leon Damas from French Guiana. Together, they developed the concept of Négritude (a Césairean neologism), presented in *L'Etudiant noir,* a journal they founded with other Black students in 1934 (Diagne, 2014). Césaire espoused Négritude so that Martinicans of African descent could dig deeply in examining the existential question, "who are we?" Because the term *nègre* was loaded with three centuries of pejorative baggage, the intent was to expropriate it and replace it with the term Négritude to purge the word of its toxicity. Thus, the aim of this self-examination was not only to fill the historical vacuum and process the psychological trauma of slavery, but also to instill pride and dignity in blackness so that people could claim a sense of identity and pride not predicated on European ideals.

> Négritude, in my eyes, is not a philosophy.... It is a way of living history within history: the history of a community whose experience appears to be... unique, with its deportation of populations, its transfer of people from one continent to another, its distant memories of old beliefs, its fragments of murdered cultures. How can we not believe that all this, which has its own coherence, constitutes a heritage? (Césaire, 2004, p. 28)

In a 1980 interview, Césaire described himself as a runaway slave: "I am a runaway slave, mentally, I am a runaway slave" (*Je suis un Nègre Marron, mentalement, je suis un Nègre Marron;* Zandwonis, 2008, para. 4). What can we make of this characterization? As discussed in Chapter 5, reactions of enslaved Africans and gens de couleur to oppression, whether sociocultural, economic, psychological, or political, ranged from subtle to defiant. Abolition granted significant freedoms to former enslaved Africans in Martinique, however, it did not end all forms of oppression, especially psychological. In post-slavery society, as a greater number of people of African descent gained access to education in Martinique, and many traveled to France to continue their studies, forms of direct resistance evolved as well. It is against this backdrop that we analogize Césaire's influence with the pen on post-slavery Martinican society to the influence of the sword of grand marronage on enslaved Africans and the threat it posed to the Plantocracy of that era.

The marrons escaped to mornes to regroup, reenergize, and gain some sense of freedom and clarity of thought, only to return to plantations under cover of night to disrupt plantation society and mobilize enslaved Africans to reassert their humanity. Césaire's sojourn in France can be viewed in a similar manner, not as an escape from slavery, but as an escape from the stifling pretensions of Martinican people of color who had a "fundamental tendency to ape Europe" (Césaire 2005, p. 19). Césaire was also concerned about negative attitudes toward Africa and African heritage and the "embarrassment" they caused to Antilleans living in France, exemplified by this comment by an Antillean, "They [Africans] are savages, we are different" (Césaire 2005, p. 28).

In the novel *The Bridge of Beyond*, Amboise, who spent seven years in France, recounts his "temptation" to leave his native Guadeloupe (a form of marronage) and realizes through his sojourn in France that the Antillean soul had been molded by colonizers as self-mutilating (Schwarz-Bart, 2013). The self-examination that physical and cultural distance afforded Amboise, and recognition of damage to the Antillean soul, is analogous to Césaire's self-examination generated during his stay in France. His concept of Négritude bloomed from this introspection. As we see later, Césaire's Négritude sowed the seeds of a quest for identity rooted in Martinicans' lived experience and history, but it did not succeed in supplanting France with Africa as a focus of identification.

A Path to Political and Legal Integration

Martinicans' quest for authentic self-definition through Négritude was juxtaposed with their drive toward continuing three centuries of cultural assimilation to French social norms. The paradox of this fused identity was relevant then, and has undoubtedly left its mark on contemporary Martinique (seen in Indian and African populations alike). Despite emancipation from slavery and Césaire's ode to Négritude, there was a strong inclination in Martinique to model French ways of life in educational and cultural practices, in Catholic religious observances, and in adopting French as the official language. This was especially true for the upwardly mobile (Butel, 2002).

It goes without saying that to identify as French, Martinicans minimized their creoleness and saw themselves through the lens of the Other, the French. This phenomenon, scrutinized further in Chapter 10, was illustrated in the film "Sugar Cane Alley."[9] The ultimate proof of belonging to the mother country was Martinican enlistment in both world wars, paying the "blood tax" or *"l'impôt du sang"* (Burton, 1995, p. 3). With cultural and social assimilation already prominent in Martinique, political assimilation was the last step for France in rectifying the maleficent legacies of colonization and slavery.

Martinique's path to decolonization seems anomalous to the

---

[9] A film about an ambitious young man in 1930s Martinique who is urged by his grandmother to seek education, learn French, and do everything he can to learn French customs so that he can escape the poverty of the cane fields. La rue cases nègres (1983), dir. Euzhan Palcy, from the novel by Joseph Zobel.

historical pattern of gaining independence and establishing a nation-state in former European colonies. Including Martinique (and other French Caribbean islands) as an integral part of France was not an idea that just sprang up after World War II. The inclination toward full political assimilation with France had been gaining strength from 1870 when universal suffrage was reinstated for formerly enslaved men. In fact, it was first proposed to France by representatives from Guadeloupe and Martinique in 1890, followed by other proposals during World War I in 1915 and after the war in 1919 (Hintjens, 1995).

Subsequent to serving in war and making the ultimate sacrifice, an editorial in a local newspaper in 1918 expressed the desire by Martinicans "... to be fully assimilated as French"[10] (Butel, 2002, p. 351). The Colonial Exhibition of 1931 in Paris, followed by celebrations of the tricentennial of Martinique's colonization and dedication of a statue of D'Esnambuc (who colonized Martinique in 1635) in Fort de France, amplified the call for political assimilation (Butel, 2002). Joseph Lagrossiliere, the mayor of Ste. Marie, speaking at a dinner in 1935 heralded the movement toward Departmentalization: "From hereforth, let the Antilles, French Guiana, and the Reunion Islands be French Departments"[11] (p.352).

Effects of World War II

World War II had a powerful effect on the socioeconomic and political climates of Martinique and France as well as the rest of the world. Examining the inter- and intra-group dynamics in both regions illuminates historical pattern of ambivalent responses to moral dilemmas. The war divided French society into two camps. One faction supported the ***Vichy* regime** under Marshall Pétain, who was a pawn of Hitler's anti-semitic, racist Nazi regime; Hitler's vile

---

[10] *... à être pleinement assimilés aux Français.*

[11] *Vivent désormais les Antilles, la Guyane, et la Réunion, en départements français.*

comment describing France as a country "bastardized by Jews and Negroes" illustrates these sentiments (Childers, 2006, p. 292). In the other camp were those who believed in liberty, fraternity, and equality and supported a free France.

The example of the *Paul Lemerle* and six other ships that sailed for Martinique from Marseilles, France in 1941 reflects French ambivalence about issues of human rights, similar to that they had shown about slavery. The *Lemerle* carried 222 passengers, all exiles, some of whom were renowned intellectuals (Claude Lévi-Strauss, André Breton, and Anna Serghers), all escaping the pro-Nazi Vichy regime. On one hand, this state-sponsored deportation of French Jews to America through Martinique was, in the words of Marcel Peyrouton, the Vichy's interior minister, humanitarian and socially responsible; on the other hand, he also saw it as a way of ridding France of the "foreigners who are overrepresented in the French nation and economy . . . taking their fill of consumer goods without producing any themselves" (as quoted in Jennings, 2002, p. 321).

Martinican society in many ways mirrored divisions in France. During the Nazi occupation of France, békés in Martinique allied with Admiral Robert, high commissioner of the French Antilles under the Vichy government, which is not surprising given the békés' historical focus on White superiority and pure bloodlines discussed in Chapter 6. Martinique's colonial government under Admiral Robert shared the xenophobia of the Vichy regime in France. The Jewish exiles sailing from Marseille were "undesirables" and most unwelcome when they disembarked in Fort de France. Martinican officials ordered the exiles to leave for another destination as soon as possible or be sent back to France. These political refugees were housed in poor conditions and had to pay hefty sums for their stay, making their challenging journey by ship seem almost palatable (Jennings, 2002).

An authoritarian with a penchant for crushing democratic

institutions such as Martinique's Conseil Général [General Council] and replacing its members with hand-picked agents (Jennings, 2001), Admiral Robert raised fears among Black Martinicans that slavery could be reinstated. Given this atmosphere, people of color in Martinique found General De Gaulle's mission to free France from the Nazis and bring liberty to all French citizens appealing, and they were keenly aware of the ideological similarity between the Nazis and the despised békés. Thus, the support of people of color for De Gaulle was an extension of their desire for political integration with Free France and equal rights, just as békés were opposed to such integration to protect their interests and maintain the status quo.

The economic ripple effects of World War II isolated Martinique from France and Europe in general. Due to Allied naval blockades, transporting and repairing machinery (and regular exports or imports) were difficult, causing a reduction of factory production that resulted in rampant poverty and food shortages. These economic strains exacerbated social tensions, which had xenophobic undertones, among poor Martinicans (mostly Blacks), particularly expressed toward the new Syrian and Lebanese immigrants (fewer than 200) who started to arrive in Martinique during the 1920s after Syria and Lebanon became French Protectorates.

These immigrants, similar to Indian indentured workers, boarded ships to "the American colonies" to build railroads and a better life for their families. Early emigrants were under the impression that they were going to the United States and did not realize that they had landed on Martinique until several weeks after their arrival. A majority of them settled in Fort de France on François Arago Street as merchants and small shopkeepers. Some became door-to-door salesmen, mostly cloth merchants (Hersilie-Héloïse, 2009). Economic hardships historically have a way of amplifying inter-group conflict, as we have seen earlier in Martinique's history with freed enslaved

Africans and indentured workers. Thus, the fraying socioeconomic fabric of Martinique prompted Césaire to call on France in 1945 to provide support in the form of a colonial solidarity fund for social welfare for the poor and to jump-start the economy. These sentiments were echoed by Communist and Socialist representatives elected to the French National Assembly after World War II from Martinique and other French colonies (Guadeloupe, French Guiana, and Réunion; Hintjens, 1995).

Even though the majority of Martinicans favored political integration with France, some feared that political assimilation would ultimately sound the death knell for a unique Martinican identity. These fears spurred advocacy for acknowledgment, preservation, and respect for Martinican history and customs. Martinicans living in France, especially educated youth, were critical of the assimilation policy, stemming from their feelings of cultural estrangement in France because of their creoleness. A small percentage of Martinicans, mostly wealthy békés, also resisted Departmentalization. Many resented their loss of influence on local judicial and economic matters that they had wielded until now. They also were wary of decisions from the central government in Paris as Martinique was 4,200 miles away with its own socioeconomic history. Unfortunately, all these concerns resurfaced after Departmentalization (Burton, 1995).

Departmentalization

In his speech to the National Assembly in February 1946, Césaire pressed for Departmentalization, claiming, "The Antilles and Reunion islands need assimilation to escape the political and administrative chaos they have been plunged into..."[12] (Assemblée Nationale Constituante, 1946, pp. 9-10). The term "assimilation" and

---

[12] *les Antilles et la Réunion ont besoin de l'assimilation pour sortir du chaos politique et administratif dans lequel elles se trouvaient plongées [...]*

its association with Césaire can easily be misinterpreted. For well over three centuries, since the expulsion of the Caribs from Martinique, France imposed its cultural and social norms on all newcomers. So when Césaire advocated that "assimilation should be the rule and derogation the exception" (Nesbitt, 2007, p. 33), he is not referring to increased "Frenchification" by psychological, cultural, and social assimilation, but to legal and political assimilation as the foundation of Departmentalization. He further clarified his use of the word assimilation as meaning something flexible, clever, and pragmatic[13] (Assemblée Nationale Constituante, 1946, p. 6).

In other words, he sought to end the system of a colonial governor in which laws and policies were enacted and interpreted by hand-picked representatives of France's head of state and the Colonial Council (elite Whites); he demanded that all French citizens, on the islands and in mainland France, be governed by the same legal and political rules. Césaire supported Departmentalization of the four former colonies of France (Martinique, Guadeloupe, French Guiana, and Reunion). He viewed Departmentalization as a path to decolonization through broad social participation and expanded power via "universal human-rights based law" (Nesbitt, 2007, p. 39). He was staunchly supported by those in the French Assembly who also stressed the geopolitical advantage to France of direct presence in the Caribbean, not colonies but French territory, especially considering the strategic position of French Guiana on the South American continent (Hintjens, 1995).

Within a year of serving as mayor of Fort de France and a deputy to the French National Assembly, Césaire's persistent, eloquent, and savvy political leadership guided unanimous passage of the Departmentalization Law in the French National Assembly on March 19, 1946. Article I of this law declared: "The colonies of Guadeloupe, Martinique, Reunion, and French Guiana will be set up

---

[13] "*une assimilation souple, intelligente et réaliste.*"

as French Departments"[14] (Loi n° 46-451 du 19 mars, 1946, article 1).

Conclusion

As noted earlier, political integration with the mother country was not the path that most former colonies chose; the majority chose to become independent states and sever political ties with European colonizers. As many scholars have pointed out, Departmentalization of French overseas colonies may seem incongruous during this period of decolonization (Murch, 1968). If the quest for self-determination revolves around securing political, social, economic, and human rights, Césaire and most Martinicans felt that the realistic path to achieving this was with France rather than apart from it. The desire to become an independent state was essentially negligible among Martinique's political leaders, based on interviews in the mid-1960s with 32 such leaders in power at the time of Departmentalization (Murch, 1968). Although Departmentalization was seen as not perfect, it seemed more likely to result in a favorable outcome than either autonomy or independent statehood; this consensus appears to continue in contemporary Martinique, as demonstrated by referenda in 2003 and 2010, discussed in Chapter 10.

Did all Martinicans of African heritage fully relate to Cesaire's Négritude movement? Or was it shrouded in ambivalence in a society whose history was obscured by the French and whose only real connection to Africa was a physical resemblance to its people? The call for revaluing aesthetics and characteristics rooted in African, rather than French, sensibilities appealed to the need of Black Martinicans to accept in themselves what was not valued by the French. Unfortunately, African sensibilities were at a significant historical and geographic distance from the average Martinican's daily experience, and thus were

---

[14] *Les colonies de la Guadeloupe, de la Martinique, de la Réunion et la Guyane française sont érigées en départements français.*

difficult to connect with wholeheartedly for many. Césaire's Négritude was also controversial because it was not entirely representative of Martinique's ethnic mosaic. "But where is the Negro in all of this? He is not there. You have him within, however. Dig deeper, and you will find him in the bottom of you, beyond all the layers of civilization"[15] (Césaire, 2005, p. 27). This call to self-examination is not directed to all Martinicans, but to Martinicans of African heritage. So, the Ariadne's thread to Africa that Négritude provided may have been relevant to people of African descent, but did not offer a way for Indian or Chinese indentured workers to reconnect to their heritage.

Ironically, Césaire's nanny (Da) of many years, who rocked him to sleep with lullabies in the Tamil language, was a descendant of an Indian indentured worker. "Let us not forget the nanny who cradled baby Aimé"[16] (Sahaï, 2008, para. 1). Although Césaire had a keen appreciation for Indo-Martinicans and the Tamil language, the focus of Négritude was the African connection. It is therefore not surprising that people with a different ethnic background would find it difficult to relate to Négritude.

Regardless of the implications of ethnic essentialism in Négritude, oppression of any kind was anathema to Césaire, whether the target was "… a Jew-man, a Kaffir-man, a Hindu-man… a Harlem-man…" (Césaire, 2001, p. 15). He acknowledged and expressed great appreciation for the Jewish predicament, historically and in the present. The concerns of Blacks in Martinique and Jews worldwide for survival as distinct groups were linked for Césaire. He did, however, draw a distinction between Jewish and Black struggles. The Israeli fight for a nation-state they can call their own, safeguarding their rights and culture, in his opinion was not the same as the Black struggle against

---

[15] *Mais où est le Nègre dans tout ça? Le nègre n'y est pas. Tu l'as en toi, pourtant. Creuse encore plus profond, et tu te trouveras au fond de toi, par-delà toutes les couches de la civilization.*

[16] *N'oublions pas la Da qui berça le petit Aimé.*

racism in the land of their birth (Miles, 2009). Simply put, Israelis are largely secure in their identity, but struggle to defend the existence of their home; Martinicans have a secure house but struggle to make themselves at home.

Although Aimé Césaire's role in the conception, promotion, and implementation of Departmentalization and the Négritude movement was not uniformly well received at home, his influence on Martinican politics and intellectuals was quite extraordinary, as we see in the next two chapters.

Martinique's political climate was inextricably bound to Aimé Césaire's political evolution; first as the Communist mayor of Fort de France and deputy of the French National Assembly in 1945, and then as the founder of the *Parti Progressiste Martiniquais (PPM)* Party in 1958. Intellectually, Fanon, Glissant, Chamoiseau, Bernabé, Confiant, Sméralda, L'Etang, and many other scholars greatly benefited from Césaire's work and legacy. "The intellectual influence of Aimé Césaire on our perception of the real Martinican is more important than once imagined"[17] (Reno, 2009, p. 19).

The following chapter discusses the ramifications of Martinique's assimilation into the French system with Departmentalization. With the political and economic concerns of most Martinicans addressed and security and stability assured, there was now space for "interior vision" and self-acceptance (Bernabé et al., 1990, p. 861). Césaire's intellectual heirs would take varied paths branching off from Négritude, which purported to connect Martinicans to the "inaccessible land" (Munro, 2008, p. 24) of Africa. The Antillanité and Créolité literary movements of the 1970s and 1980s localized and particularized Martinican identity with Caribbean colors and not solely "…with the colors of Elsewhere [i.e., France or Africa]" (Bernabé et al., 1990, p. 888). Special attention is given in the next chapter to the impact of the 1981 Socialist victory

---

[17]*L'influence intellectuelle d'Aimé Césaire sur notre perception du réel martiniquais est beaucoup plus importante que nous l'imaginions.*

in France and the "right to difference" policies of President François Mitterrand's government, which furthered the development of the Martinican Creole language and culture.

Glossary

Departmentalization - Law of 1946 that made the former colonies of France (Martinique, Guadeloupe, French Guiana, and Réunion) departments of France with the same laws and administrative structure.

Négritude - (French) Literary, philosophical, and ideological movement begun in the 1930s among Parisian university students from Africa and the Caribbean to instill pride and dignity in blackness in order to claim a sense of identity not predicated on European ideals.

usine - (French, "factory") Factory for refining sugar.

repatriation - Return of indentured workers to their countries of origin at the end of their work contracts; this was sometimes explicitly stated in contracts, and sometimes an option if the worker had saved enough money for return passage.

Armistice - Formal agreement November 11, 1917 that ended World War I between Allied powers and Germany.

"l'impôt du sang" - (French, "the blood tax") Refers to volunteers from Martinique and other French colonies in both world wars earning the right to be considered patriotic Frenchmen through their service.

Vichy **regime** - French government from 1940-1944 under Marshal Phillippe Pétain that collaborated with Nazi Germany.

Reflective Questions

1. Compared with Indian indentured workers, the contributions of Congolese and Chinese indentured workers to Martinican culture today are minimal. How would you account for this, based on your reading of this chapter and Chapter 7?

2. In this chapter Césaire was characterized as engaging in marronage. To explore this simile further, what oppressive system was he running away from? To what end?

3. The Négritude movement was considered by Césaire to be "... a voice of revolt" (Diagne, 2014, para. 8). In what ways does this description ring true?

4. Provide examples to discuss similar political divisions in Martinican and mainland French society during World War II despite their demographic differences and geographic distance.

5. Do the objectives of Négritude and Departmentalization seem antithetical or compatible? Explain your reasoning using details from this chapter.

Chapter 9

Martinique's Pluralistic Identities Today

Négritude? Antillanité? Créolité? l'Indianité?

Martinque is an old land of slavery,
of colonization and neo-colonization.
But this endless pain is a precious guide;
it has taught us the values of reciprocity and sharing.[1]

-Édouard Glissant (1928-2011) & Patrick Chamoiseau
Martinican literary figures

Abolition of slavery in 1848 spurred demands in Martinique to be French citizens with all the rights of that status. As discussed in the previous chapter, establishing the Overseas Departments of France in 1946 was seen at the time as the culmination of the struggle for equal rights. Soon after the Law of Departmentalization was passed, challenges arose because not all aspects of the French system were particularly suited to the island's culture and circumstances; 10 years after Martinique became part of France, "Departmentalist euphoria" began to fade (Chateau-Degat & Placide, 2009). Frustrations with the process were perhaps inevitable, and to conceptualize difficulties of incorporating territories into an existing nation, it is instructive to note that the legislative process of annexing Alsace-Lorraine (northeastern region bordering Germany) into France after World War I took 10 years to complete. We can only imagine the complexity of integrating

---

[1] *La Martinique est une vieille terre d'esclavage, de colonisation, et de néo-colonisation. Mais cette interminable douleur est un maître précieux: elle nous a enseigné l'échange et le partage (Glissant & Chamoiseau, 2005, para. 1).*

a territory 4,200 miles away, given the colonial baggage and an entirely different social, cultural, economic, and physical ecosystem.

The goals of liberty, fraternity, and equality were substantially attained through Departmentalization. However, the paradox for Martinique was that benefitting from being part of France was coupled with no significant power to decide how those benefits would be applied to local interests. Whether French laws and administrative structures were imposed on Martinique or modified to suit France's perceptions of the island's circumstances, the creation and implementation of these laws and structures were not under Martinican control. They seldom took local concerns into account (Burton, 1995a).

Martinicans' efforts to resolve fundamental existential questions of identity on their own terms in a Caribbean context while coping with France as the distant host community serve as the backdrop for this chapter. This chapter focuses on two main topics: the repercussions of Departmentalization on Martinique as a microcosm of France and the efforts of Martinicans to create a unique creole culture that reflects their collective narratives in an overwhelmingly French context. There is also brief discussion of how the Socialist ascent to power in 1981 facilitated efforts toward validating creole culture.

Immediate Aftermath of Departmentalization

The decision by Martinique to become a Department of France is often ascribed to two important motivations: political integration with France would circumvent the arbitrary whims of the békés and Colonial Council, as well as alleviate apprehensions about the United States, perceived as having imperial aspirations with béké-like attitudes. The combination of strategic interests in the Caribbean (specifically the Panama Canal) and fear of communism attracted serious American attention to Martinique after World War II (Childers, 2006). The powerful Communist Party in Martinique, led effectively by Aimé Césaire, mobilized the populace by focusing on the legacy of slavery and its connection to current economic deprivation.

The centennial anniversary of emancipation in 1948 posed one of the first major challenges for the new Department of Martinique. Martinicans hoped that Departmentalization would bring deeper French recognition and acknowledgment of slavery by declaring a national holiday to celebrate 100 years of freedom, including the participation of French West African representatives and the President of France, Vincent Auriol. Martinicans demanded that abolition be given at least as much attention as France gave to the tricentennial celebration of the colonization of Martinique and Guadeloupe in 1935. However, French officials considered this a local, not national, issue, and even the president chose not to participate, with the interior minister of France declaring that "the demonstrations that will take place in the Antilles will take place within a purely local context" (Childers, 2006, p. 294).

France's official response to the centennial of abolition was one of the few instances where the local context was considered in policymaking. However, one wonders how self-serving was the intent behind localizing the celebration. Certainly, the inclination to require accommodation to French regulations (including holidays) is reflective of France's historical stance on assimilation. But, the unwillingness to consider slavery as relevant to the country as a whole can be seen as equally reflective of France's historical ambivalence on the matter.

Economic and social conditions in Martinique had not markedly improved at the time of the commemoration. Békés still owned most of the land and agricultural factories, and the Black majority still constituted the main labor force on the same plantations for little pay (Childers, 2006). In the words of the U.S. Consul William H. Christensen, "The Communist Party in Martinique is preparing already for a huge celebration in 1948.... The Communist press constantly reminds its readers that they once were slaves" (Childers, 2006, p. 288). These tensions came to a head as the centennial approached, with violent clashes between the minority Whites and majority Blacks.

White Martinicans reached out to the U.S. consul for military protection and even American citizenship in the event of attacks against them. America's well-known Jim Crow laws made the prospect of supporting the békés very plausible and troubling to Martinicans of African heritage. Frustrations led to eruptions of violence against the békés. A wealthy White planter, Guy Fabrique, was brutally murdered by his enraged workers in 1948, feeding anxieties among békés (Childers, 2006). Fearing that more racial violence and unrest might erupt during the centennial celebrations, a French naval ship was on hand in Fort de France to quell any such disturbance. To everyone's relief, the celebrations took place without incident, despite the bloodshed that preceded them.

The non-White populace of French Overseas Departments (especially in Martinique and Guadeloupe) inherently trusted the French on the mainland more than wealthy Whites on the islands. When several Guadeloupean workers were accused of murdering their béké employer in 1951, they were flown to France for their trial (a considerable expense at that time) to avoid racial tension, and they were subsequently found not guilty because of insufficient evidence. This incident confirmed for many Guadeloupeans and Martinicans that France was genuinely on their side, and that békés were the oppressors. The communist newspaper *Justice* wrote, "Martinicans can count on the people of France, our surest ally, which is not to be confused with the colonialist bandits who govern here in the name of France" (Childers, 2006, p. 292).

The French Communist Party continued this staunch alliance,

supporting Aimé Césaire's candidacy as the communist mayor of Fort de France. Despite this backing and the popular sentiment among Martinicans of France as an ally, Césaire split from the French Communist Party on October 24, 1956. This was an important turning point in Martinique's ongoing effort to develop its own institutions. Césaire wrote a letter to Maurice Thorez, the general secretary of the French Communist Party, announcing his withdrawal. He felt that the voices of Blacks were drowned out in the swell of communist ideology, which was not advocating the "singularity" of the predicament of Blacks: "I am not burying myself in a narrow particularism. But neither do I want to lose myself in an emaciated universalism. There are two ways to lose oneself: walled segregation in the particular or dilution in the □ universal'" (Césaire, 2010, p. 152).

Césaire made it clear that the direction of the Communist Party and Martinique's people of color were not the same. The specific conditions of their immigration to Martinique (anthropological rupture) and current struggles with racism, disempowerment, and unemployment required them to work through these unique obstacles to build their own future because "the responsibility for this discovery belongs to no one but us..."(Césaire, 2010, p. 147). He stressed that it was important to have forums that are tailored by Black people in order to help themselves. He founded the Martinican Progressive Party (PPM) with a socialist framework in 1958; the first local party with no ties to France (Miles, 2009), created to forge Martinican political goals and identity (Miles, 2009).

Yet, Martinique's desire to experience some reciprocity from France in adapting to their concerns (or at least acknowledgment of shared interest in those needs) was not accommodated for many decades. It was not until May 10, 2001 that French parliament adopted a resolution declaring the slave trade and exploitation of non-Europeans from the 15th century onward as crimes against humanity.

In 2006, President Jacques Chirac designated the same day, May 10, as the national day to "honor the memory of the victims of slavery and commemorate its abolition" (Childers, 2006, p. 298).

Political Repercussions

Although the most powerful political figure in Martinique, Aimé Césaire, had forsaken communism, world events provoked fear in the French government that Martinique's discontent would lead to revolution. The Cold War between the United States and the Soviet Union moved closer to Martinique in 1959 with Fidel Castro's taking power in Cuba. Struggles for independence were widespread from Africa to Asia; France was fully embroiled in bloody wars with Vietnam and Algeria and was apprehensive about the deteriorating political climate in Martinique.

Centralized authority was a prominent feature of post-World War II French government, and certainly made itself felt in Martinique from the late 1940s through the 1950s. The Law of Departmentalization eliminated the position of governor in Martinique and created the position of **Prefect**, the highest representative of the French central government in Martinique (as in all Departments of France). Prefects were given wide latitude, particularly in policing, interpretation of laws, economic development, and finance (Hintjens, 1995). This position, starting with Prefect Pierre Trouillé in March, 1947 and continuing with his immediate successors, heralded a hard-line, autocratic administrative style so reminiscent of colonial governors that it hardly seemed anything had changed. The Prefect swiftly implemented opposition from the central French Government to activities deemed part of a communist movement. Labor unrest and political demonstrations were suppressed by brutal military crackdowns, such as strikes in Carbet and Basse-Pointe in 1948 and in

Ducos in 1951 (Chateau-Degat & Placide, 2009).

Although all Martinicans were full French citizens, Martinican civil servants resented the civil servants from France whom they felt enjoyed better benefits and salaries (Chateau-Degat & Placide, 2009). A law passed April 3, 1950 was intended to attract civil-service and public-sector employees to work in Martinique on expanding essential services (schools, hospitals, sanitation, roads, housing, etc.), and align Martinique with France. French *fonctionnaires* or civil servants (police, teachers, doctors, contractors, and administrators) received on average 25% to 40% more pay and benefits to compensate for "la vie chère," or the high cost of living in Martinique (Botteau, 2011).

Hostilities grew between local citizens and French civil servants; Martinicans felt that these mainland French personnel behaved no differently than their colonial ancestors who viewed Martinique as a conquered land. Social tensions between these groups, along with the major shift from an agricultural to a service and consumer-based economy ended the honeymoon period of Departmentalization. Sparks flew at even the smallest of frictions, as in the three days of uprisings over December 20-22, 1959 triggered by an altercation involving a Martinican and a Frenchman, resulting in the deaths of three young Martinicans. Following this unfortunate event, a Christmas Eve session of the General Council unanimously approved a motion for Martinicans to have more control over their own affairs, *"une plus grande participation à la gestion des affaires martiniquaises"* [greater participation in managing Martinican affairs] (Chateau-Degat & Placide, 2009, p. 115).

Social and Cultural Repercussions

The efforts to mirror the French system with all its political, social, and governmental structures in Martinique did begin with the intent of including Martinique as a kindred member of the French nation. "By giving the colonies the same institutions as metropolitan [mainland] France, assimilation little by little removes the distances which separate the diverse parts of the French territory, and finally realizes their intimate union through the application of common legislation" (Raymond Betts, cited in Hintjens, 1995, p. 25). Although this might have been the goal of Departmentalization, transplanting the French system wholesale onto Martinican soil did not automatically thrive as intended. The socioeconomic challenges faced by Martinique and its people did not facilitate this political and legal union.

However, cultural and social assimilation with the French accelerated rapidly and overtook local culture and language with unforeseen consequences. The Law of Departmentalization, intended to remedy the ills of the colonial past by bringing social security and legal rights to Martinicans, was in actuality drowning them in the Other: "Equal status as Frenchmen trumped pride of □ being Martinican'"(Miles, 2006, p. 636). Léopold Bissol, a French Guianese deputy, described the former colonies as a baby who is brought to the mother's breast for nourishment and protection, only to be smothered (Hintjens, 1995). The world became more aware of how French the Martinicans were; in other words, how powerful France was in imposing its identity and *mission civilisatrice* on the Martinican people. Regardless of political affiliation, Martinicans were "100% French," as Sheldon B. Vance, the American consul for the French West Indies in 1950, put it (Childers, 2006, p. 291). This may explain why the Négritude movement had such a difficult time taking root among the general populace of Martinique; it did, however, have support within intellectual circles.

Social mobility depended on how French one became, particularly how well one spoke French, just as it had been since emancipation. A salient aspect of this linguistic assimilation was the devaluation of the Creole language in relation to French; a constant from Martinique's beginning to the present. In spite of the ubiquitous presence of Creole on billboards, brochures, and in informal conversation, many Martinicans of a certain age vividly recounted punishments meted out by parents and teachers alike for speaking Creole in school. Creole was deemed crude and uncivilized in comparison to French. Raphaël Confiant recalls as a young student that his teacher condemned Creole as "a patois spoken by savage negros and dirty coolies" (Carter & Torabully, 2002, pp. 8-9). Bernabé et al. (1990) eloquently address the crux of this narrative, which extends beyond language as a status signifier:

> French ways forced us to denigrate ourselves: the common condition of colonized people. It is often difficult for us to discern what, in us, might be the object of an aesthetic approach. What we accept in us as aesthetic is the little declared by the Other as aesthetic.... What good is the creation of an artist who totally refuses his unexplored being? Who does not know who he is? Or who barely accepts it? (891)

Still, Creole was accepted and freely used, typically in informal situations between friends (usually of the same age) and family. Such insulation from formal French usage may well have helped preserve the Creole language for over 300 years, in much the same way that isolation of Indian indentured workers from larger Martinican society helped preserve their rituals and religious practices.

The foremost promoter of the Martinican cause, Aime Césaire, was not insulated from the influence of the French language or Western attire. One of his most impressive skills was his oratorical command of French (Reno, 1995). Césaire, the charismatic leader who always wore a suit and tie (even on an island where the temperature is always balmy), and spoke in sophisticated and eloquent French laced with subtleties and nuances comprehensible only to the well educated, without doubt rallied thousands of Martinicans to support his political agenda (Reno, 2009). The poetic eloquence that was Césaire's trademark, coupled with his protean intellect, frequently rendered complex statements that could easily have multiple interpretations..

The French language as a unifying force for the French nation was initiated at the behest of the same person who advocated establishing the colony of Martinique: Cardinal Richelieu founded the French Academy (*Académie française*) in 1635, the same year that D'Esnambuc claimed Martinique for the king and cardinal (Tapié, 1975). The purpose of the French Academy was to standardize, regulate, and maintain purity of the French language in order to bridge regional differences. Richelieu's support for the colonial enterprise, discussed in Chapter 3, and his support for the French Academy were important in promoting the glory of France and its monarchy. It is thus not too surprising that the French language not only bound France together as a nation, but also generated a deep attachment to "Frenchness" in Martinique, despite the legacy of colonialism.

Frantz Fanon is another Martinican intellectual who addressed this issue of Frenchness among post-colonial populations. Born in Fort de France in 1925 and a student of Césaire's, Fanon grew up believing that he was French, so much so that he left Martinique to fight in the Free French Army during World War II. His experience of racism during and after the war disillusioned him, and prompted him to question his identity as a post-colonial individual (Ahluwalia, 2003; Miles, 2009b). Fanon viewed the attachment of former colonial subjects to the culture of the colonizer as a psychological disorder, and successful treatment required violent revolt to reverse this power dynamic. His work as a psychiatrist in Algeria in the 1950s convinced him of the importance of revolution in relieving the symptoms of colonization. This emphasis on the necessity for violence in decolonization was based on his understanding of the role of violence in establishing the colonial relationship (Fanon, 1967/1952). His ideas, especially his focus on violent rejection of the colonizer's culture, along with his departure from his homeland, places him outside the sphere of the most influential thinkers on Martinican identity. Most academics we spoke to in Martinique only mentioned Fanon if we directly brought him up.

Transition from a Production-Based to a Consumption-Based Economy

During the 1950s, the shift from an agricultural and manufacturing economy to a consumer and civil-service economy ushered in modern urban life as seen in Martinique today. The exodus from rural plantations to cities increased, especially to Fort de France. Greater population density promoted a consumer economy. To accommodate the large influx of people, high-rise apartment complexes (housing projects), supermarkets, and other retail franchises (such as *Prisunic,* a French supermarket chain) sprang up in and around Fort de France. The number of local businesses declined; local products were not perceived as attractive as French products. Furthermore, the higher taxes and regulatory requirements of Departmentalization were a considerable strain on small local businesses.

France experienced similar economic and demographic trends during the period called "The Glorious Thirty" (*trente glorieuses,* 1945-1975). The postwar economic boom from rebuilding French infrastructure also led to increased standards of living for the lower and middle class, largely from more jobs and productivity. There was a similar shift in France of population from rural to urban settings, especially to Paris. However, France's economic growth outpaced population growth, creating a demand for workers. To ease population and economic pressures in the Overseas Departments and meet labor needs in France, Martinicans looking for jobs flocked to mainland France starting in 1960. The jobs taken by Martinicans were by and large low-level positions that were unappealing to the mainland French. (L'Etang, 2007)

In 1963, *BUMIDOM (Bureau pour le développement des migrations dans les départements d'outre-mer)* was established to encourage residents of the Overseas Departments to seek employment in France. The initial goal of the agency was the migration of 30,000 French citizens from all four Overseas Departments over three years; the actual figure far surpassed that target (Château-Degat & Placide, 2009).

> By the late 1960s, the principal French West Indian export had become... French West Indians.... By the mid-1970s, the French West Indian departments were, so to speak, all superstructure and no base, rich by virtue of the funds which, for scarcely disinterested reasons, France continued to pour into them, totally impoverished when measured by the standards of what they actually produced. (Burton, 1995a, pp. 4 and 5)

In the latter part of the 20th century, the economic, social, and political fabric in Martinique was unraveling. There was high unemployment and a drop in sugar production; furthermore, Martinique was being drowned in imported French food, fashion, appliances, and media, creating a veritable microcosm of France. By 1981, Martinique, one of the largest sugar producers in the 19th century, was left with 2 sugar factories, 18 distilleries, and a few thousand people employed in sugar production; it was growing only one fifth of its produce, with the remainder imported from France (Miles, 1985). As of 2014, there was only one sugar factory in Martinique, at Galion. Despite what may seem a dramatic socioeconomic downturn over 20 years, Martinique's per capita income and gross national product (GNP) were well above average compared with other Caribbean countries and most other countries in general because of the extensive French social safety net (Miles, 1985).

TV and other media focused on mainland French affairs, and rarely did Martinicans receive local or Caribbean news. The rapid disappearance of Creole culture, compounded by the exodus of Martinicans to mainland France, and the large number of mainland French coming to Martinique as civil servants, amplified Martinicans' dependence on France and sense of alienation (Miles, 1985). As we see in the next chapter, the brain drain from a massive emigration of young and talented Martinicans to France became a common post-Departmentalization motif. The effect of the shift to a consumer economy on the people of Martinique was disempowerment and erosion of their cultural identity, leading to a deprivation of dignity, not diet; a kind of interior void.

Socialism, Decentralization, and the Right to Difference[2]

Socialist François Mitterrand became president of France in 1981. Eighty-one per cent of Martinicans voted for Mitterrand's opponent, the incumbent Giscard d'Estaing, fearing that a vote for the socialist, with his focus on decentralization or the empowerment of local government, would be a vote for a gradual move toward an independent Martinique. Not only did the French media favor the incumbent, who supported Martinique's continued status as a

---

[2] The "right to difference" was part of the French Socialist party agenda, supported by Mitterrand (Miles, 1985). It was a call for the government to recognize and support France's sociocultural diversity.

Department, his platform maintained that Mitterrand's victory would change this status (Miles, 1985).

With Mitterrand's socialist victory, Césaire expressed optimism that Martinicans might finally be acknowledged as having their own history and culture and deserving of support to develop their community. Being the true pragmatist that he was, he also realized that this could not be achieved without allies. Césaire declared a moratorium in front of the city hall in Fort de France in May 1981, calling for Martinicans to temporarily end discussion of autonomy for Martinique and instead to revitalize the Martinican economy, culture, and identity. It was, in his words, "... not the opposite of the struggle; no, it is preparation for the struggle" (Miles, 2009b, p. 72).

In the first four years of his presidency, Mitterrand and the socialist government took several concrete measures reaffirming France's social and economic support of Martinique while granting more administrative and budgetary control to local and regional governments. In addition, unprecedented initiatives recognized and bolstered the Martinican (and that of all Overseas Departments) unique historical and cultural character and the right to difference (Christofferson, 1991). This approach, termed **Regionalization,** was intended to customize French institutions to suit Martinican circumstances, which Césaire essentially agreed with. Césaire distinguished between the goals of Departmentalization and Regionalization: Departmentalization gave Martinique the same legal and economic protections as France, and Regionalization encouraged Martinicans to develop and stimulate cultural and economic growth. He steered clear of the issue of independence for Martinique and wished that decision to be made by the Martinican people when they felt ready for it (Miles, 2009b).

France's administrative structure consists of regions subdivided into Departments, which are further subdivided into *arrondissements, cantons*, and so on. After Departmentalization, Martinique found itself in the unique position of being a region consisting of only one Department with two representative bodies, one for the region of Martinique (**Regional Council**) and one for the department of Martinique (**General Council**). This administrative model was inefficient for Martinique's local and regional decision-making process because it favored geographic representation rather than proportional representation. Mitterand's government therefore proposed to fuse the regional and the general council into one, the *Assemblée Unique.* This

> ...would have replaced the system of representation by canton by one of proportional representation; that is, instead of electing one representative for each of the island's 36 cantons, which has traditionally favored a rural, conservative electorate, there would be an island-wide vote, with each party apportioned seats based on its relative strength in the total count. (Miles, 1985, p. 68)

This proposition was ruled unconstitutional and thus went nowhere. Unfazed, Mitterand's socialist government moved forward with legislation that at least allowed proportional representation in the Regional Council while the General Council's electoral process remained the same. This reform democratized local and regional decision making by amplifying the voices of the majority of Martinicans.

As acknowledgement of the abolition of slavery in Martinique, May 22 was established as an official holiday in 1984 in Martinique to commemorate this milestone (Miles, 1985). Efforts were made to stimulate Martinican culture and, by extension, Caribbean culture. In less than a year, funding for the French Ministry of Culture was doubled (from four to eight million) and a Regional Bureau of Cultural

Affairs was formed to promote cultural diversity in the French nation (Murray, 1997). Other initiatives included greater local participation and coverage in French media, financial and organizational support for Creole language and culture, expanding educational opportunities by making the then University of the Antilles and Guiana an independent institution, no longer a subsidiary of the University of Bordeaux (Miles, 1985). In addition, special schools for the promotion of the performing and fine arts were created thanks to funding from the Ministry of Culture.

There was an attempt to improve the experience of migration to France by strengthening the ties of Martinicans in France to their home, making it easier to travel back and forth, as well as creating employment opportunities in Martinique to decelerate migration to France (Miles, 1985). It is interesting that a Creole identity seemed to be intensified by sojourns of Martinicans in mainland France and seemed greater than that of Martinicans who never left the island (Miles, 2009). The Mitterand government's emphasis on the right to difference and promoting local culture seemed to contribute to the invigoration of Martinican identity movements distinct from French culture, such as Créolité and l'Indianité toward the end of the 20th century.

Post-Departmentalization Identity Movements

The challenge of nurturing Martinican identity while being assimilated politically, economically, and socially into France (in other words, being French) is significant. This paradox is expressed eloquently by singer and songwriter Kennenga as a perception that Martinicans are "bastard children of France"[3] ("Truc de fou," 2010, verse 4). Or is the inclination to be French, despite a well-established

---

[3] *"Une enfant illégitime de cette mère patrie."*

Creole language and culture, a product of what Frantz Fanon described as post-colonial "inferiorization" created by the system of slavery (Julien, 2000, p. 157)?

The first Martinican identity movement, Négritude, predicated on racial essentialism, was an assertion of an identity centered on Martinican history and perspective as connected to pan-Africanism. As discussed earlier, although Négritude gained international recognition and momentum among the Martinican intelligentsia, the average Martinican had difficulty personally relating to African culture. Césaire's disengagement from Creole language and culture might have been because it was considered a compromise between enslaved people and their masters. Cesaire's focus was African heritage and not the joint creation of language and culture as an adaptation to the challenging new environment (Confiant, personal communication, March 17, 2014). Therefore, Négritude failed to represent the totality of Martinicans' (of all ethnicities) lived experiences.

Although most Martinicans perceived themselves as French, they obviously did not resemble the typical French person; they certainly resembled Africans, but did not perceive themselves as Africans. This dissonance between subjective cultural identification and objective appearance fostered an identity exterior to Martinican reality (Eurocentric or Afrocentric). *Antillanité* and *Créolité* were born out of the search for a multifaceted identity rooted in historical and cultural realities, or Caribbeanness.

Édouard Glissant, champion of the Antillanité movement (1965-1980s), founded *l'Institut Martiniquais d'Etudes* (Institute of Martinican Studies), a private secondary school for the promotion of the plurality of cultures in the Antilles. The Antillanité movement focused on the simile of the Martinican identity as akin to a "rhizome" or mangrove. The historical, genealogical, cultural, linguistic, and geographic roots of the Martinican people entwined together to form a lush, diverse, and self-sustaining Antillean identity. Glissant does not see Martinique's history as a definitive knowable past, but rather as a rhizome, whose interconnected roots sprout horizontally as well as vertically. This perspective confirms the experience of most people in a Caribbean context, given their largely obscured historical narratives. Antillanité's move away from the singularity of "African" or "Black" of Négritude to the plurality of "le divers" or diversity of cultures represented in Martinique was certainly more accessible to the average Martinican (Burton, 1995b; Chanson, 2005).

Glissant focused on the "functional, pragmatic" purpose of Creole; a language developed to collectively "produce" something for survival of plantation society, which eventually lost its function as plantation society waned. The disappearance or languishing of Creole is because Martinicans no longer have this "collective responsibility" (Glissant, 1989, p. 187); a generation after Departmentalization, Martinique had gone from a "self-sufficient producer" (Chamoiseau, Confiant, Bernabé, & Taylor, 1997, p. 129) to a consumer society dependent on French handouts, with most of what was consumed being imported.

Martinicans found little use for Creole outside the home, especially as assimilation increased after abolition and more so after Departmentalization. French was the language of knowledge, education, and upward mobility in Martinican society. Glissant expressed this about a typical child growing up in Martinique:

> In class he is exposed to the world of the serious, of work, of hierarchical relationships, with which he naturally associates the French language. At play, he reverts to creole, with which he associates the world of recreation, freedom, and lack of restraint. (Glissant, 1989, p. 187)

The Institute of Martinican Studies was founded in 1965 by Glissant to resuscitate Creole language and culture. In his *Caribbean Discourse,* Glissant (1989) advocated analyzing the disuse of Creole from a sociolinguistic and political perspective and exploring ways to institutionalize Creole with local pedagogy and introduce it in schools.

Ten years later in 1975, an organization was established by Jean Bernabé and other academics to standardize and promote Creole language and culture, *GEREC-F (Groupe d'Etudes et de Recherches en Espace Créolophone et Francophone)*, at the University of Antilles and Guiana. GEREC-F explored and advanced Creole language, culture, and people, with emphasis on the linguistics of French-based Creole languages. With additional support from the French government after 1981 for the study of Creole, publications and advocacy initiatives to legitimize Creole education through developing undergraduate and graduate curricula at the university increased significantly ("Déclaration de politique scientifique," n.d.; GEREC-F, 2005).

During the 1970s and 1980s there was a groundswell of work by the Institute of Martinican Studies, GEREC, and several other writers who published journals, newspapers, novels, poetry, and other works in Creole. Mitterrand's policies of Regionalization and the right to difference that supported Creole language and culture complemented these efforts. During the 1970s, many eminent *créolistes* such as Confiant were antagonistic to the French language, which they saw as eroding and crippling Creole language and culture. By the 1980s, as Creole language and literature became firmly part of Martinican culture and higher education, most writers and researchers in Creole sought to embrace French as another aspect of their identity. It is in this atmosphere that the Créolité movement emerged as a tribute to the Creole language and culture (Chamoiseau, et al., 1997); Jean Bernabé, Patrick Chamoiseau, and Raphaël Confiant, three eminent Martinican scholars, presented their manifesto *Eloge de la Créolité* at the

1988 Antillean Cultural Festival in France. This declaration focused on creative expression (especially literature) as essential to awareness and understanding of the complexity of identity in postcolonial societies.

Expanding on Glissant's Antillanité, they articulated their vision of Martinican culture as a mosaic or an "aggregate of Caribbean, European, African, Asian, and Levantine cultural elements, united on the same soil by the yoke of history" (Bernabé et al., 1990, p. 891). Confiant shares his experience of growing up in a remote town where he was exposed to multiple languages and cultures (French, Creole, African, Indian, Chinese, Syro-Lebanese; Confiant, personal communication, March 17, 2014). His experience represents the rule and not the exception in Martinique and this *"diversalité"* is at the heart of the Créolité movement and its accessibility to the average Martinican. Créolité was not limited to the Caribbean as Antillanité was; it included the island of Réunion because the essence of being creole is the ongoing braiding of various cultural narratives, which certainly applies there (Carter & Torabully, 2002). The word creole was also reclaimed as no longer exclusive to Whites born in Martinique but became inclusive of all Martinicans. The authors of the *Éloge* admit that Negritude is a significant dimension of Créolité, because the majority of Martinicans are of African descent, but it is one of many dimensions of Créolité (Chamoiseau et al., 1997). Negritude was the beginning of self-assertion and reclaiming self-respect. It is, in the words of Bernabé, "ante-creole" (Bernabé et al., 1990, p. 888).

Similar to Glisssant's rhizome metaphor describing Martinican history, the Créolité manifesto posits Martinican history as "a braided history," "diffracted but recomposed" (Bernabé et al., 1990, p. 892). Adaptations to a new environment by the various groups that came to Martinique, and their interactions and reciprocal adaptations to each other, define contemporary, collective Martinican culture.

Another identity movement that emerged in the 1980s is

l'Indianité, and the organization behind this movement was the *Association culturelle Martinique/Inde (ACMI,* or Martinique/India Cultural Association), founded by Michel Ponnamah, a Martinican of Indian heritage. On the surface, there is an apparent similarity to Négritude in that it focused on the rediscovery of Indian heritage (according to some scholars as akin to Négritude's focus on Africa). However, proponents of this movement argue that the intent is to make Martinicans of Indian descent, who have been "socially non-existent... fundamentally on the margins" (Jean Benoist, as quoted by Carter & Torabully, 2002, p. 12), more visible. As noted in the previous chapter, the Négritude movement overlooked Indian cultural narratives.

Five years after the end of Indian immigration to Martinique there were 3,700 individuals (mostly men) of Indian descent, and by 1987, only three percent of the Martinican population considered themselves as having any Indian background, because of extensive intermarriage (Smeralda-Amon, 2004). Since their arrival in 1853, the stories of Indians were obscured by the history of slavery, as Indians were wedged between the numerically dominant Afro-Martinicans and the culturally dominant French. Just as their African counterparts, Indians were also persuaded that the path to success was paved with all that was French, which resulted in the loss of much of their original culture and language.

The Indianité movement sought to acknowledge and include the contributions of Indian indentured workers to Martinique's cultural tapestry without excluding those of other groups. Some initiatives include organizing trips to India for Martinicans of Indian origin, which for most was more a symbolic gesture than a program of reconnection (although some did seek to trace their genealogical histories with little or no success). The Indianité movement also rekindled interest and pride in the religious rites and rituals of their ancestors and the material culture associated with the few remaining

Hindu temples in Martinique. Traditional Indian dance forms and Hindu practices such as Ayurvedic medicine, yoga, and other forms of meditation became more common. A body of Indo-Creole literature is being written as well, recounting the untold history and experiences of Indian indentured workers and filling a long-neglected void in Martinican history (Smeralda-Amon, 2004). To commemorate the 150th anniversary of the arrival of Indian indentured workers in 2003, a bust of Gandhi was installed on the Boulevard Charles de Gaulle in Fort de France. This gift from the Indian government provided the Indian experience in Martinique with a powerfully visible representation in the capital. As Curtius (2010) notes, "With the bust of Gandhi, it is the first time that Indianité was ceremoniously fixed in Fort de France where thus far, most of the statues followed the symbolic logic of conquest, slavery, colonization, liberation, and assimilation"[4] (p. 115).

Conclusion

By the end of the 20th century, robust discussions on Martinican-Creole identity in literary, linguistic, and cultural movements led to a more secure self-definition that embraced their full historical experience. This did not exclude Frenchness, either in habits or institutions, both of which had popular support. The much thornier question of Martinique's departmental status with its political and administrative ramifications remained unresolved, however. It was very apparent to French President Jacques Chirac's (1995-2007) administration that the structure of Martinique as a Department with a one-size-fits-all uniformity had "...perhaps reached its limits..."

---

[4] *Avec le buste de Gandhi, c'est la première fois qu'une indianite se fixe cérémoniellement à Fort de France où la plupart des statues obéissent à une logique symbolique articulée autour de la conquête, de l'esclavage, de la colonization, de la liberation, de l' assimilation.*

and the time had come to "...evolve towards a differentiated status" (Chirac, 2000, as quoted in Miles, 2006, p. 638).

Two critical political milestones in the 21st century were the 2003 non-binding consultation vote and the 2010 referendum. The consultation vote was held to assess Martinicans' interest in changing their administrative status from a Department to a Collectivity, allowing greater local control, particularly of education, public-sector employment, and economic development, including environmental issues. This change in terminology from a Department to Collectivity seemed to generate anxiety among the Martinican electorate, which feared that a change in status would lead to independence and severing ties with France, with the loss of social and financial security. The campaign against this vote, using the old Creole saying "do not buy a cat in a bag," won the day. The historic first vote on an issue concerning Martinique by Martinicans had only a 44% turn out and ended in a defeat for the proposition (by a margin of about 1,000 votes; Miles, 2006).

The 2010 referendum followed strikes and labor unrest in 2009 caused by low pay and the high cost of living. There were popular demands for an increase in the minimum wage, price cuts in essential goods and services including gas, electricity, college tuition, and staple foods. Improvements in housing, education, and cultural services were also sought. Under French President Nicolas Sarkozy, in less than a week several demands were met, especially reducing the cost of basic necessities by 20%-30% in Martinique (Clothier, 2009). During his visit to Martinique in June 2009, Sarkozy suggested a referendum by which Martinicans would decide whether to remain a Department or move toward more autonomy. He did assuage fears that autonomy would lead France to abandon Martinique:

So long as I am president of the republic, there will be no

question of independence for Martinique, of its separation from France.... Martinique is French and it will remain French, first because it wants to, but also because France wants it to. France wouldn't be France without Martinique. ("Sarkozy Offers Autonomy Vote," Caribbean Net News, June 27, 2009, para. 2)

With a 55% voter turnout, about 80% of Martinicans rejected the January 10, 2010 referendum for greater autonomy while remaining part of France (Lamy, January 11, 2010). However, in a second referendum January 24, 2010 Martinicans approved a "unique collectivity," with a new administrative structure fusing the Regional and General Councils. The **"Territorial Collectivity of Martinique"** and its Assembly was ratified by the French government on July 27, 2011 to be implemented in 2015 (General Council of Martinique, 2014, http://www.region-martinique.mq/la-collectivite-territoriale-de-martinique/le-projet/).

Sixty-eight years after Departmentalization, two revelations have emerged: First, a one-dimensional perspective on Martinican cultural identity (i.e., African, French, Indian, etc.) does not resonate with the majority of Martinicans; rather, a multi-dimensional perspective rooted in their collective history and environment seems more appropriate to them. Second, applying France's administrative structures to Martinique may have created equal rights under the law, but was unable to address Martinique's economic, cultural, environmental, and political concerns.

Ultimately, it is clear that few Martinicans were (or are) interested in severing ties with France, for fear that eventually they would be thrown on their own resources without monetary support from France. The paradox of wanting to be assimilated into France (culturally, politically, and economically), yet unable to chart their own course because of assimilation is something Martinicans have had to grapple with throughout the 20th century. There is perhaps a way out of this conundrum, as we have seen with the second referendum of 2010. The next and concluding chapter provides an overview of contemporary Martinique as it prepares for its new status as a Territorial Collectivity in the context of its distinctive historical and cultural paradigm.

Glossary

prefect - (French, *"préfet"*) Appointed chief administrator of a Department of France.

fonctionnaire - (French) Individual with a specific function, especially in civil service.

Académie Française - (French) Association of 40 scholars established in 1635 by Cardinal Richelieu to preserve the purity of the French language and establish standards of proper usage.

BUMIDOM (Bureau pour le développement des migrations dans les départements d'outre-mer) - French government agency to encourage Martinicans to come to the French mainland to work, as well as periodically return to Martinique.

Regionalization - Policy of François Mitterand's government of providing support for local and regional control of cultural and social programs.

Assemblée Unique - (French) Proposed revision to combine the Regional Council and General Council of Martinique into one body elected proportionally; defeated in the non-binding vote of 2003.

Antillanité - (French) Cultural, literary, artistic, and political movement developed in the 1960s associated with Édouard Glissant and René Ménil that focused on the pluralistic nature of Antillean identity in contrast to Négritude's racial essentialism.

Créolité - (French) Predominantly literary movement founded in the 1980s by Jean Bernabé, Raphaël Confiant, and Patrick Chamoiseau that expanded Antillanité's concept of multiple cultural elements in post-colonial identities with an emphasis on the development and use of the Creole language.

GEREC-F (Groupe d'Etudes et de Recherches en Espace Créolophone et Francophone) - (French) Scholarly association founded in 1974 at the University of the French West Indies to advance the study of Creole language, culture, and people with emphasis on the linguistics of French-based Creole languages.

l'Indianité - (French) Indian cultural and literary identity movement of the 1980s, explored by scholars such as Jean Benoist, Ananda Devi, Patrice Domoison, Gerry L'Etang, and Juliette Sméralda to reclaim the historical and cultural narratives of indentured workers of Indian descent in Martinique and other French colonies.

Association culturelle Martinique/Inde (ACMI) - (French) Founded in the 1980s by Michel Ponnamah to help Martinicans of Indian descent rediscover their heritage; influential in the beginning of the *Indianité* movement.

Territorial Collectivity of Martinique - Administrative structure allowing more local autonomy and control than a Department.

Reflective Questions

1. Explain why there were fears of communism taking over in Martinique and why, despite the significant role of communists in local politics, Martinique was unlikely to become communist.

2. Discuss the evolution of the Creole language in Martinique from a denigrated patois to a subject in Martinican secondary and post-secondary curricula.

3. Departmentalization shifted Martinique from a production-based to a consumption-based economy. What are some of the benefits and drawbacks of this shift?

4. Have French presidents from Mitterand to Sarkozy fostered responsible actions of the mère patrie, or mother country? Provide examples for and against.

5. Discuss the difference between Négritude and the identity movements in Martinique after Departmentalization.

6. Wanting to be both different from and the same as the French is the paradoxical situation of Martinicans. Discuss this paradox in light of Martinique's history.

Chapter 10

One Martinique, Multiple Voices

> *First and foremost, I am Martinican.*
> *I am French by law, but Martinican in my heart.*
> *I am both French AND Martinican!*
>
> —Law students of Christine Warner
> University of the French West Indies, Martinique

"Culture is not as fragile as we sometimes think; its essential soul is hardy and durable" (Chinua Achebe, cited in Julien, 2000, p. 166). Chinua Achebe's words ring true in Martinique. Since the 1600s with the arrival of the French pioneers, against all odds, the Caribs and other groups that made Martinique their home have succeeded in transmitting elements of their cultural identities in a few significant forms. Be it through religious and spiritual practices, patronyms, food, clothing, music, folktales, or fishing and hunting, such aspects of culture emblematize the collective heritage of these dispersed groups.

A strong argument can be made that Martinique (and the Caribbean as a whole) is representative of contemporary globalization: "In a sense, we are in the vanguard of a world wide movement" (Chamoiseau, Confiant, Bernabé & Taylor, 1997, p. 141). Martinican identity is a mosaic reflecting the world's major cultural groups— European, African, Amerindian, and Asian. As seen in preceding chapters, no single group of people or aspect of the island's history speaks to the depth of the experiences of contemporary Martinicans. Martinican society cannot and should not be studied through a single lens lest the intricacies and profundity of its kaleidoscopic vistas be reduced to trivialities. Martinique is largely a pluralistic society trying to validate the journeys and cultural narratives of all its cultural groups.

Thus, through this book we have attempted to provide a comprehensive interdisciplinary framework to chronicle and understand the development of Martinique's complex braiding of culture, language, and identity. The contexts of emigration outlined in this book (voluntary, involuntary by force, or voluntary under demanding circumstances) and the adaptive responses of Caribs, French, Africans, and Indians to each other over 377 years were the mediators of cultural evolution in Martinique.

This chapter begins by suggesting some potential avenues for future research, given the interdisciplinary breadth that this island of 436 square miles offers. Following that, we trace Martinique's journey toward a pluralistic society through the revitalization of its mosaic culture. Reaffirmation of the importance of the Creole language in this journey is also presented. Finally, this chapter presents a snapshot of contemporary Martinique through the voices of various Martinicans reflecting on their history, language(s), culture, and identity. The diversity of their voices is representative of the tributaries of cultural narratives that flow into the river of Martinican society.

Future Research

Martinique's rich history and the narratives of its people as topics for research are hardly exhausted by issues explored in this book. Our intentions were to provide a solid examination of the arc of Martinique's story in the framework of emigration and resettlement. The scope of this project precluded more detailed analysis of topics deserving further study. Some of these topics are outlined below, though it is far from an all-encompassing list.

Political movements and organizations in Martinique post-departmentalization, with the exception of Aimé Césaire's PPM (*Parti Progressiste Martiniquais*), have not been examined in detail. The Territorial Collectivity of Martinique and Assembly ratified by the French government on July 27, 2011, to be implemented in 2015, changes Martinique's status. The variety of political perspectives and influences that will guide the exercise of greater local autonomy bears more scrutiny.

Since 1980, **ASSAUPAMAR** *(l'ASsociation pour la SAUvegarde du PAtrimoine MARtiniquais)* and other such organizations have tirelessly advocated environmental awareness and activism regarding sustainable development. ASSAUPAMAR's principal objective is to highlight Martinique's economic dependence on outside resources and help promote its abundant diverse resources and collective heritage to ultimately attain economic and energy self-sufficiency for all Martinicans.

It is striking that Frantz Fanon, the internationally known writer and anti-colonial scholar born in Martinique, was not frequently mentioned by Martinicans during our visits there. Although there is a substantial body of work on his relevance to decolonization and diasporas, especially for people of African heritage, Fanon's legacy in Martinique is not as influential as that of Césaire or Glissant. Consideration of Fanon's ideas on the psychological effects of cultural assimilation and their relevance to contemporary Martinican society presents a range of research possibilities.

We noted in the Preface that works on Martinique in English are far fewer than French resources. In order to increase availability of the profound and prolific research by Martinican scholars, more translations from French are needed so that access to research from Martinique is expanded beyond the Francophone world.

From an anthropological perspective, exploring efforts to resuscitate the Carib legacy in Martinique, both cultural and genealogical, is a promising applied academic project. Such a project would connect the work of organizations such as ASSAUPAMAR and Karisko[1] and further highlight the interdisciplinary nature of research on Martinique. In addition, the contributions of lesser-known ethnic groups to contemporary Martinican culture, such as of the Chinese and the Syro-Lebanese, is yet another research avenue to be pursued.

An examination of Martinique's history and cultural evolution through the visual and performing arts would be a productive line of inquiry for researchers interested in these fields. Artistic expression in Martinique has taken various forms throughout its history and expanded considerably since the 1980s.

Another important research topic would be an examination of the self-imposed isolation of the béké minority. This wealthy group owns the majority of the land in Martinique and continues to wield considerable economic power.

Last, but far from least, comparing Martinique's history and cultural evolution to that of the other Francophone islands in the Caribbean and Indian Ocean is an important avenue for interdisciplinary research. Comparative studies of Martinique and other Anglophone, Hispanophone, and Dutch Caribbean islands in the contexts of emigration and resettlement could provide a wealth of multidimensional research opportunities.

Journey toward a Pluralistic Society

The French approach to colonization as an obligation to impose their culture was intended to provide the foundation of a common identity in Martinique: French identity. The comparative success of this approach could account for the lack of a unique Martinican identity

---

[1] A Martinican organization founded to reconnect Martinicans to their Carib heritage through various cultural, athletic, anthropological, and archaelogical projects.

recognizing other cultural roots, which was not deemed necessary or worthy of inspection by Martinicans in general until the Négritude (1940s) and Antillanité (1960s) movements. The proclamation of the right to difference and the decision by President Mitterand in the 1980s to acknowledge Martinique's history of slavery was a turning point in the development of Martinique's pluralistic society. Subsequently, promoting Martinique's multiple histories through educational and cultural institutions facilitated rediscovery and exploration of all its narratives. Thus, validating the entirety of cultural contributions to Martinican society, not just those of the French, is central to the evolution of modern Martinican identity.

"We have a society where debris and traces have survived... little traces of India, of Africa, and of Europe.... It is always a composite reality, uncertain, fluid, fluorescent. We are a mobile mosaic..."[2] (Chamoiseau, quoted by Chinien, 2008, para. 9). The desire of Martinicans to explore and recover cultural roots is not interested in obscuring or devaluing any one root in favor of another, nor is it based on an essentialist wish to identify with an original cultural source, be it African, Carib, French or Indian. Instead, Martinicans (particularly the intelligentsia) seem to focus on the "debris and traces" to redefine their identity as a "composite and fluid" narrative. The challenge of diversity in any pluralistic society lies in balancing a sense of cohesiveness among members with valuing varied circumstances and viewpoints. Since the Antillanité and Créolité movements there is a growing interest in retracing and validating diverse points of reference for cultural heritage in Martinique. We now focus on the contemporary status of Martinique's traditionally neglected cultural narratives, those of Caribs, Africans, and Indians.

Ethnographic and archeological research on Carib contributions

---

[2] *On a une société où subsistent des débris, des traces... ce sont de petites traces d'indianité, des traces d'africanité, des traces européennes.... C'est toujours une réalité composite, incertaine, fluide, fluorescente. Nous sommes dans une mosaïque mobile....*

to Martinican society and Antillean culture in general has proliferated recently. Although the genealogical connection of Martinicans to Carib ancestors is not as strong as to African and Indian forbears, such studies indicate that there are Martinicans with Carib ancestry today. University-level research and teaching have been focusing on Carib civilization, resulting in numerous scholarly publications (Rosaz, personal communication, March 19, 2014).

In an effort to recapture some of the self-sufficiency and debrouillard spirit of their Carib, African, and Indian ancestors, there is a movement in Martinique to revive the "creole garden," which combines the agricultural traditions of the Caribs and the subsistence gardens of the enslaved Africans (discussed in Chapter 5) with a renewed appreciation of the island's biodiversity. Martinicans living in apartments and high-rises are encouraged to grow herbs and plants with medicinal properties on their roofs and balconies (Belrose, 2010; Berard, 2014; Saint-Louis, personal communication, October 10, 2014). This trend is growing stronger, especially in urban areas following the 2009 unrest, and is particularly important now in Martinique, where imported food and energy are at staggering levels. Over 90% of Martinique's food and almost 95% of its energy is imported, despite being situated in a tropical environment with ample resources to be self-sufficient (Rosaz, personal communication, March 18, 2012).

In an effort to reduce the disconnect between Martinique and the rest of the Caribbean, the organization Karisko sponsored an ambitious re-enactment of the long-ago voyages undertaken by the Caribs between the Antillean islands. Highlighting ties of Caribbean people to Carib heritage was a major goal of these expeditions, which began in 2008. The lore of navigation, skill of rowing, and cultural traditions and camaraderie associated with these voyages were all ways of acknowledging and authenticating the Carib presence in Martinique (Berard, 2014).

Considering that the vast majority of Martinicans have ancestors from Africa, African cultural motifs are not as conspicuous as French mannerisms, language, food, clothing, and Catholicism. The limited number of scholarly works on Africa at the only institution of higher education in Martinique, the University of the French West Indies in Fort de France, provides a glaring example. Approximately 1,200 of the over 120,000 volumes in the university library relate to Africa, which seems incongruous given Martinique's heritage (Sméralda, personal communication, March 19, 2014; Saint-Louis, personal communication, October 10, 2014). The legacy of over two centuries of slavery and over three centuries of French colonialism has unequivocally effaced most original African cultural expressions and history. For too long, much of the history of the involuntary immigration of Africans to Martinique has been glossed over in the Martinican educational system in favor of French history. This neglect of non-French cultures is eloquently expressed by Martinican singer Kennenga:

> I learn about the history of great men from this far-away country.... I have the impression that I am not being told everything, A big piece is missing from my history.[3]
> (Kennenga, 2010, verses 3-4)

The pervasive African influence on music, dance, discourse, storytelling, and quimboiserie in Martinique is readily apparent to the casual observer. Winston Berkeley, a well-known local musician who lectures at the university, pointed out that *Tambour Bélé* music

---

[3] *J'apprends l'histoire des grands hommes de ce pays lointain....*
L'impression qu'on ne me dit pas tout,
De mon histoire on m'a caché un grand bout.

incorporating African drumming techniques, often accompanied by dance, and other kinds of Antillean music, such as *Zouk,* have clear African origins. African drumming was used by runaway slaves as a means of coded communication among themselves and with the enslaved on the plantations to coordinate resistance against the slave-owners (Winston Berkeley, personal communication, March 19, 2012). In a similar vein, another practice with African roots, quimboiserie, was also a tool of resistance to slavery and is a constant throughout Martinique's history. Healing through spiritual rituals and medicinal herbs is prevalent in contemporary Martinique and cuts across class lines (Corteggiani, 1994).

The transmission of African traditions through storytelling has the hallmark of call and response, such as *Yé Krik, Yé Krak,* seen in the film "La Rue Cases-Nègres" (Palcy, 1983). Such expressions that start, punctuate, continue, and end storytelling sessions have been an integral part of Martinican culture. Storytelling, music, and dance formed the hub around which slave communities were organized, as discussed in Chapter 5. Martinican folktales developed also as a symbolic and cathartic representation of plantation society; animals frequently characterized hierarchical layers in this society. Lessons to successfully negotiate the hierarchy to attain a better life reinforced the ethic of debrouillardism. *"Débouya pa péché"* [It's no sin to be a debrouillard] and a host of other proverbs relating to this tradition have carried over into contemporary Martinique.

Another aspect of verbal discourse found in Martinique today is the "t'chip" vocal sound. From our conversations with Antillean academics,[4] it appears that this sound is used during informal conversations and is found throughout the African diaspora and in Africa. This sound, sometimes short, sometimes long, is usually accompanied by a facial expression conveying feelings such as

[4] Personal communications from the Winthrop-King Institute Conference at Florida State University, October 21-22, 2014.

agitation, frustration, disapproval, etc. All the practices mentioned in the preceding pages were brought to Martinique by enslaved people from West and Central Africa and were the rare aspects of daily life not completely under the master's control.

The identity movement of *l'Indianité* has begun spreading its influence throughout Martinique. We met individuals on each of our trips who not only identified with their Indian ancestry, but also expressed a fervent desire to travel to India to understand where their ancestors came from. Anthropologist Patrice Domoison has been working tirelessly over the past decade to preserve and transmit ceremonies and cultural practices from India on the former plantation of Ste. Marie located in the region of La Trinité. As caretaker of the temple, he frequently opens this place of worship to the Indian community and educates Martinicans and other visitors about the narratives of the 25,000 or so Indian indentured workers who came to Martinique to work on the plantations after the abolition of slavery.

Since the 2003 sesquicentennial commemoration of the arrival of Indian indentured workers to Martinique, several scholarly and literary works (including four that were published that year) have entered Martinique's literary canon. Furthermore, celebratory expositions promoting and recognizing the Indian heritage so painstakingly preserved by their ancestors have been held. The Indianité Days *(Les journées de l' Indianité)* celebrated in Basse-Pointe and St. Pierre in May by organizations such as ACMI (*L'Association Culturelle Martinique Inde*) and the dance troupe Savana Savita are examples of such celebrations ("Savana Savita...," 2013; Town of Basse-Pointe n.d. http://www.mairie-basse-pointe.fr/?q=node/140). As noted in Chapter 9, there are also efforts to organize "genealogical tourism" for those traveling to India to rediscover family connections. However mixed their ancestry, Martinicans of Indian heritage invariably describe themselves as Martinican.

Efforts to reconnect with Carib, African, and Indian backgrounds should not be seen as attempts to reconstitute an ethnic identity or community, but as a desire to reconnect with little-known aspects of their history and to give voice to their stories that have been silenced and obscured. In contrast, the békés still live apart, and their behavior reflects their heritage as plantation owners in a slave society. They are said to have little awareness of contemporary Martinican society because of this self-imposed isolation from the rest of Martinique (Rosaz, personal communication, March 19, 2014).

Language as a Key to Martinican Pluralistic Culture

Creole expressions are unmistakably heard in Martinique, especially among the young. Flyers, brochures, billboards, and commercials in Creole are seen everywhere. Salutations and casual conversations among Martinicans in creolicized French (*français créolisé*) or gallicized Creole (*creole françisé*) are not uncommon. Our experience talking with university students and local Martinicans indicates that the majority speak Creole and expect to pass it on to their children. They also mentioned that their parents often resorted to Creole to express frustration or anger; others spoke of using Creole in a jocular vein or to express endearments to friends and family.

Teachers of Creole in Martinique from preschool to elementary school have been certified to teach the language and culture, which is provided a couple of times per week. At the middle- and high-school level, Creole is optional, but it is possible to major in Creole at the university. In 2000, the GEREC group established the equivalents of a B.A., M.A, and Ph.D. in Creole, and the following year, the CAPES (French national teacher certification exam) was approved for Creole by the French Ministry of Education (Confiant, 2009). Recently there seems more interest among Martinicans to learn and use Creole more broadly, but unfortunately there are not yet enough qualified teachers to make it more than an elective. It will take at least a generation at the present pace of certification for Creole to become a mandatory school subject (Saint-Louis and Bernabé, personal communication, March 19, 2014).

Although Creole is gaining recognition, we see two major obstacles for the future of Creole: first, the "Frenchification" or "decreolization" of Creole and second, its status vis-à-vis the French language. In regard to the first obstacle, as Marie-José Saint-Louis, a translator and Creole educator notes, there are efforts to arrest adulteration of Creole by French, primarily through a proliferation of literary works as well as translations into Creole. Television programs launched in 2007 and 2008 to teach correct ways to read, write, and speak Creole have been remarkably successful (Saint-Louis, personal communication, March 19, 2014). Martinican intellectuals working to reinvigorate Creole (including but not limited to Jean Bernabé, Raphaël Confiant, Michel Dispagne, and Marie-José Saint-Louis) are optimistic about the survival of Martinican Creole, but they are less sanguine about the quality.

Most students we spoke to had never read a book in Creole, primarily because they found the orthography challenging. Translations of popular French works, such as Saint-Exupéry's *The Little Prince*, into Creole intend to broaden the use of Creole from purely oral to literary as well. Marie-José Saint-Louis spoke of her motivation for this work: "I take real pleasure in translating these works [into Creole], first, because it makes a direct connection with the Martinican readership. And second, because one day they will be able to participate in valorizing and expanding the use of our regional language, Creole."[5]

---

[5] *J'ai chaque fois un réel plaisir à traduire ce genre de texte, et la première raison c'est que ces textes sont en connexion avec les lecteurs du pays. La deuxième raison, c'est qu'ils pourront, un jour ou l'autre, participer à la valorisation et la diffusion de notre*

(Interview with Caraïbéditions on the publication of *The Little Prince* in Martinican Creole, 2010).

Recognition of Creole as a legitimate language has not completely effaced the long-held perception that French is superior because it was the language of the master. This stigma about Creole is a complicated obstacle to overcome. Not too long ago, parents forbade children from speaking Creole at home; even when parents spoke Creole, children were required to respond in French. Martinicans perceived that Creole interfered with their children's ability to master French, which was deemed necessary for success, and thus they disparaged Creole. Michel Dispagne, a professor of Creole, recalls being harshly punished by his teacher, with the full support of his parents, for using Créolisms in school (Dispagne, personal communication, March 17, 2012). Although Creole was created by both the French and the enslaved Africans, it is viewed with more ambivalence by descendants of former enslaved Africans and indentured workers than by descendants of the French Plantocracy. Some have made the argument that békés in Martinique speak Creole among themselves with less stigma than the non-White community (Confiant, personal communication, March 17, 2014).

The continued stigmatization of Creole is evidenced by various conversations, observations, and anecdotes. When asked "In what language would you say 'I love you' to a romantic partner? French or Creole?" most students we spoke with responded that they would use French and not Creole because it was a "prettier language," it was the "language of a gentleman," or simply because using Creole might make one appear "unrefined." American college students spending an alternative spring break in Martinique in 2011 discovered rapidly that local vendors at the market in Fort de France took a dim view of the students practicing their newly learned Creole expressions. On one occasion, a vendor retorted to a student, "Why are you speaking to *langue régionale, le creole.*

me in Creole? You think I cannot speak good French?" Spencer Nehrt, an American student teaching English at a primary school in Trinité (2013-2014), noted that in his experience Creole was mostly limited to outside the classroom (hallways and playgrounds) and only spoken in the classroom during Creole lessons (Nehrt, personal communication, March 19, 2014). The Martinican singer Kennenga alludes to the same phenomenon in his song "*Truc de fou,*" in which he mentions children speaking Creole among themselves in hushed tones at school, providing a further indication of Creole's inferior status (Kennenga, 2010).

France has been connected to Martinique since 1635, and almost one-third as many Martinicans live in France as on the island. Nevertheless, Creole language and culture does not appear to have penetrated mainland French society, indicating the low value that the French place upon it. (Bernabé, personal communication, March 18, 2014). And yet, all Martinicans today express themselves in French with ease, and in most situations the majority readily set aside Creole in favor of French. However, French has sometimes been transformed to accommodate the Creole spirit as Confiant attests. "I write in a French that I invented because Metropolitan French is not able to completely express my creole sensibilities"[6] (de Saint Périer, 2012, para. 9).

It is striking that in a study conducted between 1873-1874 on the Creole language, Turiault (1874) observed, "The Creole that the [b]lacks of the Antilles speak is a mis-pronounced, corrupt French mixed with Negro words and expressions. In this language one can also recognize words of Carib origin..."[7] (p. 402). Explaining the pragmatics behind the genesis and development of this language, he accounts for its fragmented and distorted nature for French audiences.

[6] *J'écris dans un français que j'ai inventé parce que le français de l'Hexagone ne peut exprimer tout à fait ma sensibilité creole.*
[7] *Le créole que parlent les noirs qui habitent le Antilles est du français mal prononcé et corrompu, mélange de mots et d'expressions nègres. Dans ce langage on rencontre aussi des noms d'origine caraibe….*

However, Turiault does acknowledge the "originality" involved in the structure of Creole and urges his French readers not to regard it with "so much disdain" (Turiault, 1874, p. 402).

To better understand this dynamic, a brief review of Creole's development as the "language of compromise" from Chapter 3 to facilitate communication between masters and the enslaved is useful. At the beginning of colonization, enslaved Africans were valued and a sought-after precious commodity, however, over time with the expansion of the slave trade, the number of the enslaved increased greatly, making them more affordable. This demographic shift, with the enslaved vastly outnumbering the Whites, contributed to the development of Creole, as discussed in Chapter 1. As the colonists became wealthy, an architecture of dominance emerged with a clear hierarchical system that relegated cultural features associated with enslaved Africans, including Creole language, to subaltern status (Bernabé, personal communication, March 19, 2013).

When plantation owners spoke Creole, it was from the vantage point of a master communicating with subordinates; perhaps this function of Creole as a status indicator accounts for less stigma among békés than other groups in Martinique. Martinicans have made significant strides since the 1970s in developing a written and literary dimension to Creole, a language based on African intonations and imagery, not only to anchor their identity and reduce this stigma, but also to propel the diverse elements of Martinican culture into the 21st century.

One Martinique, Multiple Voices

Based on our numerous conversations with Martinican university students, it is apparent that they are keenly aware of their dual identity and, for the most part, these students readily affirmed both their French and Martinican identities and are quite comfortable with that duality. Our observations seemed consistent with their assertions. Engaging university students in a conversation about what is French about being Martinican was not difficult because they are constantly exposed to mainland French media and mores. They may be acutely cognizant of their "non-Frenchness," yet articulating what is non-French about being Martinican was much more challenging. After some reflection, all the students were able to identify and proudly speak of the various strands of their braided culture. This suggests that, although Frenchness may be at the forefront of these students' minds, other aspects of their cultural matrix were not automatically available and had to be pondered. In general, the younger generation of Martinicans appears balanced in their synergy of cultural inputs, albeit struggling to express that clearly. The exception to this was their skillful and effortless infusion of Creole into daily conversations.

Not everyone in Martinique displays this same level of comfort with all aspects of their heritage and history, particularly regarding the history of slavery. In her article "Statues Don't Die in Fort de France," Anny Curtius (2008) sheds light on the importance of statues in the capital Fort de France; some have been desecrated and new ones installed. One example worth pointing out is the statue of Joséphine, Napoleon's empress. It was erected in 1859 and was the first statue in Fort de France. There is a strong belief in Martinique that because of Joséphine's influence, slavery was reinstated by Napoleon in 1802 after its abolition in 1794. In 1991, this statue was found decapitated and vandalized with red paint dripping from her neck, signaling the same end that Marie-Antoinette met at the guillotine after the French Revolution. Today, it is probably the most visited statue in Martinique. This story of betrayal by Joséphine, a Martinican, infuriated some Martinicans, and destroying the statue was how they coped with the painful memory of slavery (Curtius, 2008).

Figure 25. Statue of Empress Josephine in Fort de France, 1851 lithograph. (Courtesy of the Beinecke Lesser Antilles Collection, Burke Library, Hamilton College, NY)

Although Martinique's rich culture has produced world-renowned intellectuals such as Césaire, Fanon, and Glissant, and the island enjoys good education and healthcare in an idyllic setting, some scholars regard Martinique as a neo-colony, primarily because of its dependence on France. No more than 13% of its revenue is self-generated or comes from what Martinique produces; the rest is provided by France. Even the sugar and banana plantations (the few that remain), once the backbone of the Martinican economy and society, now hire immigrants from Haiti and St. Lucia to work them. Thanks to great financial support from France, Martinicans in general enjoy a standard of living that is high compared with most Caribbean islands.

Figure 26. The statue of the Empress Josephine in 2014. (Photo by the authors.)

For example, there are more kilometers of road per capita than in France. The average replacement rate for automobiles is once every decade in France, but Martinicans replace their cars every two years. Car ownership is widespread regardless if one is employed. As even the casual visitor to Martinique notices, cars clog the roads at all hours of the day (Confiant, personal communication, March 17, 2014)! There is concern among Martinican intellectuals that they are trapped in artificial luxury coming from unearned wealth. The painful reality is that if France severed its ties with Martinique, Martinicans would die of hunger or be forced to emigrate because it is now a consumer society that produces very little. This is the albatross that they feel hangs around their necks (ASSAUPAMAR, Confiant, & Rosaz, personal communications, 2013 and 2014).

One of Aimé Césaire's worries in the latter part of his life was his anguish over the increasing number of mainland French civil servants in Martinique, further entrenching French mores and institutions. Correspondingly, there is a tide of Martinican migration to France, as mentioned earlier. Césaire's fear, expressed by his famous phrase "genocide by substitution" (Miles, 2009b, p. 66) was echoed by several scholars we spoke with. Unlike Césaire, whose awareness of his identity came after meeting Senghor in Paris, the average Martinican has no such concerns about identity.

There is a perception among the Martinican intelligentsia, who have worked to preserve and promote Martinican culture, that most Martinicans don't identify with the culture of their ancestors and still feel alienated in their own land (Saint-Louis, personal communication, March 19, 2014). These Martinicans are immersed in French language, fashion, food, politics, and mannerisms and seem at ease in a European context, aware of current events in France and its European neighbors despite the fact that they live a few thousand miles from Europe. Ironically, as Confiant points out, their knowledge of neighboring islands (especially non-French speaking) is quite limited, and they seem insulated from their non-Francophone Caribbean neighbors.

There is another school of thought that this alienation is a necessary phase for Martinique, given the complexity and trauma of its nearly 380-year history. Reiterating Césaire's and Glissant's ideas, some in Martinique call for patience during this period of alienation, which they feel needs to be experienced, and "digested" by all Martinicans. The economic, social, and cultural crises that Martinique faces are an inevitable part of this growth process according to proponents of this perspective. The conclusion one can draw from this view is that "optimism about Martinique's future" is warranted (Rosaz, personal communication, March 18, 2012). Curiously, the sense of alienation that Césaire stressed in the 1940s is echoed today in Martinique by the singer Kennenga (2010), who deals with his sense of alienation by looking to the future but not forgetting the past. This coping strategy echoes the responses of many of the university students we spoke with and, in our opinion, gives credence to the optimism expressed above.

Most Martinicans we spoke with realize that one positive aspect of creolization and cultural hybridization is the minimal likelihood of interethnic conflict. Unlike Guadeloupe (and other Caribbean islands such as Trinidad), extensive miscegenation and assimilation has led to the mixing of ethnic groups that distinguishes Martinique from other islands. Furthermore, the number of Indians (about 25,500), the second largest group after Africans, was less than on some other islands of the Caribbean, notably Trinidad and Guyana. As a result, Martinicans with ancestral ties to India number no more than a few thousand, mostly hybridized. Thus, the small communities that are of Indian descent seldom clash with the majority who are of African descent. This may explain why Martinicans do not foresee any civil wars or religious conflicts in the immediate future (Bernabé and Rosaz, personal communications, March 18 and 19, 2014).

> From here onwards, all Gods of the Universe are present within the Creole man: the God of the Whites, the God of the Blacks, and the Gods of India without disregarding certain beliefs inherited from Carib mythology. This phenomenon is the first of its kind in all of human history.[8] (Confiant, 2004a, para. 6)

The ceremonial recognition of the Islamic saint Nagour Mira by the Indians discussed in Chapter 7 and the continuing practice of quimboiserie by all Martinicans are further examples of harmonious religious syncretism. Although Martinique clearly is still establishing its identity, the majority of Martinicans, no matter where in the social order, do not see a path to a Martinican pluralistic society being achieved through factionalism or interethnic violence. They may be "torn between several languages, several histories, caught in the torrential ambiguity of a mosaic identity," but to "prevent creative death," Martinicans have chosen to embrace their mosaic identity "in all its complexity" (Bernabé et al., 1990, pp. 902-903). As one of the students mentioned, "We're close-knit, even though we have our problems."

---

[8] *Désormais, en l'homme creole cohabitent tous les dieux de l'Univers: le Dieu des Blancs, le Dieus des Noirs et les Dieux de l'Inde, sans oublier certaines croyances héritées de la mythologie amérindienne. C'est la toute première fois dans l'humanité que se produit un tel phénomène.*

Glossary

ASSAUPAMAR - (l'ASsociation pour la SAUvegarde du PAtrimoine MARtiniquais) Activist group working to preserve Martinique's environment and cultural heritage in relation to self-sufficiency.

Bélé - Martinican dance and music based on West African drumming rhythms.

Zouk - Martinican and Guadeloupean music with a fast tempo.

Reflective Questions

1. Some postcolonial theorists posit that Martinicans are "psychologically sick" in the way they have internalized being French. Discuss evidence for and against this idea based on your readings.

References

Ahluwalia, P. (2003). "Fanon's Nausea: The Hegemony of the White Nation." *Social Identities, 9*(3), 341-356. DOI: 10.1080/1350463032000129966

Aldrich, R. (2002). "Imperial mise en valeur and mise en scène: Recent Works on French Colonialism." The Historical Journal, 45(4), 917-936.

Allaire, L. (1981). "On the Historicity of Carib Migrations in the Lesser Antilles." *American Antiquity, 45,* 240-42.

American Journeys Collection (2003). *Journal of the First Voyage of Columbus: Document No. AJ-062.* Wisconsin Historical Society Digital Library and Archives. [online] Available at: <americanjourneys.org/pdf/AJ-062.pdf >.

Arciniegas, G. (1946). *Caribbean: Sea of the New World.* New York: Alfred A. Knopf.

Assemblée Nationale Constituante (February 26, 1946). *Annexe du procès-verbal de la séance du 26 février, 1946.* [online] Available at: <http://www.assemblee-nationale.fr/histoire/images/rapport-520.pdf>

Assemblée Nationale du France (1946). Loi n° 46-451 du 19 mars 1946 tendant au classement comme départements français de la Guadeloupe, de la Martinique, de la Réunion et de la Guyane française. [online] Available at: <http://www.legifrance.gouv.fr/affichTexte.do?cidTexte=JORFTEXT000000868445>

Baber, W. L. (1985). Political Economy and Social Change: The Bissette Affair and Local-Level politics in Morne-Vert." American Ethnologist, 12(3), 489-504.

Baker, P. (1995). "Some Developmental Inferences from Historical Studies of Pidgins and Creoles." In J. Arends (Ed.) *The Early Stages of Creolization* (pp. 1-24). Philadelphia: John Benjamins.

Bannerjee, R. (2009). "The *Kala Pani* Connection: Francophone Migration Narratives in the Caribbean Writing of Raphael Confiant and the Mauritian Writing of Ananda Devi." *Anthurium: A Caribbean Studies Journal,* 7(1). [online] Available at: <http://anthurium.miami.edu/volume_7/issue_1/bannerjee-kalapaniconnection.html>

Beckles, H. McD. (1997). "Capitalism, Slavery, and Caribbean Modernity." *Callaloo, 20* (4), 777-789.

Belrose, V. H. (2010). *Le jardin créole à la Martinique.* Fort de France, Martinique: Parc Naturel Régional de la Martinique.

Berard, B. (2014). "De l'archéologie précolombienne au patrimoine antillais: La patrimonialisation des héritages amérindiens en Martinique et en Guadeloupe." *Outre-mers, 102*(382-383), 237-251). [online] Available at: <https://hal-uag.archives-ouvertes.fr/hal-01020219>

Bernabé, J., Chamoiseau, P., Confiant, R., & Khyar, M. B. T. (1990). "In Praise of Creoleness." *Callaloo, 13*(4), 886-909.

Bernabé, J. (2013). *Prolégomènes: à une charte des créoles.* Paris, France: L'Harmattan.

Benoist, J., Desroches, M. L'Étang, G., & Ponaman, G.-F. (2004). *L'Inde dans les arts de la Guadeloupe et de la Martinique: Héritages et innovations.* Matoury, French Guiana: IBIS ROUGE.

Berry, J. W. & Sam, D. L. (1997). "Acculturation and adaptation." In J.

W. Berry, M.H. Segall, & C. Kagitcibasi (Eds.), *Handbook of Cross-Cultural Psychology: Vol. 3, Social Behavior and Applications* (2nd ed., pp. 291-326). Boston: Allyn & Bacon.

Beuze, L. R. (1998). *Entraves et liberté, deux siècles de lutes pour être libres.* Fort de France, Martinique: Musée Régional d'Histoire et d'Ethnographie de la Martinique.

Botteau, S. (2011). "Être fonctionnaire dans les DOM-COM...Un «Eldorado»?" *TERRITORIAL-Éditions Carrières Publiques,* 1-7.

Boucher, P. P. (2008). *France and the American Tropics to 1700: Tropics of Discontent?* Baltimore: Johns Hopkins University Press.

Boucher, P. P. (1992). "The Island Caribs: Present State of the Debate." *Terrae Incognitae, 24,* 55-64.

Browne, K. E. (2002). "Creole Economics and the Debrouillard: From Slave-Based Adaptations to the Informal Economy in Martinique." *Ethnohistory, 49* (2), 373-403.

Browne, K.E. (2004). *Creole Economics: Caribbean Cunning under the French Flag.* Austin: University of Texas Press.

Burton, R.D.E. (1995a). "The French West Indies *à l'heure de l'Europe:* An Overview." In R.D.E. Burton & F. Reno (Eds.), *French and West Indian: Martinique, Guadeloupe, and French Guiana Today* (pp. 1-19). Charlottesville, VA: University of Virginia Press.

Burton, R.D.E. (1995b). "The Idea of Difference in Contemporary French West Indian Thought: Négritude, Antillanité, Créolité." In R.D.E. Burton & F. Reno (Eds.), *French and West Indian: Martinique, Guadeloupe, and French*

Guiana Today (pp. 137-166). Charlottesville, VA: University of Virginia Press.

Butel, P. (2002). *Histoire des Antilles françaises*, XVIIe-XXe siècle. Paris, France: Tempus Perrin.

Caraïbéditions (2010). Interview with Marie-José Saint-Louis [online] <http://www.potomitan.info/bibliographie/petit-prince.php>

Carter, M. & Torabully, K. (2002). *Coolitude: An Anthology of the Indian Labour Diaspora*. Ann Arbor, MI: Anthem.

Césaire, A. (2001). *Notebook of a Return to the Native Land*. (C. Eshleman & A. Smith, Trans.). Middletown, CT: Wesleyan University Press. (Original work published 1939)

Césaire, A. (2004). *Discours sur le colonialisme, Discours sur la Négritude*. Paris: Présence Africaine.

Césaire, A. (2005). *Nègre je suis, nègre je resterai. Entretiens avec Françoise Vergès*. Paris, France: Albin Michel.

Césaire, A. (2008). "Négritude, Africa and Black History" (P. Bolland, Trans.). [online] Available at: <http://www.humaniteinenglish.com/spip.php?article898> (Original work published 1987)

Césaire, A. (2010). "Letter to Maurice Thorez (C. Jeffers, Trans.)." *Social Text*, 28(2), 145-153. DOI 10.1215/01642472-2009-072

Champeaud, G. (2001). "The Edict of Poitiers and the Treaty of Nerac, or Two Steps towards the Edict of Nantes." *The Sixteenth Century Journal, 32*(2), 319-334.

Chamoiseau, P. (1995). *Créole Folktales* (L. Coverdale, Trans.). New York: The New Press.

Chamoiseau, P., Confiant, R., Bernabé, J., & Taylor, L. (1997). "Créolité Bites." *Transition, 74,* 124-161.

Chanson, P. (2005). "Identité et altérité chez Édouard Glissant et Patrick Chamoiseau, scripteurs visionnaires de la parole créole." [online] Available at: <http://www.potomitan.info/chamoiseau/identite.php - 1>

Château-Degat, R. & Placide, L.-G. (2009). "Les émeutes de Décembre 59, un tournant historique." In T. L'Etang & A. Lucrèce (Eds.), *Les Cahiers du Patrimoine (*No. 27, pp. 104-119)*: Révoltes et luttes sociales en Martinique:* Fort de France, Martinique: Musée Régional d'Histoire et d'Ethnographie.

Chatman, S. L. (2000). "'There are no slaves in France': A Re-examination of Slave Laws in Eighteenth Century France." *The Journal of Negro History, 85*(3), 144-153.

Chilcoat, M. (2004). "In/Civility, in Death: On Becoming French in Colonial Martinique." *boundary 2, 31*(3), 47-73.

Childers, K.S. (2006). "Citizenship and Assimilation in Postwar Martinique: The Abolition of Slavery and the Politics of Commemoration." *Proceedings of the Western Society of French History, 34,* 282-299. [online] Available at: <http://quod.lib.umich.edu/w/wsfh/0642292.0034.018/--citizenship-and-assimilation-in-postwar-martinique?rgn=main;view=fulltext>

Chinien, S. P. (2008). «Une identité, c'est une histoire que l'on se raconte»: Entretien de Patrick Chamoiseau avec Savrina Parevadee Chinien (2e volet) sur la question de la diversité des cultures en Martinique.»[online] Available at: <http://www.africultures.com/php/index.php?nav=article&no=7311 -

sthash.BmIb01cm.8jbePBqf.dpuf>

Christofferson, T. R. (1991). *French Socialists in Power*, 1981-1986. Newark, DE: University of Delaware Press.

Cicéri, E. & Hartmann, A. (1851). *Album Martiniquais*. Paris : Lemercier.

Clothier, P. (2009). "Martinique's Tough Choice. *Prospect, 163*. (October 16). [online] Available at: <http://www.prospectmagazine.co.uk/magazine/martiniques-tough-choice>

Confer, V. (1964). "French Colonial Ideas before 1789." *French Historical Studies, 3*(3), 338-359.

Confiant, R. (1995). *Contes Creoles des Amériques*. Paris: Stock.

Confiant, R. (2003). "Cultural Diversity as a New Utopia." [online] Available at: <http://www.potomitan.info/atelier/utopia.html>

Confiant, R. (2004a). "Dictionnaire des croyances et pratiques magico-religieuses du monde   creole." [online] Available at: <http://kapeskreyol.potomitan.info/guides/magico.html>

Confiant, R. (2004b). *La panse du chacal*. Paris: Mercure de France.

Confiant, R. (2009). "Le créole, cette langue orpheline." [online] Available at: <http://www.potomitan.info/confiant/creole.php>

Cook-Darzens, S. & Brunod, R. (1999). "An Ecosystemic Approach to Improving Mother-Infant Attachment in a Caribbean Matrifocal Society." *Contemporary Family Therapy, 21*(4), pp. 433-452.

Corteggiani, B. (January, 1994). "Foi et magie sur l'île créole." *Peuples Du Monde, 268,* 6-7. Available at:
<http://jbcorteggiani.com/wp-content/uploads/2011/09/peuples.pdf>

Crouse, N. M. (1940). *French Pioneers in the West Indies,* 1624 – 1664. New York, NY: Columbia University Press.

Crouse, N. M. (1966). *The French Struggle for the West Indies, 1665-1713.* New York: Octagon.

Crystal, D. (2007). *How Language Works: How Babies Babble, Words Change Meaning, and Languages Live or Die.* New York : Avery.

Curtius, A. D. (2008). "A Fort-de France les statues ne meurent pas." *International Journal of Francophone Studies, 11*(1), 87-106.

Curtius, A. D. (2010). "Gandhi et Au-Béro, ou comment inscrire les traces d'une mémoire indienne dans une negritude martiniquaise." *LEsprit Créateur, 50* (2), 109-123.

Davenport, F.G. (1917). *European Treaties Bearing on the History of the United States and Its Dependencies to 1648.* Washington, DC: Carnegie Institution of Washington.

Debien, G. (1996). "*Marronage* in the French Carribean." In R. Price (Ed.), *Maroon Societies: Rebel Slave Communities in the Americas* (pp. 107-134). Baltimore: Johns Hopkins University Press.

Déclaration de politique scientifique du GEREC-F (n.d.). [online] Available at: <http://www.potomitan.info/travaux/declaration.htm>

Delphin, L. & Roth, P. (2009). *Une Terre, une plante, une people—A Land, a Plant, a People.* Trois-Ilets, Martinique: Maison de la Canne.

de Saint Périer, L. (2012). "Raphaël Confiant: 'Les Syro-Libanais sont le sixième peuple fondateur du peuple Martiniquais.'" [online] JeuneAfrique. com. Available at: <http://www.jeuneafrique.com/Article/ARTJAWEB20120903121622/liban-syrie-martinique-douard-glissant-martinique-raphael-confiant-les-syro-libanais-sont-le-sixieme-peuple-fondateur-du-peuple-martiniquais.html>

Desroches, M. (1996). *Tambours des dieux: musique et sacrifice d'origine tamoul en Martinique.* Montreal: L'Harmattan.

Diagne, S. B. (2014). "Négritude." In E. N. Zalta (Ed.), *The Stanford Encyclopedia of Philosophy,* Spring 2014 Edition. [online] Available at: <http://plato.stanford.edu/archives/spr2014/entries/negritude/>

Dobie, M. (2004). "Invisible Exodus: The Cultural Effacement of Antillean Migration." *Diaspora: A Journal of Transnational Studies, 13*(2-3), 149-183.

Dubois, L. & Garrigus, J.D. (2006). *Slave Revolution in the Caribbean, 1789-1804: A Brief History with Documents.* Boston: Bedford/St. Martin's Press.

Elisabeth, L. (1972). "The French Antilles." In D.W. Cohen & J.P. Greene (Eds.), *Neither Slave nor Free: The Freedman of African Descent in the Slave Societies of the New World.* Baltimore: Johns Hopkins University Press (pp. 143-171).

Elisabeth, L. (2009). "Présyndicalisme." In T. L'Etang & A. Lucrèce (Eds.), *Les Cahiers du Patrimoine* (No. 27, pp. 54-59): *Révoltes et luttes sociales en Martinique:* Fort de France, Martinique: Musée Régional d'Histoire et d'Ethnographie.

Etienne, J. (2003). "La littérature en langue créole du 17ᵉ siècle à nos jours

(No. 27, pp. 32-39). [online] Available at: <http://www.potomitan.info/ bannzil/litterature.html>

Fanon, F. (1967). *Black Skins, White Masks* (C.L. Markmann, Trans.). New York: Grove Press. (Original work published 1952).

Ferguson, J. (2008). *A Traveler's History of the Caribbean,* 2nd ed. Northampton, MA: Interlink Publishing Group.

Flandrina, M. (2009a). "L'affaire Bissette (1823-1827)." In T. L'Etang & A. Lucrèce (Eds.), *Les Cahiers du Patrimoine:* (No. 27, pp. 32-39): *Révoltes et luttes sociales en Martinique:* Fort de France, Martinique: Musée Régional d'Histoire et d'Ethnographie.

Flandrina, M. (2009b). "L'insurrection de la Grande Anse en 1833-1834." In T. L'Etang & A. Lucrèce (Eds.), *Les Cahiers du Patrimoine* (No. 27, pp. 40-49): *Révoltes et luttes sociales en   Martinique.* Fort de France, Martinique: Musée Régional d'Histoire et d'Ethnographie.

Gamess, R. and Gamess, Y. (2003) *De l'Inde à la Martinique: le droit d'exister.* Fort-de-France, Martinique: Désormeaux.

Garcia-Ramirez, M., de la Mata, M. L., Paloma, V., & Hernandez-Plata, S. (2011). "A Liberation Psychology Approach to Acculturative Integration of Migrant Populations." *American Journal of Community Psychology, 47,* pp. 86-97. DOI: 10.1007/s10464-010-9372-3.

Garraway, D. (2005). *The Libertine Colony: Creolization in the Early French Caribbean.* Durham, NC: Duke University Press.

Gautier, A. (2000). "Les familles esclaves aux Antilles francaises, 1635-1848." *Population (French   Edition), 55e* (6), 975-1001.

Geggus, D. (1983). "Slave Resistance Studies and the Saint Domingue Slave Revolt: Some Preliminary Considerations (Paper #4)." *LACC Occasional Paper Series (1981-1990).* Paper 3. [online] Available at: <http://digitalcommons.fiu.edu.laccops/3>

Geggus, D. (1989). "Racial Equality, Slavery, and Colonial Secession during the Constituent Assembly." *The American Historical Review, 94* (5), 1290-1308.

Geggus, D. (2001). "The French Slave Trade: An Overview." *William and Mary Quarterly, Third Series, 58* (1), 119-138.

General Council of Martinique website(2014). "La collectivité territoriale de Martinique: Le projet." [online] Available at: <http://www.region-martinique.mq/la-collectivite-territoriale-de-martinique/le-projet/>

GEREC-F: Groupe d'Études et de Recherches en Espace Créolophone et Francophone (2005). [online] Available at: <http://www1.univ-ag.fr/gerec-f/>

Glissant, É. (1989). *Caribbean Discourse: Selected Essays.* (M. J. Dash, Trans.). Charlottesville, VA: University of Virginia Press.

Glissant, É. & Chamoiseau, P. (2005). "De loin." [online] Available at: <http://www.potomitan.info/articles/deloin.php>

Golovko, E. (2005). *"The Making of Identity, the Making of a Language: On Some Linguistic Consequences of the Russian Colonization in Siberia." In: N. Crawhall and N. Ostler, (Eds.), Creating Outsiders: Endangered Languages, Migration, and Marginalization.* Proceedings of the Ninth Conference of the Foundation for Endangered Languages, Stellenbosch, South Africa (pp. 31-36).

Gray, J.G. (1983). "The Origin of the Word Huguenot." *The Sixteenth Century Journal, 14* (3), 349-359.

Gullick, (1980). "Island Carib Traditions about Their Arrival in the Lesser Antilles." In R. Bullen (Ed.), *Proceedings of the 8th International Congress for the Study of Pre-Columbian Cultures in the Lesser Antilles* (pp. 464-472). Tempe, AZ: Arizona State University Press.

Héber-Suffrin, P. (2014). *Un marin, un martiniquais, notre grand-père.* Paris: L'Harmattan.

Hersilie-Héloïse, E. (2009). "'Les 'Syriens' de Martinique." [blog] Available at: <http://vivrauxantilles.canalblog.com/archives/2009/07/28/14547908.html>

Hintjens, H. (1995). "Constitutional and Political Change in the French Caribbean." In R.D.E. Burton & F. Reno (Eds.), *French and West Indian: Martinique, Guadeloupe, and French Guiana Today* (pp. 20-33). Charlottesville, VA: University of Virginia Press.

Hodson, C. & Rushforth, B. (2010). "Absolutely Atlantic: Colonialism and the Early Modern French State in Recent Historiography." *History Compass, 8* (1), 101-117. DOI: 10.1111/j.1478-0542.2009.00635.x

Hoffman, P.E. (1980). *The Spanish Crown and the Defense of the Caribbean, 1535-1585: Precedent, Patrimonialism and Royal Parsimony.* Baton Rouge, LA: Louisiana State University Press.

Hubbard, V. K. (2002). *A History of St. Kitts: The Sweet Trade.* London: Macmillan Caribbean.

Hulme, P. (1986). *Colonial Encounters: Europe and the Native Caribbean.* London:

Methuen.

Icart, J.-C. (2007). "La traite négrière et son abolition: Une tranche de l'histoire mais pas du passé." [online] Available at: <http://www.potomitan. info/ayiti/traite.php>

Jayawardena, C. (1968). "Migration and Social Change: A Survey of Indian Communities Overseas." *Geographical Review, 58* (3), 426-449.

Jennings, E. (2002). "Last Exit from Vichy: The Martinique Escape Route and the Ambiguities of Emigration." *The Journal of Modern History, 74* (2), 289-324.

Julien, E. (2000). "Terrains de recontres: Césaire, Fanon, and Wright on Culture and Decolonization." *Yale French Studies, 98,* 149-168.

Kelly, K.G. (2008). "Creole Cultures of the Caribbean: Historical Archeology in the French West Indies." *International Journal of Historical Archeology, 12,* 388-402. DOI: 10.1007/s10761-0080058-6

Kennedy, M. (1960). "The Bissette Affair and the French Colonial Question." *The Journal of Negro History, 45*(1), 1-10.

Kennenga, E. (2010). "Truc de fou" [recorded by E. Kennenga] On E.K. Trip [Mp3 file]. Fort de   France, Martinique: B Caribbean.

Labat, J.-B. (1742). *Nouveau voyage aux isles de l'Amerique.* Paris: Ch. J. B. Delespine. [online] Available at: <https://archive.org/details/ nouveauvoyageau04laba>

Lamy, R. (2010, January 11). "French Guiana, Martinique Reject Autonomy Proposal." *Seattle Times.* [online] Available at: <http://seattletimes.

com/html/businesstechnology/2010762689_apcbmartiniquefrenchg
uianaautonomy.html>

Lavollée, P. (1841). *Notes sur les cultures et la production de la Martinique*. Paris: Imprimature Royale.

L'Etang, G. (2003). "De l'héritage culturel congo, indien et chinois à la Martinique." Paper presented at La Maison franco-japonaise de Tokyo, April 24, 2003. [online] Available at: <http://www.potomitan.info/travaux/heritage.php#1>

L'Etang, G. (2007). "Article 74: Pour commencer à en finir avec notre mendicité arrogante." [online] Available at: <http://www.potomitan.info/matinik/art74.php>

L'Etang, G. (2011a). "Littérature martiniquais et mythologie." [online] Available at: <http://www.potomitan.info/gletang/litterature.php>

L'Etang, G. (2011b). "Nagour Mira: Une figure islamique dans l'hindouisme tamoul de la Caraïbe." [online] Available at: <http://www.potomitan.info/articles/nagour.php#1>

L'Etang, G. & Permal, V. (1994). "Zwazo: Récit de vie d'un prêtre hindou, commandeur d'habitation à la Martinique." [online] Available at: <http://www.potomitan.info/ki_nov/inde/zwazo.php - 1>

Meslien, S. (2009). "1665, guerre contre les nègres marrons de Martinique." In T. L'Etang & ALucrèce (Eds.), *Les Cahiers du Patrimoine* (No. 27, pp. 6-9): *Révoltes et luttes sociales en Martinique*. Fort de France, Martinique: Musée Régional d'Histoire et d'Ethnographie.

Miles, W. F. S. (1985). "Mitterrand in the Caribbean: Socialism (?) Comes to

Martinique." *Journal of Interamerican Studies and World Affairs, 27* (3), 63-79.

Miles, W. F. S. (1995). "Deja Vu with a Difference: End of the Mitterrand Era and the McDonaldization of Martinique." *Caribbean Studies, 28* (2), 339-368.

Miles, W. F. S. (2006). When Is a Nation 'A Nation'?: Identity-Formation within a French West Indian People (Martinique)." *Nations and Nationalism, 12* (4), 631-652.

Miles, W. F. S. (2009a). "Aimé Césaire as Poet, Rebel, and Statesman." *French Politics, Culture, & Society, 27* (3), 1-8. DOI: 10.3167/fpcs.2009.270301.

Miles, W. F. S. (2009b). "Metaphysical Considerations Can Come Later, But the People Have Children to Feed": An Interview with Aimé Césaire." *French Politics, Culture, & Society, 27* (3), 63-75. DOI: 10.3167/fpcs.2009.270308.

Miller, C.L. (2008). *The French Atlantic Triangle: Literature and Culture of the Slave Trade.* Durham, NC: Duke University Press.

Montaigne, M. (2012). "Of Cannibals." In W.C. Hazlitt (Ed.) *The Complete Essays of Michel de Montaigne* (Chapter XXX, C. Cotton, Trans.). Project Gutenberg: <http://www.gutenberg.org/files/3600/3600-h/3600-h. htm - link2HCH0030> (Original work published 1877)

Munford, C. J. (1986). "Slavery in the French Caribbean: A Marxist Analysis." *Journal of Black Studies*, 17(1), 49-69.

Munro, M. (2008). "Avenging History in the Former French Colonies." *Transition*, 99, 18-40.

Murch, A. (1968). "Political Integration as an Alternative to Independence in the French Antilles." *American Sociological Review, 33* (4), 544-562.

Murray, D. A. B. (1997). "The Cultural Citizen: Negations of Race and Language in the Making of Martiniquais." *Anthropological Quarterly, 70* (2), pp. 79-90.

Naidoo, L. (2007). Re-negotiating Identity and Reconciling Cultural Ambiguity in the Indian Immigrant Community in Sydney, Australia." *Anthropologist Special Issue, 2,* pp. 53-66.

Nesbitt, N. (2007). "Departmentalization and the Logic of Decolonization." *L'Esprit Créateur, 47* (1), 32-43. DOI: 10.1353/esp.2007.0026.

Nicolas, A. (2009). "A l'origine du mouvement ouvrier martiniquais." In T. L'Etang & A. Lucrèce (Eds.), *Les Cahiers du Patrimoine* (No. 27, pp. 60-75): *Révoltes et luttes sociales en Martinique:* Fort de France, Martinique: Musée Régional d'Histoire et d'Ethnographie.

Palcy, E. (Producer & Director). (1983). "La Rue Cases-Nègres." [Motion Picture]. Paris, France: NEF.

Palmer, V. V. (1996). "The origins and authors of the Code Noir." *Louisiana Law Review,* 56(2), 363-407. [online] Available at: <http://digitalcommons. law.lsu.edu/lalrev/vol56/iss2/5>

"Patrimoine de la Martinique — Les Habitations (2014)." [online] Available at: <http://www.zananas-martinique.com/martinique-patrimoine/ habitations.htm>

Peabody, S. (1996). *"There Are No Slaves in France": The Political Culture of Race and Slavery in the Ancien Regime.* London: Oxford Press.

Peabody, S. (2002). "'A Dangerous Zeal': Catholic Missions to Slaves in the

French Antilles, 1635-1800." *French Historical Studies, 25* (1), 53-90.

Peabody, S. (2004). "'A Nation Born to Slavery': Missionaries and Racial Discourse in Seventeenth Century French Antilles." *Journal of Social History, 38*(1), 113-126. DOI: 10.1353/jsh.2004.0099

Petit Jean Roget, J. (1980). *La société d'habitation à la Martinique: Un demi-siècle de formation, 1635-1685.* Lille, France: Université de Lille III.

Pillai, S. K. (2005). "Indian culture in Guadeloupe and Martinique." [online] Available at: <http://independent.academia.edu/SureshPillai/ Papers/392416/Hindu_Indian_cultural _ D i a s p o r a _ i n _ F r e n c h _ Caribbean_islands_of_Guadeloupe_and_Martinique>

Ramakrishnan, M. (2013). "French, African, and Indian Cultural Narratives in Martinique: The Architecture of Shifting Social Hierarchies from 1848-1884." *International Journal of Interdisciplinary Cultural Studies, 7* (2), 27-26. [online] Available at: <http://ijicst.cgpublisher.com/product/pub.268/ prod.9>

Ramakrishnan, M. (2012). "Preservation and Loss of Elements of Native Language: Resettlement in Martinique." *Proceedings of the Asian Conference on Language Learning, September, 2012.* [online] Available at: <http://iafor. org/Proceedings/ACLL/ACLL2012_proceedings.pdf>

Ramassamy, D. (2012). "6 Mai 1853–6 Mai 2012: 159 ans de présence indienne en Martinique." [online] Available at: <http://www.potomitan. info/matinik/occultation.php>

Reno, F. (1995). "Politics and Society in Martinique. In R.D.E. Burton & F. Reno (Eds.), *French and West Indian: Martinique, Guadeloupe, and French Guiana Today* (pp. 34-47). Charlottesville, VA: University of Virginia Press.

Reno, F. (2009). "Aimé Césaire ou l'ambivalence féconde." *French Politics, Culture & Society*, 27(3), 19-23. doi:10.3167/fpcs.2009.270303

Revauger, J.-P. (2002). "The Influence of Culture and of Institutional Factors in Social Policy: French Social Policy in Martinique." *Social Policy & Society*, *1*(4), pp. 285-292. DOI: 10.1017/S1474746402004025

Riddell, W. R. (1925). "Le Code Noir." *The Journal of Negro History*, *10* (3), pp. 321-329.

Roberts, W. A. (1942). *The French in the West Indies*. New York: Bobbs-Merrill.

Rouse, I. (1963). "The Caribs." In J. Steward (Ed.), *Handbook of South American Indians* (vol. 4, pp. 547-548). New York: Coopers Square.

Sahaï, J.-S. (2008). "Aime Cesaire : Adagio pour la Da." [online] Available at: <http://cqoj.typepad.com/chest/2008/04/la-noble-da-t-1.html>

Sala-Molins, Louis (1998). *Le Code noir ou le calvaire de Canaan*. Paris: Presses Universitaires de France.

"Sarkozy Offers Autonomy Vote for Martinique" (June 27, 2009). *Caribbean Net News*. [online] Available at <http://www.caribbeannewsnow.com/caribnet/martinique/martinique.php?news_id=17 354&start=0&category_id=34>

Savage, J. (2006). "Unwanted Slaves: The Punishment of Transportation and the Making of Legal Subjects in Early 19th Century Martinique." *Citizenship Studies*, *10* (1), 35-53. DOI: 10.1080/13621020500525928

Savage, J. (2007). "'Black Magic' and White Terror: Slave Poisoning and

Colonial Society in Early 19th Century Martinique." *Journal of Social History, 40* (3), pp. 635-695.

"Savana Savita sur la route de l'Inde." (March 3, 2013). [online] Available at: <http://www.martinique.franceantilles.fr/loisirs/sortir/savana-savita-sur-la-route-de-l-inde-197176.php>

Schloss, R. H. (2007). "The February 1831 Slave Uprising in Martinique and the Policing of White Identity." *French Historical Studies, 30* (2), pp. 203-236. DOI 10.1215/00161071-2006-025.

Schloss, R.H. (2009). *Sweet Liberty: The Final Days of Slavery in Martinique.* Philadelphia: University of Pennsylvania Press.

Schmidt, N. (2012). *Slavery and Its Abolition, French Colonies, Research and Transmission of Knowledge.* The Slave Route Project, UNESCO. [online] Available at: <http://www.unesco.org/new/fileadmin/MULTIMEDIA/HQ/CLT/pdf/Nelly_Schmidt_Eng_01.pdf>

Schoelcher, V. (1842). *Des colonies françaises:Abolition immediate de l'esclavage.* Paris: Pagnerre. [online] Available at: <http://gallica.bnf.fr/ark:/12148/bpt6k84499k>

Schwarz-Bart, S. (2013). *The Bridge of Beyond* (B. Bray, Trans.). New York: New York Review Books. (Original work published 1972)

Shukla, S. (2001). "Locations for South Asian Diasporas." *Annual Review of Anthropology, 30,* 551-572.

Singler, J. V. (1995). "The Demographics of Creole Genesis in the Caribbean: A Comparison of Martinique and Haiti." In J. Arends (Ed.), *The Early Stages of Creolization* (pp. 1-24). Philadelphia: John Benjamins.

Sméralda-Amon, J. (2004). "La problématique de l'indianité dans le contexte Martiniquais." [online] Available at: <http://www.indereunion.net/IREV/amon/amon1.htm>

Sméralda-Amon, J. (n.d.) "Interview with *Indes Reunionnaises.*" [online] Available at: <http://www.indereunion.net/actu/amon/interamon.htm - Interview>

Smith, R. S. (2013). "African and French Cultural Narratives in Martinique: The Architecture of Social Dominance from 1635-1848 (Part 1)." *International Journal of Interdisciplinary Cultural Studies, 7* (1), 35-44. [online] Available at: <http://ijicst.cgpublisher.com/product/pub.268/prod.8>

Sutherland, N.M. (1988). "The Crown, the Huguenots, and the Edict of Nantes." In: R.M. Golden (Ed.), *The Huguenot Connection: The Edict of Nantes, its Revocation, and Early French Migration to South Carolina.* The Netherlands: Springer.

Sweeney, J. L. (2007). "Caribs, Maroon, Jacobins, Brigands and Sugar Barons: The Last Stand of the Black Caribs on St. Vincent." *The African Diaspora Archeology Network Newsletter.* [online] Available at: <http://www.diaspora.uiuc.edu/news0307/news0307.html>

Tapié, V.-L. (1975). *France in the Age of Louis XIII and Richelieu* (D. McN. Lockie, Trans.). New York: Praeger.

Taylor, D. (1949). "The Interpretation of Some Documentary Evidence on Carib Culture." *Southwestern Journal of Anthropology, 5,* 380-381.

Thaniyayagam, X. S. (1968). "Tamil Migrations to Guadeloupe & Martinique, 1853 to 1883." Paper presented at the Second International Conference of

Tamil Studies, Madras, 1968. [online] Available at: <http://tamilnation.co/diaspora/guadeloupe.htm>

Thomas, H. (1997). *The Slave Trade: The Story of the Atlantic Slave Trade, 1440 -1870.* New York: Simon & Schuster.

Tomich, D. (1990a). "'Liberté ou mort': Republicanism and Slave Revolt in Martinique, February 1831." *History Workshop, 29,* 85-91.

Tomich, D. (1990b). *Slavery in the Circuit of Sugar: Martinique and the World Economy, 1830-1848.* Baltimore: Johns Hopkins University Press.

Town of Basse-Pointe Website (n.d.). [online] Available at: <http://www.mairie-basse-pointe.fr/?q=node/140>

Trouillot, M.-R. (1992). "The Caribbean Region: An Open Frontier in Anthropological Theory." *Annual Review of Anthropology*, 21, 19-42.

Townley, G., Kloos, B., Green, E. P., & Franco, M. M. (2011). "Reconcilable differences? Human Diversity, Cultural Relativity, and Sense of Community." *American Journal of Community Psychology, 47,* pp. 69-85. DOI: 10.1007/s10464-010-9379-9.

Turchetti, M. (1991). "Religious Concord and Political Tolerance in Sixteenth-and Seventeenth-Century France." *The Sixteenth Century Journal, 22* (1), 15-25.

Vamarasi, M. (2008). "The Critical Role of Language in the Construction of Rotuman Diasporic Identity." *Refereed Papers from the 3rd International Small Island Cultures Conference, Institute of Island Studies, University of PEI, June 29-July 2, 2007.*

Yelvington, K. A. (2001). "The Anthropology of Afro-Latin America and the Caribbean: Diasporic Dimensions." *Annual Review of Anthropology, 30,* pp. 227-260. DOI: 0084-6570/01/1021-0227.

Zandwonis, D. (2008, April 17). Aimé Césaire: "Je suis un Nègre Marron." *Carib Créole News.*   [online] Available at: < http://www.caraibcreolenews.com/ news/martinique/1,199,17-04-2008-aime-cesaire-quot-je-suis-un-negre-marron-quot-.html> (Originally published in *Journal Guadeloupéen,* 10 April, 1980.)

Index